The Biblical Seminar

Series Editor
David E. Orton

JUDAISM IN ANTIQUITY

JUDAISM IN ANTIQUITY

Political Development and Religious
Currents from Alexander to Hadrian

Benedikt Otzen

Translated by
Frederick H. Cryer

jst
1990
jsot press

Translated from the Danish
*Den antike jødedom. Politisk udvikling og
religiøse strømninger fra Aleksander den Store
til Kejser Hadrian* (København: G.E.C. Gad, 1984)
Copyright © G.E.C. Gad, 1984

This translation copyright © 1990 Sheffield Academic Press

Published by JSOT Press
JSOT Press is an imprint of
Sheffield Academic Press Ltd
The University of Sheffield
343 Fulwood Road
Sheffield S10 3BP
England

Printed in Great Britain
by Billing & Sons Ltd
Worcester

British Library Cataloguing in Publication Data

Otzen, Benedikt
     Judaism in antiquity: political development and
     religious currents from Alexander to Hadrian.
     (Biblical seminar Series: ISSN 0226-4984; v.7).
     1. Jews. Social life, to 1983
     I. Title II. Series III. Den antike Jødedom. *English*
     909'.04924

     ISBN 1-85075-197-8
     ISBN 1-85075-090-4pbk

CONTENTS

PREFACE

As the subtitle indicates, this book attempts to describe the historical and religious developments of Judaism in the centuries immediately before and after the time of Christ. The importance of the period will be evident to all, for it is here that Jewish and European history meet, so to speak: Christianity arises out of the Jewish milieu in Palestine and becomes a decisive factor in European culture and spiritual life for centuries to come. Christianity is a product of Judaism, and we cannot understand Early Judaism without knowing its Jewish background. In this book we shall concentrate exclusively on Judaism; we shall try to follow the political, social, and religious trends in Jewish culture and society, and we shall track the connecting lines between these various sectors of Early Judaism.

The Danish edition was published in 1984. In the translation I have corrected some errors from the original edition, and I have made a number of changes in the Bibliographic Notes: some Scandinavian titles have been removed, and several English and German publications have been added, including some published since the writing of the Danish edition. The final section on Apocalyptic has its own character and is based on a series of lectures that I delivered at the Swedish Theological Institute in Jerusalem in 1981. Nevertheless, I regret that I did not for the final presentation of the section notice the fine English book on the subject from 1982, Christopher Rowland's *The Open Heaven*.

The Jewish literature from the period is rich: the Old Testament book of Daniel, the Apocrypha and Pseudepigrapha, the writings of Josephus, and some early rabbinic texts. From the two Jewish groups that break with the religious community in Jerusalem, the Qumran sect and the young Christian church, we have the Qumran texts and the New Testament, collections which in a special way throw a sharp sidelight on Early Judaism. In the Appendix (pp. 225-34) the reader will find some short items of information concerning 'Jewish Writings from Antiquity'. Here the translations are mentioned from which I quote. All biblical quotations are from *The New English Bible. Mishna* is quoted from Danby's English translation, other rabbinic texts from the secondary literature. In the Bibliographic Notes at the end of the various sections of the book I have listed sources and secondary literature. Most of the titles represent books which I have used and which readers may also find useful.

Finally, I want to thank three friends and colleagues: Fred Cryer, M.A. (Oxon.), who accepted the onerous task of translating from Danish; Bent Rosendal, Ph.D., who has drawn the beautiful map; and Dr Per Bilde, the Scandinavian expert on Josephus, who has read the manuscript and given me many valuable suggestions.

Aarhus University B.O.
Denmark
January 1990

Map of
Roman Palestine

PART I

JEWISH SOCIETY, POLITICALLY AND SOCIALLY CONSIDERED

Every culture has its heights—epochs which signify new beginnings, in which internal forces and external influences collaborate to create something wholly new. We have grown used to regarding the history of European culture as a sort of wave motion consisting of the classical period, when the Greeks and Romans founded what we now understand to be European culture, followed by the Middle Ages, which has been regarded as a sterile time without creative energies, and finally the Renaissance, the time of rebirth, namely the rebirth of classical culture, merging with new and modern ideas. The Renaissance has for good reasons been regarded as a highpoint in European history when that Europe was formed which we know today.

Similar considerations apply to Israelite-Jewish culture. It, too, had its highpoints, and the 300-400 years which we shall examine here may reasonably be regarded as a phase of cultural development which was superior to both what came before and what followed it. It was in many respects a revolutionary, and hence transitional, period, during which the external political events were many and violent. Social currents developed apace, and Jewish religion experienced extraordinary influences from foreign cultures and religions, yet managed, nevertheless, to retain its own peculiar character. It was a revolutionary, transitional period, but by the same token a period which was richly creative, during which the cultural and religious phenomenon of Judaism assumed the form in which we know it today. In these senses this span of time reminds us of the European Renaissance.

What we shall attempt to come to grips with here are the decidedly new features in ancient Jewish religion and culture which made their appearance in these years. At the same time, though, we shall attempt to perceive these new features in Early Judaism in relation to the ancient and classical religion and culture of Israel, with respect to both startling innovations and further developments—or, if you will, the 'rebirth' of ancient motifs and conceptions. However, this concentration on the spiritual life of Early Judaism must not be allowed to obscure the importance of then-contemporary political and social developments. Precisely in the context of Judaism the connection between the political and the religious is indissoluble. Both the religions of classical Israel and of Early Judaism may be described as national in character. The reason for this is that the concept of Israel as Yahweh's chosen people, and as the people whose right to the possession of Palestine was guaranteed by God, has always been deeply rooted in both the Israelite and the Jewish religious consciousness. Accordingly, there was always an intensive interaction between political and religious developments in Jewish society; the one facet cannot be understood without reference to the other. Political events triggered religious reactions, and religious attitudes initiated certain chains of political action. Thus it is both natural and necessary that our account will begin with some sections which concentrate on political and social features in antiquity.

Classical Israel existed for only a short period as an integral quantity. It was first with King David around 1000 BC that an Israelite state *per se* arose, an empire consisting of a central Israelite kingdom extending throughout Palestine, plus a number of vassal states in the surrounding regions. All of it was unified under the reign of a single dominant personality. David's son Solomon managed to equip the state with a centralized government and a corps of administrators, in addition to a sort of national cultus centring on the new temple in Jerusalem. However, all this collapsed after Solomon's death around 930 BCE. The vassal states won their independence and, still worse, the Israelite kingdom proper was divided up, so that in the subsequent centuries Israel consisted of two independent states, the northern and southern kingdoms, which went their own separate ways.

The northern kingdom had a complicated history. For long periods of time it was under pressure from the neighbouring Aramean states in Syria. It also experienced countless internal conflicts in which coups and regicides were the order of the day, and, although at times the kingdom possessed considerable political power, it never attained political stability. In cultural and religious terms the northern kingdom was characterized by its openness to Canaanite-Phoenician culture, which was well established in the Phoenician coastal cities farther to the north. This meant that the ancient Israelite worship of Yahweh was at times only weakly represented in important circles in the northern kingdom.

By way of contrast, the southern kingdom, which was called Judah, was far more stable in political terms, as the dynastic principles remained successful there; for 400 years heirs of David occupied the throne in Jerusalem. The government was unconditionally centralistic, so that the country was ruled in every respect, also religiously and culturally, from the capital city of Jerusalem. It was here that the version of Yahwism was developed which became determinative for the later Jewish understanding of what belief in Israel's god, Yahweh entailed.

Around the middle of the first millennium BCE world history was witness to the formation of great empires in the Mediterranean region; this epoch was to last for over a thousand years. Around 750 BCE in northern Mesopotamia the Assyrians became the first real world power. They were replaced by the Babylonians in southern Mesopotamia around 600 BCE, and already, by c. 540 BCE, they in turn had given way to the third wave of world conquerors, the Persian, emanating from southern Iran. With the career of Alexander the Great around 330 BCE the Greeks achieved world domination, and, finally, from the first pre-Christian century until the beginning of the Middle Ages, the Romans controlled the entire Mediterranean basin.

Obviously, the two Israelite mini-kingdoms were unable to assert their independence in the face of such gigantic powers. In fact the northern kingdom of Israel had already gone to its doom in 722 BCE, when the Assyrians captured the capital city of Samaria, dissolving the kingdom into a number of provinces, and incorporating them into their empire. The southern kingdom suffered a similar fate in 587 BCE; this time it was the Babylonian king Nebuchadnezzar who captured Jerusalem, destroyed the temple of Solomon, and assimilated the province into his giant empire.

These two sequences were superficially similar. There were, however, some decisive differences which were influential for centuries, and we shall therefore concern ourselves with them here. Both the Assyrians and the Babylonians undertook deportations of parts of Israelite society in connection with their conquests. The deportees consisted above all of administrators, priests, leading citizens, and artisans; they were removed in order to excise possible sources of rebellion. However, we should note that the Assyrians also transported deportees from other conquered lands and resettled them in northern Palestine, so that in the course of time a semi-heathen population evolved in the region. Nothing of the sort took place in the case of Judah, about 130 years later. Admittedly, the Babylonians did deport some thousands of Judeans to Babylon, but outside of that they left the country largely in peace. Yet another fact is important in this connection, namely that the deportees from the two kingdoms seem to have had very different attitudes towards their common Israelite heritage. This is immediately intelligible when we consider the above-mentioned differences between the northern and southern kingdoms in the time subsequent to David. Whereas the deportees from the northern kingdom were simply assimilated into their new surroundings, those from Judah had only a single goal: to retain their inheritance from their fathers; to adhere to the worship of Israel's traditional god, Yaweh; to reject all heathen influence; and to utilize the time of their exile to enable them to understand their hard fate until they could ultimately return. At the same time, the Judeans who remained in Palestine were only to a moderate degree subject to foreign religious influences during this critical period. All things considered, there were excellent prospects for the continued development of Judean religion and culture.

The Judeans (or Jews) in Babylon were relatively free, and naturally some of them were assimilated into the heathen milieu. But by and large the small Jewish congregation retained its closed character, and as early as around 540— only fifty years after the fall of Jerusalem—they were given the opportunity to return to Palestine. The occasion was the defeat of the Babylonians by the Persian king Cyrus en route to establishing his world-engulfing empire. This event marked the foundation of the Persian monarchy, and a few years ago the late Shah of Iran managed, with great pomp and circumstance, to celebrate the 2,500th anniversary of the monarchy—at the last instant before it fell.

The Persian empire survived longer than did any of the other ancient empires except that of the Romans, and in geographical extension it exceeded them all. Cyrus, Cambyses, Darius, Xerxes and the other Great Kings managed to maintain their grip on an empire that stretched from Thrace in the west to the Indus River in the east, and they did so for more than 200 years. They were able administrators, and they conducted a wise policy of tolerance with respect to their many subject peoples, so that the temptation to rebel was modest at best. Those Jews who remained behind in Babylon—and they were very probably the majority of the deportees and their descendants—formed the nucleus of the eastern Jewish Diaspora, so important later on. In many ways Babylon was to be the spiritual locus of power for Judaism in the following centuries. It was from Babylon that renewing and reforming currents emanated towards Jerusalem, embodied in such figures as Ezra and Nehemiah in the fifth century BCE.

Developments in Palestine remained nevertheless decisive. The return from exile after 540 BCE seems mainly to have included the leaders of the people. They re-established the cult and rebuilt the temple, which was eventually finished in 516 BCE. A central administration was organized in Jerusalem, although we can hardly speak in this connection of a Jewish 'state'. Rather, it was a question of a modest little district called Judea which, to begin with, was subject to the authority of the provincial governor in Samaria, who in turn was subject to the Persian satrap in Damascus. This tiny Jewish district consisted only of Jerusalem and the outlying land to a distance of 20-30 km. What was important, however, was not the size of

the diminutive district, but the special status it received within
the empire thanks to the Persian policy of religious tolerance.
The district of Judea became a 'temple state', consisting of the
temple city and its surrounding areas. The temple was under
the special protection of the Persian king; he contributed
economically to its rebuilding, and the high priest was allo-
cated a degree of authority sufficient to render Judea's
position unusual; later it became independent in relation to the
province of Samaria. We do not know too much about the
development in Judea in Persian times; reforms which
originated in the eastern Diaspora have been mentioned, and
in general the Persian period seems to have been a peaceful
time when the Jews were allowed to look after themselves, on
the condition that they paid their taxes.

Bibliographic Note to pp. 7-12
The Old Testament sources bearing on this period are 2 Kgs 17–25,
certain sections of the prophetic corpus, particularly Jeremiah 26–29
and 34–45, as well as Ezra, Nehemiah, and the *Antiquitates* (Book 10)
of Flavius Josephus. However, the use of Old Testament source
materials is not without its problems; only a critical approach to the
texts permits us to approximate the actual historical situation. See
such modern histories of Israel as, for example, J. Bright, *A History
of Israel* (2nd edn, London, 1972); J.H. Hayes and J.M. Miller,
Israelite and Judaean History (Philadelphia, 1977); S. Herrmann, *A
History of Israel in Old Testament Times* (London, 1975); I have myself
dealt with the later periods of Israelite history in *Israeliterne i
Palästina* (3rd edn, København, 1988), pp. 264-324. The Persian period
is described thoroughly in *The Cambridge History of Judaism*, Vol. I:
Introduction; The Persian Period (Cambridge, 1984) (with a biblio-
graphy, pp. 401-46). The exceptional position of Judea in the Persian
empire is treated by H.G. Kippenberg, *Religion und Klassenbildung
im antiken Judäa* (Göttingen, 1978), pp. 54-77.

Chapter 1

THE POLITICAL DEVELOPMENT

Alexander the Great, the Ptolemies and the Seleucids

It will be recalled that Alexander the Great conquered the entire Persian empire with extraordinary speed around 330 BCE. This achievement was in and of itself impressive, but its decisive significance proved to be that it created the basis for a cultural encounter between East and West which was to be of the greatest importance for the religious and cultural development of the whole of the Middle East, a development which also, of course, included the Jews.

Seen from this vantage-point, the fact that Alexander's empire fell apart after his death is 323 BCE is unimportant. The gates between East and West had been opened once and for all, and the conquered territories which were the inheritance of Alexander's generals became the objects of powerful Greek influence. Among the new states that arose at this time, mention need only be made of the Ptolemaic kingdom in Egypt and the Seleucid kingdom in Syria and Mesopotamia (which at times also included Asia Minor). The border between these two kingdoms lay at Tripoli in southern Syria, and for 100 years, that is, between about 300 and about 200 BCE, Palestine was dominated by the Egyptian Ptolemies. Once again we are not well informed about conditions in Palestine; Josephus is not expansive about the period, while the *Letter of Aristeas* and *3 Maccabees* are more informative, but mainly in legendary form. A number of Egyptian papyri contain some scattered information about property relationships, administration and trade. In general the period seems to have been poor in exciting events, in spite of the fact that several conflicts between the Ptolemies and the Seleucids affected Palestine.

The Ptolemies never installed a governor in Palestine. As a result the high priest retained his influential position and even became the Jews' representative to the Ptolemaic king in Egypt. The high priest was by birth the leader of the Jewish Council of Elders which was composed of members of the most prestigious members of the priesthood, and of representatives of the old aristocratic families. In many respects the Jews were self-governing; they had received the right 'to live according to the laws of the fathers', as it was later expressed. With a wise and cautious high priest as leader the Jewish community was sometimes able to obtain considerable concessions from its foreign rulers. Nevertheless, the Ptolemies insisted on asserting their influence wherever necessary, and the relationship between Egypt and Palestine was regulated through a number of Egyptian administrators who were posted to Palestine. These figures were answerable directly to the central government in Alexandria. They seem primarily to have served the ministry of finance, and in this capacity their main task was to collect taxes and to develop trade links with the north. Furthermore, the Egyptian military garrisons in the country had their own chiefs who were responsible for maintaining law and order in their respective districts.

All in all, the situation seems to have been acceptable for both parties. It was nevertheless to prove unstable; after the middle of the century the power of the high priest and the Council of Elders was diminished in a way which offers us some insight into the important changes which were then taking place in the social structure of the country. What happened was that the high priest Onias II had difficulties with the Ptolemies, after which they deprived him of his authority as the connecting link to the central administration in Alexandria, and gave it to a certain Joseph, son of Tobias, a half-Jew from the region east of the Jordan, who had previously been the lessee of the Ptolemaic collection of taxes in Palestine.

Joseph's career is symptomatic; behind it we can glimpse the new upper class that was emerging in Palestine in these centuries. The old Jewish aristocracy consisted of the higher reaches of the priesthood and of the oldest, most prestigious families—the ones who, as previously mentioned, held the power in the Council of Elders in Jerusalem. Now a new upper class was emerging; it was a monied aristocracy of parvenus, many of whom had only a slender connection with Jewish tradition and culture. The reason this was possible was a determinative change in the physiognomy of the country, a change which was to prove of paramount importance for the country's social and, in the long run, cultural and religious evolution. During the centuries after Alexander the Great cities were erected throughout the hellenistic kingdoms, each of which had the status of *polis*, like the classical Greek free city state. Some of these were newly founded cities and some were older communities which had obtained this new form of government. These cities functioned as military centres and as trading colonies in the new empires. Their original upper classes were, at least in the beginning, composed of ethnic Greeks and of peoples from the surrounding countries; they were administrators, military leaders and traders. But in the course of time a considerable number of Jews also entered these cities, obtaining a share in the local wealth and joining the upper classes themselves. The special character of such cities came from their democratic form of government, which was an absolute novelty in the Orient, and they became disseminators of the new hellenistic culture and of the hellenistically orientated syncretistic religions.

As we have observed, it was money and material wealth which upheld the new upper class in these cities; indeed, wealth and economic advancement were altogether characteristic of the Palestinian *polis*. The locations of such cities were hardly accidental; rather, they were situated at strategically important sites, so that the surrounding area could be controlled militarily. By the same token, however, they were also situated along the caravan routes and in the shipping ports, so that the important transit trade between East and West, which in precisely this period experienced unprecedented growth, conferred vast wealth upon these cities.

We shall mention here the names of the most important Palestinian free cities, and it should be noted that not all of them had achieved *polis* status in Ptolemaic times. Some of them derive, as their names suggest, from Seleucid or even Roman times. In the nature of things, most of them are

located on the Mediterranean coast and in the territory east of
the Jordan, where the important caravan route, the King's
Highway, ran from the far south up to Damascus. On the
coast, for example, we find Gaza, Ashkelon, Ashdod, Jabneh,
Jaffa, Straton's Tower (later Caesarea), Dora and Ptolemais
(Accho). East of the Jordan we find a group of cities which
made up the so-called Decapolis: Hippos, Gadara, Abila, Pella,
Gerasa, Philadelphia (modern Amman), Skythopolis (ancient
Beth Shean west of the Jordan) and others. Finally, in the
interior of the country: Samaria, Sepphoris, Antipatris,
Tiberias, Marissa and several others.

Returning to the Tobiad called Joseph, who attained such
considerable power in third-century BCE Palestine, we might
say that Joseph was a product of the new *polis* system. He was
a new, 'modern' type within comtemporary Jewish society:
open—almost opportunistic—to foreign influence; greedy for
money and power, ruthlesss, and above all, intelligent and
supple in his dealings with those in positions of power. The
same phenomenon recurred two centuries later when the
half-Jewish Herod, from strongly hellenized southwestern
Palestine, attained kingship over the Jews by appropriating
Roman culture and securing the favour of the Romans. In
any case, we must not underestimate the significance of the
new social and cultural phenomenon of the Greek *polis* in
Palestine, and we shall repeatedly return to the importance of
the new cities for the social and cultural development of
Jewish society in Palestine.

A decisive change in the political balance of the great powers
occurred in the years around 200 BCE, when the Ptolemies
were no longer able to hang on to Syria and Palestine. The
Ptolemaic army was crushed by the Seleucid king Antiochus
III in a major battle near the sources of the Jordan in
northern Palestine. The Seleucid assumption of power in
Palestine introduced a phase in the history of Judaism which,
in terms of drama and tumultuous events, stood in shattering
contrast to the previous peaceful centuries under the Persians
and Ptolemies.

Should we attempt to arrive at some perspective on the
historical developments during the following centuries, the
undertaking could be either simple or complicated. It would be

quite complicated if we wished to produce a detailed picture of the course of events. With, above all, the writings of the Jewish historian Josephus, the books of the Maccabees, and the many Greek and Latin accounts of the Seleucids, we practically suffer from an *embarras de richesses* in comparison with earlier centuries. We could accordingly follow the Seleucids' path to power through their many wars with the Ptolemies, as well as the extremely complicated intrigues around the Seleucid throne in the second century BCE. Likewise, we might attempt to describe the struggles for power in Jerusalem, in which a variety of high priests figured prominently. It would also be possible to plot out, month by month and year by year, the Jewish struggle for independence under the Maccabees after 170 BCE, and we could try to describe the changing attitudes of the latter Hasmonean kings towards the religious groups which had arisen within Judaism. The complicated familial relationships of the Herodean line would naturally also prove relevant; and, finally, we could attempt to explore the Roman thrust towards the east in the last pre-Christian centuries, their administrative dispositions in Palestine up to 135 CE, and so much more. An account containing even a merely reasonable amount of detail on this period would easily fill a book by itself.

However, as implied above, it can also be done more simply. It is not my intention in these pages to offer detailed accounts of the history of the Near East and specifically of the Jews during the centuries in question. I shall instead confine myself to sketching an outline of the history of the Jews during this period, and against this historical background I shall attempt to account for the social relationships and the cultural and religious developments of the period. In other words, the rich historical materials will not be exhaustively explored, and it could doubtless be said that in so doing we are taking a shortcut. But I would subscribe absolutely to the elegant, even if somewhat circumstantial, remarks of the author of 2 Maccabees (2.24-32) when he feels himself obliged to defend to the reader his decision to offer only an abbreviated account of the Maccabean campaigns.

Before we proceed to our account of the historical events, it might first be useful to consider from a bird's-eye view the more important facets of the Early Jewish period. Such a view reveals that the period is framed by two revolts, that is, attempts by force of arms to achieve political and religious freedom for the Jews. At the beginning, in the 160s BCE, we have the Maccabean revolt against the Seleucids in Syria; the revolt was thoroughly successful, and the Jews in fact achieved both political and religious freedom. At the end of the period we find the revolt against the Romans in the 60s CE. It ended catastrophically; that is, Jerusalem was destroyed, the temple was burned to the ground, and what might be termed the Jewish nation was never the same again after 70 CE. However, the Jewish religion triumphed and continued to survive. If we look at these two revolts in the same perspective, we perceive links between the two events which are of considerable importance.

The political freedom achieved via the first revolt was quite considerable, not only throughout the Hasmonean period in the second and first centuries BCE, but also under Herod the Great at the beginning of the Roman period and until the time of the birth of Christ. However, the struggle also had to do with religious freedom; or, more correctly, the orthodox had to do battle for the right to shape Judaism in a way they found congruent with the true Jewish tradition. This struggle was unceasing, whether the opponents were hellenized Jews, Hasmonean kings, illegal high priests, Herod and his sons, or the Roman procurators. This concentration on the question of the essence of the faith, which began during the first revolt, necessarily continued throughout the entire period. But this in turn meant that when catastrophe arrived, in the form of the unsuccessful revolt against the Romans around 70 CE, Judaism had already been through a prolonged purification process. In the course of this process some solutions had been reached regarding the relationship between state authority and religion. For this reason, the Jewish religion did not collapse when the Jewish state fell. Among other things, we shall examine this purificatory process; we shall attempt to make out just how strong the tensions were which plagued Judaism in this period, and to see how many new features entered into the Jewish religion while retaining the central tradition.

We paused previously around 200 BCE, when the Syrian Seleucids assumed power over Palestine. Everything began very well; Antiochus III tried to woo the Jews with benevolence, so that the first three years were tax-free. He paid for the restoration of property which had been destroyed by war. Priests and the upper echelons of the adminstration received permanent tax-free status, and in general the Jews received as much local autonomy as conditions permitted. However, Antiochus had forgotten to guard all the exits, and the Romans soon began to manifest their presence on the western horizon and to disturb the brief idyll. With their victory over the Seleucids at Magnesia in western Anatolia in 190 BCE, the Romans had leaped over the Bosporus and begun their series of conquests in Asia, moving continuously eastwards in the course of the next centuries. The Jews felt no immediate sign of the approach of the Romans, but one unpleasantness did occur: their tax-free status was over! The Seleucids were obliged to pay enormous taxes to the Romans, and they naturally milked the money from their occupied provinces, including, of course, that of the Jews.

Of more serious import was the fact that the Jews gradually forfeited the considerable autonomy they had received from Antiochus III. The immediate reason for this seems to have been the strong internal tensions within the Jewish population which led to virtual civil war conditions in the 170s. Some of these internal contradictions were at cross-purposes with one another; there was a Ptolemaic party and a Seleucid one; then there was the powerful family of the Tobiads in the region east of the Jordan, and the no less powerful high priestly Oniad line in Jerusalem; there was the old, heritable aristocracy, versus the new 'monied' aristocracy; and, finally, there was the new Greek-orientated or hellenistic reform party, whose natural opponent was the conservative 'old-Jewish' party.

The last-mentioned contrast was probably the most important of them all, and it is possible to feel its presence underlying all the others. The ultimate question was whether Judaism's further development would be determined by the hellenizing reform party or by the 'old-Jewish' faction. This entire problem, which was to be of such moment for Judaism during the centuries in question, was the result of the previous mentioned cultural encounter between East and West. The new cultural current which resulted from this encounter is usually termed 'hellenism', and it was, evidently, very much a composite phenomenon. It is difficult, if not simply impossible, to provide a satisfactory description of hellenism in all its complexity. Moreover, it is difficult for us to regard hellenism objectively. It may be understood negatively, that is, as a phenomenon of cultural disintegration—an indication of the submersion of ancient cultures—and so regarded as a decadent hybrid culture. This was, for example, the opinion of the Danish scholar, Vilhelm Grønbech. Alternatively, it is possible to understand hellenism positively, that is, as a creative cultural factor which had emerged from the serendipitous encounter between the best features of western and eastern culture. Seen in this light, Christianity may be held to be the noblest fruit of hellenism, as Johann Gustav Droysen maintained, who published the first comprehensive account of hellenism in the 1830s.

But no matter how one comes to understand hellenism, it remains clear that the understanding of human existence which was characteristic of hellenistic culture was as different from that of the old Israelite-Jewish culture as may be imagined. Greek philosophy and the Greek understanding of society and of the individual's relationship to it were frequently associated, sometimes quite curiously, with oriental myths and religious systems. Thus the Jew was confronted with an attitude towards life which must have seemed wholly strange to him: ranged against the belief in Providence which was characteristic of ancient Israelite (and more recent Jewish) thinking was a doctrine of fate which was frequently connected with astrological speculation. Likewise, where old Israelite and Jewish faith understood Yahweh, the God of Israel, as creator and lord, hellenism contained an ambiguous understanding which eventually developed into a true dualism. According to this dualism the soul rightly belonged in the divine world, but it was confined within the earthly envelope of the body here in the created world. Thus the soul longed for salvation and to be allowed to return to its heavenly origins. Such a view deprived the created world of significant content; existence could only consist of fleeting phenomena, and in consequence one either fled from the world via the mystery religions, or else immersed oneself in sensual indulgence.

We shall meet hellenism later on as a cultural phenomenon and as a religious quantity in a number of different connections. Here it will suffice to note how the new cultural current divided the Jewish population, and how the Selucids' political measures towards Jerusalem and Jewish society were interwoven with divisive tendencies, leading to the events which characterized a large part of the second century BCE and were important for Judaism's later development.

Of the kingdoms which arose after the death of Alexander the Great, that of the Seleucids was by far the largest, but it was also the most heterogeneously composed. The Seleucid kings were therefore obliged to utilize a variety of political systems in order to keep their empire unified. As far as we can see, the diverse subject regions enjoyed varying degrees of status within the Seleucid empire. The most characteristic of these was the previously mentioned establishment of free cities, which were formed after the model of the Greek *polis*. Hundreds of such free cities (or city-republics) were established in the Seleucid empire; we have already mentioned a number of the Palestinian ones, some of which were established as early as Ptolemaic times. The mere fact of the extremely mixed populations of the free cities, which included Greeks and other non-Jews, endowed these cities with an exceptional position. We should note that their status as free cities varied according to their respective character, but it was at all events typical of them that they were largely autonomous, and that their social outlook was notably *democratic*. These cities were actually governed by the people via the popular assemblies, councils, and magistracies.

However, groupings of the original inhabitants of the asiatic lands, naturally delimited from one another by virtue of their respective languages, prehistories, and geographical locations, made up national units within the Seleucid empire, each of which was styled an *ethnos*, a people. Often the type of government within such a unit was *aristocratic*, which is to say that the government was in the hands of a small group which in reality represented, for example, the higher levels of the priesthood and the old hereditary aristocracy.

Finally, it was also possible for a region with more arbitrary delimitations to comprise, within the Seleucid empire, what we today would term principalities. A territory of this kind was subject to a local prince, a *dynastes*, and the type of government was *monarchical*. The prince was obliged to pay his taxes to the Seleucid Great King; he may also have had to supply the latter with troops, but otherwise his sovereignty within his domains was absolute.

In which of these three ways was the relationship of the Jews to the Seleucids regulated? No simple answer will suffice; it is probably characteristic of the Jews' complicated relationship to their rulers that in fact their status changed several times. However, it is clear, at least to begin with, that the Seleucids regarded the Jews as an *ethnos*, a national group, This accords with the fact that during Ptolemaic and Seleucid times the government of Jewish society was aristocratic, power being concentrated in the Council of Elders, where the high priest was the leader of the representatives of the upper class.

Thus the high priest became the central figure in Jewish society. His functions were both religious and political, and his position cannot have been an enviable one. The office was, at least in theory, heritable within certain lineages; in reality, the choice of each new high priest had to be ratified by the Seleucid king, and, as we shall see below, the office became a pawn in the political chess game. The high priest was at all events bound to be loyal to the reigning Seleucid. At the same time the Jews regarded him as their spiritual and political leader. This ambiguous rôle contained the seeds of conflict within it, and indeed, the difficulties which arose after 175 BCE, when a new king, Antiochus IV Epiphanes, took the throne, concerned the office of high priest.

A complicated intrigue took form around this important office, and in the flickering configurations, all the previously mentioned oppositions are discernible. The high priest Onias III, who was deposed after 175, represented, on the religious front, the conservative, old-Jewish line, and on the social one, an ancient and prestigious family of priestly nobles, presumably accustomed over time to securing the high priestly position for its heirs. In addition, there are indications that the family's sympathies inclined more to the Ptolemies than to the Seleucids. Jason, Onias's successor in the office, was also descended from the Oniad line, although he had what were clearly hellenizing ideas. There are indications that he attempted to obtain *polis* status for Jerusalem; at all events, we do know that he encouraged the establishment of a number of Greek institutions in the city, such as a *gymnasion*, which was not only a novelty to the Jews, but also a monstrosity.

However, the first decisive break came a few years later, when Antiochus awarded the office to a certain Menelaos. He, too, was a warm adherent of the new hellenistic culture and, unlike the Oniads, he was a faithful supporter of the Seleucids. But Menelaos had a fatal flaw, namely that he did not belong to any of the lineages which, according to Jewish law, were entitled to assume the high priestly office. Moreover, he does not even appear to have belonged to Jerusalem's old aristo-cracy; he was a parvenu who had perforce to rely on the support of the Tobiads.

The appointment of Menelaos in defiance of the law naturally enraged orthodox Jews, and no doubt many sup-ported Jason when he attempted to regain his office by attacking Jerusalem with an army of mercenaries. In short, civil war as such had broken out, and this proved more than Antiochus was prepared to tolerate. He reappointed Menelaos to the office of high priest and at the same time made Jeru-salem subject to Seleucid administration. In this wise the relationship of Jewish society to the Seleucids had decisively changed. Previously, Jerusalem had enjoyed a special, inviol-able status as a temple-city and centre of the Jewish *ethnos*; now it was virtually subjugated to a new, Greek *polis*. Jeru-salem was bisected in a remarkable manner when Antiochus ordered the construction of a strongly fortified section of the city, called Acra, 'the Citadel', alongside the ancient temple city. Acra was accorded *polis* status, and its military was to dominate the city. It was in part a military colony, but it was also a residence for immigrant Greeks and pro-hellenistic Jews.

This arrangement drove a wedge among various groupings within Jewish society, so that the gap which had already existed between pro-hellenistic citizens on the one hand and the old fashioned orthodoxy on the other now became fully apparent. The former group saw the new order as a change in the right direction; that is, towards the evolution of all Jerusalem into a Greek *polis*, governed on democratic principles and liberated from the insular Jewish élite and the power of the priesthood. One can well imagine that many representatives of the leading circles, who were sufficiently well educated as to have made acquaintance with hellenistic culture, may have thought along these lines. Many were doubtless fascinated by the novelty involved, while others may have seen the possibility of securing trade advantages through a closer association to the West. One may well ask just why so many members of the priesthood saw any reason to advance a cause which would inevitably reduce the importance of the temple and the power of the priesthood. Or would this inevitably have been the outcome?

This is far from certain. When Jerusalem and the temple were compassed within the newly erected *polis*, the temple became the common cult site for both Jews and non-Jews. The Jews could still worship their God, Yahweh, in the temple; at the same time, Greeks and apostatized Jews dwelling in the Acra were able to worship in the same temple, as the latter had, in fine sycretistic fashion, identified Yahweh, the ancient god of the temple, with Zeus. Thus, in the plans of the hellenists the Jerusalem temple had been removed from its isolation and received a new, cosmopolitan importance as other ancient and famous local sanctuaries in the Seleucid empire had done. Thus they may have held that this development would, in the long run, be to the advantage of the priesthood. However, the orthodox Jews bitterly resented the pollution of the temple. A reaction had to come, and it was not long delayed.

The Revolt, the Maccabees and the Hasmoneans

The reorganization of Jerusalem's situation took place in 168 BCE. It was a victory for the hellenists, who had now tasted blood and consequently aimed at a complete change of the religious life of Palestinian Jewish society. In this connection it is vital to understand that the extensive innovations undertaken by the authorities at the expense of the Jews in 167 BCE were largely inspired by hellenistic circles within Judaism itself. The matter is frequently depicted as if it was Antiochus Epiphanes who was the author of all the various evils in question, and that the violent suppression of Jewish religion which took place in the 160s was solely the result of his 'uninhibited passion', as Josephus puts it. In recent times, however, we have become aware of the unreasonable extent to which Josephus, Maccabees and Daniel attempt to place all blame at the feet of the Seleucid ruler. In reality, Antiochus can hardly have been more than fleetingly concerned with the internal situation in Jerusalem, and he was no doubt a tool in the hand of the hellenizing Jews. That this procedure backfired to the extent that it did after the king had carried out the various reforms and prohibitions, so that in the end he was compelled to deal harshly with the recalcitrant elements in the population, is another matter entirely. Admittedly, Antiochus was no saint, but it would be reasonable to suppose that although the prohibition against the practice of the Jewish cult, which is reflected in 1 Macc. 1.41-51, was actually signed by the king, it was most probably composed by the high priest Menelaos and his adherents among the hellenized Jews in Jerusalem.

That this was most likely the actual course of events has been demonstrated by the Jewish scholar Elias Bickermann in his work on the Maccabean revolt, which appeared in 1937. Bickermann emphasizes the fact that the prohibitions in question apply solely to the Jewish society of Jerusalem and the tiny Jewish state in her environs, but not to Jews in any other part of Antiochus Epiphanes' kingdom, nor to the Samaritans, who were as fully bound by the Mosaic Law as the Jews themselves. There are many other indications pointing in this direction, and Josephus, who does not otherwise assign much that is creditable to Antiochus, does happen to cite the claim of the Syrian general Lysias that it was Menelaos who was the author of the whole problem, in that he had convinced Antiochus to force the Jews to abandon the faith of their fathers (*Ant.* 10.384). In other words, it was not the case, despite the claim of 1 Macc. 1.41-42, that Antiochus wished to foster a unified culture or religion within his empire. The problem was rather, as noted in 1 Macc. 1.11, that the hellenists in Jerusalem regarded the Jews' tendency to isolate themselves, culturally and religiously, as a hindrance to progress and development. The wish to break out of this isolation and be accepted into the society of nations, that is, to distance themselves from a form of life which the Greeks could only regard as barbarous, was the ultimate impetus behind the efforts of the Jewish hellenists.

Their procedure was radical indeed. The prohibitions which they cause to be enacted intervened deeply in the Jewish cult and lifestyle: the prescribed temple sacrifices were done away with and replaced by sacrifices upon a new, heathen altar; observance of the Sabbath and the festivals was forbidden; the laws governing ritual purity were violated through the use of swine and other unclean animals for the sacrifices, and participation in such sacrifices was made obligatory; the circumcision of newborn males was forbidden, as was the possession of copies of Jewish sacred writings.

Many Jews disobeyed the prohibitions and suffered martyrdom if they did not manage to flee into the desert. Malcontents gathered around the priest Mattathias, and the military leadership was given into the hands of his son, Judas Maccabaeus.

Thus, in principle, what took place was a civil war between two factions within Judaism itself. However, the Seleucid king did not dare allow the war to proceed unchecked, and Syrian reinforcements were sent to deal with the rebels. Both the books of Maccabees and Josephus tell us, in the most exciting way possible, about the Maccabean wars against the Syrian overlords. It was a guerilla war of the first order, and the military achievements of the Maccabees were astonishing. In a series of battles Judas defeated first one Syrian general and then another, so that he was ultimately able to invest the temple region of Jerusalem in December, 164, and then to reconsecrate the temple, which had lain desecrated for three years.

It should be mentioned that it was during these critical years that the book of Daniel, the youngest of the books of the Old Testament, was written. The remarkable vision sequences in the work, which are assigned to Daniel and projected back to the days of Nebuchadnezzar, describe these developments up to the culmination of the crisis in the light of apocalyptic insight. We shall later return to the book of Daniel.

The prohibitions against the Jews' free practice of religion were subsequently revoked, so that the rebels in fact obtained their immediate aim. The war, however, continued. The Syrian troops continued to occupy the Acra, that is, the *polis* section of Jerusalem, and the Seleucids continued to support the hellenistic party, who were still in control of the office of high priest. Menelaos' successor as high priest was named Alcimus; he was a Seleucid puppet who slew the Maccabean rebels where opportunity offered, and who desecrated the temple yet again. Thus the struggle to determine whether the hellenists, backed by the Seleucids, or the Maccabees, were to dominate Jewish society was doomed to continue. Judas won numerous victories, but finally fell in 161 in a battle south of Jerusalem. Eleazar, one of his brothers, was killed in another battle, having been crushed by a fallen war elephant. The leader who was to carry on the war effort was yet another brother, Jonathan. This figure was perhaps not as great a tactician as Judas; on the other hand, he understood the art of diplomacy. Thus he allied himself with the Romans and exploited the internal divisions within the Seleucid empire so well that he achieved the office of high priest in Jerusalem. This took place in 153 BCE, and the event may be said to signal the victory of the Maccabees over the hellenists.

Nevertheless, the war continued! And this time the ultimate goal was the total dismantling of the Seleucid yoke. A third brother, Simon Maccabaeus, was so successful that he managed to dislodge the Syrian garrison from the Acra in 142; he also obtained freedom from taxation, and was able to style himself 'prince of the Jewish people'. Thus the *polis* arrangement in Jerusalem was terminated, and the third type of organization employed by the Seleucids came into play: the Jewish society became a 'principate' under the monarchical leadership of a *dynastes* (later in the century they used the title 'king'). However, by this time the position of the Seleucids had become so weak that the subordination of the 'prince' to the Seleucid king was purely a matter of form, and it was characteristic of the new situation that it was the Roman senate which ratified Simon's new status. Roman influence was in the ascendant—a sign of things to come!

Simon was the last of the sons of Mattathias; he was also the first person who managed to combine the office of high priest with the secular hegemony in Jerusalem. He founded a dynasty which managed to control both offices for about eighty years, until the Roman occupation of Palestine. The dynasty in question is called 'Hasmonean', after the Maccabean family name, and its two most important representatives were John Hyrcanus (135-104) and Alexander Jannaeus (103-76). Both were talented military leaders, and after the conclusion of the struggle for independence they sought new objectives, such as expanding the Jewish rump-state of Judea through conquests in the other more or less Jewishly populated parts of Palestine, which the Seleucids were no longer able to retain.

To the south the Hasmonean conquests included *Idumea*, the southern half of the ancient Israelite state of Judah, which had in post-exilic times been occupied by Edomites encroaching from the territory east of the Jordan. The Jewish element of the population of Idumea was by this time thin on the ground. By the same token, the hellenistic influence was strong, particularly in the western part of the region, where such sizable *poleis* as Marissa and Adora were situated. John Hyrcanus accordingly attempted the 'enforced Judaization' of the populace. It is difficult to say whether this entailed the compulsory circumcision of all males in the area, but everyone was certainly obliged to pay tax to the temple in Jerusalem and to the Hasmonean king. No matter how much Idumea was ultimately integrated into the kingdom, it is significant that it was the rich, half-Jewish Antipater family who held the actual power in the region. Later, when Herod the Great, the pre-eminent representative of the family, acceded to the throne in Jerusalem, Idumea became an important component within the national unit.

The situation was somewhat similar in *Perea* in the territory east of the Jordan, which the Hasmoneans also conquered. Here, too, there seem to have been but few Jews, while the hellenistic influence from the many *poleis* was pronounced. It was here we encountered the wealthy Tobiad family which exercized so great an influence during both Ptolemaic and Seleucid times. After the incorporation of the region, Jewish immigration to the area east of the Jordan was continuous.

The two most interesting of the regions conquered by the Hasmoneans are in the north: Samaria and Galilee. Taken together they cover the main part of the ancient Israelite northern kingdom, and it has been described previously how this region was partially settled by non-Israelites from Syria and Mesopotamia in conjunction with the Assyrian conquests around 700 BCE. During the Persian period the relationship between the newly established mini-state of Judea and that of *Samaria* was particularly strained. The tension between Judeans and Samaritans was further exacerbated around 300 BCE by two factors: already Alexander the Great had constituted the town of Samaria as a Greek military colony with the status of a *polis*, and it was perhaps around the same time that the Samaritans established their own sanctuary on Mount Gerizim. Although any Israelite would have been forced to admit that the Samaritans were more Jewish than heathen (the Pentateuch was and remains the sacred canon of the Samaritans), it was also clear that their variety of Judaism did not conform to the Jerusalemite norm. Furthermore, the Jerusalemites could only regard the establishment of a sanctuary on Mount Gerizim as a schismatic act. According to a view which had won great popularity in the time around the Babylonian exile, a sacrificial cult of the God of Israel could only be legitimately maintained in Jerusalem. Thus all right-thinking Judeans were obliged to distance themselves from the Samaritans, and in spite of the 'enforced Judaization' which took place under the Hasmoneans the view has prevailed up to the present according to which the Samaritans—however few they may be—are a sect.

The last-mentioned of the areas conquered by the Hasmoneans was *Galilee*, immediately to the north of Samaria. It is difficult to evaluate properly the relationship between Galilee and Judea and Jerusalem. Earlier scholarship held that Galilee was a predominantly non-Jewish region from as far back as the 700s BCE until Hasmonean times. On this theory, the region came increasingly under Jewish influence throughout the Roman period as a result of the Hasmonean attempts at Judaization; that is, if one does not wish to claim, as the Nazi scholars did, that the region remained non-Jewish, so that it was possible to maintain that Jesus of Nazareth was a non-Jewish Arian!

However, if one critically examines the available sources today, one is inclined to see the problem in a different light: no doubt there was always a very mixed population in Galilee, since even in remote antiquity the region was interpenetrated by caravan routes and lay completely open to contact with the Phoenician coastal cities in a way that was quite different from the mountainous Judea. By the same token, however, there were always many Jews, so that it was by no means a striking event when in the course of the second century CE it was precisely Galilee that became the Jewish centre in Palestine. In other words, the Hasmonean efforts to 'Judaize' Galilee were scarcely as decisive as has been maintained.

Finally, there were the Greek *poleis*. The Hasmoneans deprived them of their privileges and attempted to erase their Greek features. The Hasmonean goal was clearly the establishment of a unified Jewish state, and it may fairly be said that by 100 BCE they had achieved much of what they intended, as their empire comprised the whole of classical Palestine and was approximately as large as that of David and Solomon had been. Little Judea, together with Jerusalem, which contained the temple, court, central administration, and the Council of Elders, enjoyed the same dominant position as in the era of David, and at least in theory (that of 'Judaization') the whole kingdom was populated by the Jewish *ethnos*. Theory is one thing, however, and practice another, and in reality it proved difficult to reconcile a number of disparate provinces which had remained separate for 800 years, each of which had run its own independent, evolutionary course for as long. The density of the actual Jewish population, which is to say, of those who felt themselves to be truly attached to the temple in Jerusalem, and who accordingly paid the temple tax, varied markedly from province to province, from temple-dominated Judea to schismatic Samaria.

Moreover, the Hasmoneans had other problems as well. It was mentioned previously that Maccabean wars had, or eventually received, two goals: religious freedom and national freedom. It was this very ambivalence which characterized the internal conflicts which subsequently developed. At the onset, unity was complete; in their struggles against the hellenistic reform plans and religious repression the Maccabees received support from Jews across a broad front. 1 Macc. 2.42ff. refers to 'the company of the Hasideans' (that is, the pious) and 'all they that fled from the evils' as the support groups of the Maccabees. But already after the year 164 BCE, when the temple had been reconsecrated and the Jews had recovered their religious rights, the Hasideans felt that there was no good reason to continue the struggle. And this conviction was intensified in all those whose sole motivation was to obtain religious freedom when the Seleucids made Alcimus high priest in 162 BCE. In spite of the fact that he later proved to be a scoundrel, this figure had the decisive advantage over his predecessor, Menelaos, that he belonged to the correct high-priestly lineage. Thus the Hasideans had actually attained what *they* desired, and to them the idea of continuing the struggle against the Seleucids might, in the worst possible cases, have led to the loss of the very right to religious freedom for which they had so laboriously battled.

Furthermore, it became a real burden on the relationship between the old allies, the Maccabees and the Hasideans, when Jonathan Maccabaeus assumed the high priestly office in 153. This was a fatal miscalculation on the part of the Maccabees, as they had as little right to the office in question as the once so abominated Menelaos! This established an oppositional relationship which continued throughout the entire period of the Hasmoneans, which is to say, until the Romans took power. Whereas this oppositional relationship was one of a number of factors which weakened Hasmonean rule during the first pre-Christian century, it also helped to strengthen the Hasidic movement, which we shall encounter later in the forms of Pharisaism and Essenism.

To the pious, the development of Maccabean, and, later, Hasmonean rule provided textbook examples of the fact that power corrupts. The Hasmoneans developed a secularized and ultimately tyrannical government, which speedily departed from the ideals of the struggle for freedom and sought only gain and position. It is ironical that as early as in the reign of John Hyrcanus the Hasmoneans had to seek the support of the aristocratic party, which was later called Sadducee. The irony lies in the fact that in this party we find a number of representatives of that upper class which had formed the hellenizing party early in the century, and which the Maccabean forefathers of the Hasmoneans had risked everything to combat. However, in political terms the Hasmoneans were pure pragmatists; to them the goal of creating an independent Jewish empire under a strong Hasmonean line legitimated the means chosen to achieve it.

The Hasideans were the ones who had suffered most and sacrificed most during the Maccabean wars, and their opposition to the Hasmoneans exposed them to persecutions which were no less savage than those prompted by Antiochus Epiphanes. Josephus relates that during persecutions enacted by Alexander Jannaeus around the change of the century, 50,000 orthodox Jews were the victims of Hasmonean massacres, although the figure may be unreliable. Conditions improved first on the death of Alexander Jannaeus in the 70s BCE. By this time portions of the Hasidic movement had consolidated into Pharisaism, which was so well rooted in the population that the Hasmoneans saw the advantages of maintaining a good relationship with this significant group.

The Hasmonean dynasty collapsed through a meaningless civil war waged by the two sons of Alexander Jannaeus in the 60s BCE. This time the Seleucids were entirely unable to restore order to the scene in Palestine. The Romans, however, who had already penetrated into Syria, could do so. In 63 BCE Pompey was able to take Jerusalem without much trouble, so that Palestine was to remain subject to the Roman eagle for several centuries.

Bibliographic Note to pp. 13-32
Above all, the following ancient texts inform us about the events between Alexander the Great and Pompey: the 1 and 2 Maccabees and Josephus, *Ant.* 11.304-14.73 (shorter exposition in Josephus, *Bell.* 1.31-151). Daniel 11 deals with the first part of the period in visionary form.

Further sources, more or less fragmentary, are mentioned in E. Schürer, *History of the Jewish People,* ed. Vermes & Millar, Vol. I (Edinburgh, 1973), pp. 63-120. In addition to the Jewish sources, the Roman and Greek historians are also relevant. The course of events from the time of Alexander is accounted for in several modern histories of Israel, e.g., M. Noth, *The History of Israel* (2nd English edn; London, 1960); *The World History of the Jewish People,* I, 6-7 (Jerusalem, 1972-75); J.H. Hayes and J.M. Miller, *Israelite and Judaean History* (Philadelphia, 1977), as well as in presentations of the history of Early Judaism (some of which, however, only cover developments from the Seleucid era): Schürer's work mentioned above; P. Schäfer, *Geschichte der Juden in der Antike* (Neukirchen, 1983); D.E. Gowan, *Bridge between the Testaments* (Pittsburgh, PA, 1976); A.R.C. Leaney, *The Jewish and Christian World 200 BC to AD 200* (Cambridge, 1984); H. Jagersma, *A History of Israel from Alexander the Great to Bar Kochba* (London, 1985); B. Reicke, *The New Testament Era* (London, 1978); E. Lohse, *The New Testament Environment* (London, 1976); Shaye J.D. Cohen, *From the Maccabees to the Mishnah* (Philadelphia, 1987).

My assessment of the conflicts leading up to the Maccabean rising is dependent upon E. Bickermann, *The God of the Maccabees* (Leiden, 1979) and on M. Hengel, *Judaism and Hellenism* (London, 1973); the same problems are treated in V. Tcherikover, *Hellenistic Civilization and the Jews* (Philadelphia, 1959); T. Fischer, *Seleukiden und Makkabäer* (Bochum, 1980); and K. Bringmann, *Hellenistische Reform und Religionsverfolgung in Judäa* (Göttingen, 1983). The Hellenistic *poleis* in Palestine are listed and treated in Schürer, *History,* vol. II, pp. 85-183, and in A. Paul, *Le monde des Juifs à l'heure de Jésus* (Paris, 1981), pp. 125-45, 187-210. The geographical conditions in connection with the Hasmonean conquests: M. Avi-Yonah, *The Holy Land* (Grand Rapids, 1966), and esp. the problems of Galilee: S. Freyne, *Galilee from Alexander the Great to Hadrian* (Wilmington and Notre Dame, 1980), and of the Samaritans: H.G. Kippenberg, *Garizim und Synagoge* (Berlin, 1971). There is a rich literature on hellenism as a political and cultural phenomenon; see e.g., W.W. Tarn and G.T. Griffith, *Hellenistic Civilisation* (3rd edn; London, 1952); F.W. Walbank, *The Hellenistic World* (Glasgow, 1981); M. Grant, *From Alexander to Cleopatra. The Hellenistic World* (New York, 1982); Vilh. Grønbech, *Der Hellenismus* (Göttingen, 1953).

The Romans and Herod the Great

Now the reason the Romans were interested in Palestine was most likely (as it certainly was in the case of Pompey) that they had already begun to entertain thoughts of acquiring Egypt, which was indeed incorporated into the empire in the succeeding decades. Prior to this event, however, Palestine formed the southeastern border of the Roman empire and was under the control of the legate of the province of Syria. Hyrcanus, a son of Alexander Jannaeus, managed to win the favour of Pompey and so received the high priesthood, though not the royal title.

History had repeated itself: after a brief period of freedom, the Jews were once more in the clutches of a world power. The Romans' grasp on their eastern possessions was firm, so that repeated attempts by various members of the Hasmonean line to attain power were in reality insignificant. A good sense of balance was required to serve under the Romans during this period, particularly around 50 BCE, for during these troubled years Caesar and Pompey vied with one another for power. The leading Jews had to take care to support the right candidate, thereby ensuring retention of the limited degree of self-government in their possession. Hyrcanus managed this feat; after the death of Pompey he went over to Caesar's side with alacrity, and the latter rewarded him with the title of 'ethnarch' (leader of the people). Of course, Caesar knew precisely what he was doing. Superficially, it might seem as though in addition to his high-priestly office Hyrcanus had now achieved political authority over the Jewish portion of the populace. However, Caesar was eminently familiar with the slogan *divide et impera*. Thus while he generously awarded Hyrcanus his impressive title, he simultaneously made Antipater 'procurator' of Judea.

In Antipater, Hyrcanus had acquired a competitor with whom he could not deal. Antipater was no less than the father of the man who was to become the later Herod the Great. They were Idumeans, which is to say that they belonged to the half-Jewish half-Edomite population in southern Judea. In the days of Alexander Jannaeus, the family had already risen to prominence in Idumea. Now, under Antipater, its power extended into Judea. Antipater installed the young Herod as governor in Galilee, and when the Roman political constellation once again shifted, Hyrcanus was unable to keep abreast of the changes, so that Herod and his brother were able to assume the political leadership of the Jewish territories. The Hasmonean Hyrcanus had once again to make do with the high-priestly title. This, however, made no great odds, as Hyrcanus had never been able to actualize his nominal political power with respect to Antipater and Herod. Parenthetically, we can add that he suffered the unfortunate fate of falling into the clutches of one of his nephews, eager to carve his own path to the power and dignity of the high priesthood. This he achieved by cutting off Hyrcanus' ears, since the maimed were ineligible for the office.

At the close of the 40s BCE it had become apparent that the role of the Hasmoneans was finished, and that the future belonged to Antipater and Herod. The latter were wealthy, and thus able to offer the appropriate bribes to the Roman politicians; moreover, both were dynamic and possessed political will to an extent never matched by the latter Hasmoneans. Finally, they apparently also had a sixth sense which kept them from transgressing against the Romans. They exercised their virtuosity in playing off the various interests in the Roman camp against one another, thus achieving considerable advantages, not only for themselves, but also for the Jews in Palestine.

After the death of Antipater, it was incumbent on Herod to overcome one last obstacle before he could assume the position to which he thought himself entitled. The Parthians, that is, the Iranian people who had taken power in Mesopotamia after the Persians, and who blocked the Roman advance towards the east for centuries, forced their way into Syro-Palestine around the year 40, and helped install the last Hasmonean pretender on the throne. The Romans had to withdraw, and Herod with them. This, however, proved to be Herod's chance, for when he arrived in Rome as a refugee, the Romans promoted him to the kingship of Judea. Admittedly, this was a coronation of a somewhat conditioned character, since the crown and throne belonged to Herod on the understanding that he would have to expel both the Hasmoneans and the Parthians! However, the Romans had correctly recognized that this clever and ambitious man could be useful in solving the problems of the eastern border of their empire.

After three years, in 37 BCE, Herod occupied the throne in Jerusalem as a 'client king' of the Romans.

When Pompey had conquered Palestine twenty-five years earlier, he had divided the Hasmonean kingdom into two jurisdictions: the Jewish *ethnos* were accorded the regions regarded as predominantly Jewish, namely the part of Judea surrounding Jerusalem, a part of Idumea to the south, Perea immediately east of the lower course of the Jordan, and finally Galilee. The rest had been restored to the hellenistic *poleis*, which the Hasmoneans had attempted to expunge as political quantities. What the Romans now gave to Herod consisted in the first instance of the four Jewish territories of Judea, Idumea, Perea, and Galilee. However, Herod knew how to remain in Roman favour, and in the course of the next two decades he achieved sovereignty over the whole of Palestine as well as substantial areas in the territory east of the Jordan. His empire was larger than the Hasmonean rule had ever been. Moreover, his relationship to the Romans was such that his kingdom enjoyed as many privileges and as much freedom as the system permitted. He governed independently of the provincial governor in Syria, and was not obliged to quarter and supply the Roman troops. He had his own army and complete sovereignty in domestic matters. On the other hand, he had no right to conduct an independent diplomacy outwards, and was obliged to make his army available to the Romans as occasion demanded. Finally, his right to issue coinage was also limited.

Herod's diplomatic astuteness achieved for the Jews the maximum that could be otained from the Romans. It was no doubt his ambition to recreate a Jewish empire within the framework of the Roman empire, an empire that would equal that of David and Solomon, and in fact he succeeded in large measure. In many respects Herod's reign was a new golden age in which the comfortable relationship with the Romans brought about considerable development in international trade, an increased standard of living for everyone in the kingdom, stable internal relations, greater esteem in the world at large; in short: everything went very well indeed.

Why then does posterity recall Herod as a tragic figure? It is not only because early Christian legends characterize him as the evil villain whose scurrilous designs ultimately miscarry. No, the tragic aspect resides primarily in Herod's split personality, which, though consisted of intelligence, courage, and a degree of magnanimity, was coupled with something primitive and brutal. Moreover, there was also his strained relationship with the Jews. To them, Herod was never more than a parvenu, the descendant of degenerate Edomites from the wild desert regions beyond the Dead Sea, possessed of no true relationship to Jewish culture and religion. The Jews despised him as the born aristocrat disdains the nabob. Had the Jews been able to acknowledge Herod's good side, his bad qualities may not have come to the fore. As things developed, however, he was forced to answer the Jews' disdain with contempt and barbaric cruelty. This pattern proved to be self-reinforcing, so that a kingdom which could have been brilliant and illustrious degenerated into a tyranny of the worst sort.

This situation was not ameliorated by the fact that Herod was an open, warm adherent of hellenism. His admiration was surely unfeigned, although it was no doubt also clear to him that a positive attitude towards western culture made things easier for anyone who desired to win Roman acceptance. The orthodox Jews saw in many of Herod's measures a repetition of those efforts at hellenization which had sparked off the Maccabean revolt 150 years earlier. Furthermore, although Herod's construction of a new and beutiful temple to Yahweh in Jerusalem no doubt pleased many sincere Jews, they cannot have been as enthusiastic for his donation of funds to a temple of Apollo in Rhodes, or for his construction of temples in Samaria and Caesarea, dedicated to the emperor Augustus. Like earlier hellenists, Herod probably saw his mission as the unification of Judaism with the new spiritual movements emerging out of the West, in order to fit his kingdom organically into the Roman empire.

The hellenistic free cities in Palestine enjoyed a renaissance under Herod. Already Pompey had restored their rights, and Herod supported them powerfully by rebuilding and enlarging many of them. Cities with *polis* status, such as Samaria, Caesaraea, Antipatris, and Phasaelis contain the most extensive construction projects of this period. Herod saw an advantage to be won by creating a balance between the

Jewish *ethnos* and the Palestinian-hellenistic *poleis*. He would
be able to strengthen his own position if he could play both
quantities off against one another; he seems to have learned
the principle of 'divide and rule' from his Roman friends. And,
of course, if things fell through in Palestine, it could only be
useful to have friends with a common cause in the hellenistic
poleis of the neighbouring lands. Thus we note that Herod
contributed financially to the establishment of a sports
facilities in Tripoli and Damascus, to defensive works in
Byblos, to theatres in Sidon and Damascus, to roads in Antioch,
and so on. A true cosmopolitan had come to power in
Jerusalem!

In may ways, Herod is reminiscent of King Solomon, who
also had a weakness for external pomp, but who knew the
value of international connections in his efforts to create a
great and powerful Israel. But the Israelites had been prepared to forgive Solomon his many errors; he, of course, was
the son of the unforgettable David.

The Jews' relationships to Herod remained discordant.
They were never blinded by the outward brilliance that
surrounded him, and an eruption of open conflict was a
constant threat. The Hasmoneans still enjoyed prestige in the
popular eye, but then, Herod never underestimated their
dangerous potential. Herod's construction of the numerous
defensive works and fortresses round about the country (one
thinks of Masada, Herodion, Hyrcania, Machaerus, etc.) was
not solely directed against external enemies; if occasion arose,
they could easily have been directed against internal threats.

Although Herod had married into the Hasmonean line, the
tensions with this old royal line persisted and ultimately
developed into a bloody family drama. There would be no point
in listing the many members of the family who fell victim to
Herod's mistrust. There is no doubt that his suspiciousness
was pathological, although it is equally clear that in many
cases it was not unmotivated. It is likely that the only reason
the Hasmoneans refrained from attempting a coup was that
the Romans obviously preferred Herod.

Herod's ire affected more than just the members of the
Hasmonean line, however; he waged a stubborn struggle with
those who had earlier been accounted the leaders of Jewish

society. He dispensed the office of high priest according to his own pleasure; if a given high priest fell from Herod's good graces, he was simply removed and replaced by yet another. Herod had nullified the old aristocratic Council of Elders already when he assumed power. His procedure in this instance was firm and characteristic of Herod: he had forty five of the most eminent Jewish leaders executed on the pretext that they supported the Hasmoneans. The men in question were most probably the nucleus of the Council of Elders, or Sanhedrin, as it was called at the time, and it is obvious that this organ remained without influence throughout the rest of Herod's reign.

Moreover, not only the Council, but also the old family-based aristocracy, which had previously had difficulties trying to hold its head up in the face of pressure from the Hasmonean monarchy, was weakened under Herod's absolute government. Against this, the new monied aristocracy who were mentioned previously, came into the ascendant. We shall later discuss the relationship between these two aristocratic groups and their relationship to the Sadducees. At all events, it was entirely natural for Herod to seek the support of these *nouveaux riches*. Many of them came from the Diaspora, but they were particularly recruited, as mentioned above, from the hellenistic free cities. In fact Herod himself derived from a similar milieu in southwestern Palestine, a region which had been strongly influenced by foreigners, and in which attachments to Jewish culture and religion were weak.

Herod was obliged, nevertheless to take account of the Pharisees, who had gradually developed into a power factor in Jewish society. They were dangerous to Herod in that, unlike most other Jews, they would have preferred a purely Roman regime in the land to Herod's despised monarchy. Eventually they got their wish with the Roman procuratorial government in the first century CE.

The Sons of Herod, the Procurators, and the two Rebellions

Herod's later years were full of incendiary feuds with the sons of his various marriages. He managed to execute three of these sons and, in consequence, changed his will all of three times before he finally died in 4 BCE. The last will was recognized by the Romans; according to its terms the empire was to be divided among three sons. The central part of Palestine, consisting of Idumea, Judea, and Samaria, went to Herod Archelaus. Another son, Herod Antipas, received Galilee and the southern part of the territory east of the Jordan (Perea), while a third son, Philip, received the northern part of the territory east of Jordan.

Herod Antipas and Philip retained their territories until the close of the 30s CE, although their status in the Roman system was lower than their father's had been; they were not kings, but 'tetrarchs'—literally, rulers of a quarter of a kingdom. They lacked the dynamism of their father, but knew how to steer a careful course between the Romans and the leaders of the Jewish communities in their districts. Both were helle-nistically influenced and so built cities bearing Greek characteristics (e.g. Tiberias and Caesarea Philippi). It was in the kingdom of Herod Antipas that both John the Baptist (Perea) and Jesus of Nazareth (Galilee) were active around the year 30; Herod Antipas was responsible for the death of John the Baptist.

The possessor of the bulk of Palestine, and bearer of the slightly more elevated title of 'ethnarch' (prince of people) was, then, Herod Archelaus. The most interesting detail known about him is the fact that he had already disappeared around 6 CE, having been deposed by the Romans and exiled to Gaul. Subsequently, his kingdom, the central Jewish region in Palestine, received a completely different status from the northern and eastern parts. It did not receive a new ruler from the line of Herod, but was subjected immediately to the rule of a Roman *procurator* (or *praefectus*, during the first decades of the period). This arrangement, which was only interrupted by Agrippa's brief monarchy in the 40s, was to have fateful consequences for the Jews later on in the century.

All else aside, Herod and his sons had shown considerable understanding of the Jews' special character; above all, they had known that it was not worthwhile to provoke the populace unnecessarily. Likewise, the Romans were tolerant in principle and often went to considerable pains to avoid controversy. However, the lower ranks of the Roman functionaries had a particular lack of sympathy for the Jews' preoccupation with religious regulations and ceremonies, not to mention their willingness to face death rather than transgress them. Such stubbornness, in the case of what the Romans held to be subordinate matters, merely served to irritate them. Much depended on the functionary in question, and confrontations frequently ended in disaster. There were a considerable number of procurators, of whom Pontius Pilate, who held office in the 30s, was one. The gospels reckon him to be of quite noble character, while the Jewish tradition has only the harshest account of him; clearly, he was unnecessarily provocative. The functions of the procurator included seeing to military affairs in Palestine, tax-collecting and, in certain cases, legal matters. But of course his authority entitled him to intervene arbitrarily, offering rich possibilities for conflict.

As mentioned above, the northern and east-Jordanian parts of Palestine were ruled by the Herod-sons until the close of the 30s. After a short period under direct Roman rule these regions, soon followed by Idumea, Judea, and Samaria, were transferred to the authority of Agrippa I, a grandson of Herod the Great who had had the wit to keep on good terms with the emperors Caligula and Claudius. Yet again Palestine was assembled under the rule of a single king; his empire was virtually as large as that of Herod the Great. Moreover, Agrippa was both a pious and a good man who stood well with the Pharisees and the leading Jews. At the same time, he was severe against the heathens and the Christians; but that is quite another matter. His reign lasted only a few years, as he died in 44 CE. The book of Acts (12.19-23) has preserved one of the legends concerning his death.

Palestine returned to the rule of the Roman procurators, and in the course of the score of years from 44 to 66 CE the relationship between Jews and Romans became increasingly tense. The final rebellion occurred in 66, and was the culmination of a long number of conflicts and collisions. There were many reasons for the conflict: the Romans' economic exploitation, the tensions between the Jews and the Greek-influenced mixed populace of the larger cities, infringements both great and small of the Jews' religious rights, the ignorance of the Roman officials, and last but not least, the strong growth of Jewish liberation movements through the century. The immediate cause of the outbreak of rebellion was relatively modest, but the procurator Florus over-reacted, and once things had begun to snowball there was no stopping the process. The Romans sent General Vespasian to deal with the rebels, and there was nationwide conflict. Later, we shall have occasion to study the rebellious movements more closely, so we shall not now follow the course of events which led to the suicide in the fortress of Masada, in 74 CE, of almost a thousand partisans, who preferred to take their own lives rather than fall into Roman hands.

The event which contributed most decisively to the breaking of Jewish resistance was the fall of Jerusalem and the destruction of the temple in 70 CE. Vespasian was by this time emperor of Rome. Thus it was his son Titus who conquered and plunged the city. It was also this event which decisively changed the Jews' situation in Palestine. The temple was destroyed, and has never been rebuilt. On its former site is the Islamic Dome of the Rock; only the western external wall of the ancient temple enclosure, known as the Wailing Wall, has been preserved by the Jews through the centuries as a holy place. With the disappearance of the temple the Jewish temple cult, which had been one of the strongest pillars in Jewish religious life, ceased once and for all. This led to a shift in the centre of gravity of Jewish religion, a factor to which we shall return.

At the same time there occurred violent realignments of the social pattern in Palestine. Almost overnight the large Jerusalem priesthood lost its importance; it suddenly lacked all social function, and accordingly had no position. Furthermore, the Council, the aristocratic body which was at the same time the highest religious and legal organ in Jewish society, both in and beyond the borders of Palestine, and which expressed Roman acknowledgment of at least some sort of self-government, was dissolved. Palestine became an 'imperial province' under the rule of a 'legate' with the rank of senator. The temple-state, together with its special rights which had been traditional since Perisan times, no longer existed. This meant that from this time forward the Palestinian Jews stood in the same relation to the Romans as did the Jews of the Diaspora elsewhere in the Roman empire. New and more severe taxes were imposed, and, to add insult to injury, the Romans continued to collect the Jewish temple tax, but sent the monies received on to the temple of Jupiter at the Capitol in Rome! The Roman military outposts in the country were heavily increased, and the 10th Legion was established permanently in Jerusalem. Moreover, as the quartering of the troops was at Jewish expense, this, too, was an extra burden.

Extensive Roman confiscations of land primarily affected the upper classes, who not only lost their power in the Council, but were exploited as well. The lower classes were also harshly affected, at least the small landowners among them. Many of these were merely copyholders on their lands, and were easily expelled via confiscations, imposts and taxes. Those who probably did best out of the situation were the artisans and tradesmen of the middle class, as the many Romans who came to the country offered them some advantages.

The scribes were a small, yet significant element in the middle class. Some of them had been associated with the Council and had to leave Jerusalem. However, they settled in Jabneh/Jamnia on the Mediterranean coast and there founded a 'rabbinical academy', which later assumed the religious functions of the Council. In the next century the rabbis moved up into Galilee, and it was in their ambit that the spiritual centre of Judaism came to reside. The rabbis represented the Pharisaic movement; superficially, their tiny assembly seems merely a modest replacement for temple and Council. However, their importance is not to be underestimated; it was they who determined the future course of Judaism; that is, they ensured that the Law became central to Jewish religious life. Furthermore, it was the rabbis whose discussions strove for an authoritative interpretation of the Law, and ultimately of the whole of the Old Testament, once they had delimited the Jewish Bible around 100 CE and determined which writings were to be accorded canonical status. We shall return to all these problems later.

The Jews had learned nothing from their many troubles, and there were several revolts among the Diasporan Jewish communities in the years 115-117, during the reign of Trajan.

We know nothing about the causes of these disturbances, but they seem not to have been directed against Roman rule, consisting instead of conflicts between Jews and non-Jews in Egypt, Cyrene (in north Africa), and Cyprus. These conflicts developed into open warfare, with the result that the Romans were forced to intervene. Christian and Roman historians preserve some information about these events, and they seem to have been violent in the extreme. Dio Cassius relates, in connection with the situation in Cyrene, that the Jews murdered 220,000 citizens, and maintains that

> they would eat the flesh of their victims, make belts for themselves of their entrails, anoint themselves with their blood and wear their skins for clothing; many they sawed in two, from the head downwards; others they gave to wild beasts, and still others they forced to fight as gladiators (*Rom. Hist.* 68,32).

This (let us hope, exaggerated) description is probably evidence of the growth of anti-Semitism in the latter part of the ancient period (Dio Cassius wrote sometime after 220 CE). There was also a rebellion in Mesopotamia, which the Romans crushed with great brutality.

Palestine seems not to have been affected by the otherwise violent currents of Trajan's reign. On the other hand, a rebellion did occur from 132-135 CE, during the reign of Hadrian, and eventually spread throughout Palestine. The occasion seems to have been provided by a Roman plan to rebuild Jerusalem as a military colony, Aelia Capitolina, in connection with which they intended to construct a temple of Jupiter on the former site of the Jewish temple. The rebellion was every bit as comprehensive as the one sixty years earlier, and it had an extra dimension, in that it was led by Simon Bar Cochba, the 'Son of the Star', whom great numbers in the Jewish population revered as the Messiah. On this occasion there was no Josephus to write the history of the war, and we are only poorly informed by the rabbis and later Roman and Christian authors. One thing, at least, is certain: the rebellion was suppressed after three years, the situation of the Jews deteriorated yet again, and the Romans denied them access to

Jerusalem, which thus became a purely Gentile city, complete with imperial statue and temple of Jupiter.

Bibliographic Note to pp. 33-45
The sources which supply us with knowledge concerning Roman rule in Palestine until Hadrian consist primarily of Josephus' *Antiquitates* (from 14.74 to Book 20) and *Bellum* (from 1.152 to Book 7), as well as his autobiography; they give a very detailed account of the period up to 74 CE. Also to be consulted are the texts in Schürer, *History*, Vol. I (cf. note p. 33). Many passages in the New Testament throw light upon some decades in the first century CE, although the reports concerning Herod the Great in Matthew 2 have the character of legends. Most of the modern works mentioned in the note on p. 33 cover this period as well. See also: W.W. Buehler, *The Pre-Herodian Civil War* (Basel, 1974); E.M. Smallwood, *The Jews under Roman Rule* (Leiden, 1976); M. Grant, *The Jews in the Roman World* (London, 1973); A. Schalit, *König Herodes. Der Mann und sein Werk*, (Berlin, 1969); S. Perowne, *The Life and Times of Herod the Great* (London, 1956); S. Perowne, *The Later Herods* (London, 1958); Y. Yadin, *Masada* (London, 1966); Y. Yadin, *Bar Kochba* (London, 1971); P. Schäfer, *Der Bar-Kokhba-Aufstand* (Tübingen, 1981). Literature about the first Jewish uprisings is listed below, p. 135. On Josephus, see: Per Bilde, *Flavius Josephus between Jerusalem and Rome* (Sheffield, 1988).

Chapter 2

THE SOCIAL PATTERN

Palestine

In a well-known passage in his apologetical work, *Contra Apionem*, Josephus underlines the excellence of the law of Moses and shows how a society which, through the ages, has been based on the Mosaic ordinances, surpasses all other types of society. Some people, as he says, have a monarchical form of government, in which all power resides in a king; others bow to the rule of an oligarchy, that is, a 'rule by the few' in which power is distributed among the members of a single social class; and finally, there are others who have adopted a more democratic type of government, and so, as Josephus expresses the matter, have given political power to the masses. But not the Jews, as he goes on to say; Moses was not attracted to any of these types of government; rather, he devised a constitution for which Josephus can find no better word than *theokratia*, a divine government 'placing all sovereignty and authority in the hands of God'.

Josephus probably coined the word 'theocracy' himself, and in so doing, was doubtless aware that he was expressing a Jewish ideal of a divinely guided society rather than depicting any social reality. After all, one must recall the vast importance of the monarchy throughout Israel's history. Yet, as far as the post-exilic and early antique periods are concerned, scholars often characterize Jewish society as having a theocratic government. The monarchy disappeared with the Babylonain exile. With the re-establishment of the Jewish state of Judea after the return, in the little district around Jerusalem to which we have so far referred as the 'temple state', it was the priesthood, and, above all, the high priest, who became primary in Jewish society both in and outside Judea.

Of course, it makes sense to describe such a priestly government as a theocracy. Nevertheless, one does not have to dip
very far down into the Persian period to discover a development towards a type of government which is far more adequately described by what Josephus termed an oligarchy; that
is, rule by a chosen few. By this is meant, of course, the Council
of Elders in Jerusalem the institution which we encountered
in the previous chapters. In principle at least, this institution
possessed all religious, juridical and political power in Jewish
society, within the limits which had been established by the
real wielders of power. As we have already seen, the Council
consisted in the first place of the 'high priests'—the leading
elements of the priesthood; in the second rank was a group of
elders: representatives of ancient and prestigious families; in
the third place were the scribes, who were legal and theological experts. In Roman times the Council was composed of
seventy-one members.

Although this Council of Elders was dominated by the
priests (the high priest was traditionally the chairman), it is
clear that the *upper class* as such tended to expand its grasp.
Obviously, the Council consisted quite exclusively of the upper
class. The Council was an aristocratic government, in which
high priests and elders were in control, thanks to their origins
and familial influence. Only the scribes possessed their seats
by virtue of their expertise, but their position was simply
administrative. Thus the formation of the Council was not a
reflex of some tendency towards democracy. Nor should we
imagine that there was any popular demand for enlarged
suffrage. Just as Jewish familial structure was patriarchal, its
social structure was correspondingly aristocratic.

Furthermore, it was not only in Jerusalem that the upper
class was in control. Lesser councils of elders were formed out
in the Jewish provinces. Their membership consisted of the
rich and important in a given village or district; admini-
stratively they were subordinate to the Great Council in
Jerusalem.

It was not always easy for the Council of Elders and thus for
the upper class to retain power. We have already seen how the
Ptolemies and the Seleucid rulers appointed royal administrators in Palestine whose prerogatives were both military

and financial. A strong royal official, combined with a weak high priest, was able to reduce the power of the Council of Elders considerably. And this was no less intolerable when the royal official happened to be a half-caste Jew from the new *polis*-upper class, as the cases of the Tobiad Joseph and, later, Antipater and Herod, so clearly illustrate.

Things became complicated in a different way during the Hasmonean period, when the Hasmonean rulers assumed both royal and high-priestly honours at one and the same time. A conflict between monarchical and oligarchical principles was inevitable, and in the end it was the Council of Elders which gave way to the absolutist tendencies of the Hasmonean government. The upper class seems to have been divided, in that the ancient hereditary aristocracy lost ground, while the new monied aristocracy, plus some elements of the priesthood, formed the Sadducee party, which proved to be so influential during the reign of the latter Hasmoneans. Something similar seems to have occurred during the rule of Herod, who apparently saw his advantage in weakening both the priestly and ancient hereditary aristocracies in the Council of Elders, preferring to surround himself with people of cosmopolitan views from the new upper class. Under the Roman procurators of the first century CE the old upper class also had difficulties asserting itself. The Sadducees and Pharisees dominated the Council of Elders, and the influence of the Pharisees grew continuously.

In other words, the 'theocracy' was a debatable quantity. In reality, Palestinian social development in this period was quite uneven. We note a continual tension between oligarchical and monarchical tendencies, while more democratic prompting may be glimpsed both in the middle class Pharisaic party, and in the various partisan and rejuvenatory movements which appeared during these centuries.

We shall nevertheless dwell for a short time on the upper class. We have already mentioned the priestly aristocracy. The designation 'high priests' refers not only to the incumbents in the office of the high priest, but also to previous high priests and high-priestly families, and in the last instance to a sizable group of eminent priests, each of whom was responsible for certain areas within the temple administration. These individuals were drawn from the ranks of priestly noble families, and were among the wealthiest people in Jerusalem. Their duties in connection with the temple were largely ceremonial, but their participation in the Council of Elders extended their power far into the profane realm. Primary among these was the high priest. In spite of the fact that his power was severely curtailed at times, as was that of the Council of Elders, the high priest enjoyed an exalted position in the eyes of the people. The office was hereditary, and its ancient, historic origin endowed it with an aura which not even Herod could remove. A strong personality could accomplish much in that office, with respect both to the people and to the wielders of power.

While the priestly aristocracy was homogeneous in both professional and economic terms, the profane aristocracy, the quantity we have referred to as the hereditary aristocracy, was more highly differentiated, even though it was true in most cases that their wealth and prestige were anchored far back in time. Whereas previously it had been the case that wealth was indissolubly connected with land ownership, it was characteristic of this period for many members of the aristocracy to increase their wealth by participation in international trade, now flowing into Palestine. Not least because of the many hellenistic *poleis*, Palestinian trade was flowering as it had not since the days of king Solomon, when external trade was a royal privilege. At this time, however, there arose an entire subclass of merchants in Jewish society. This extensive trade consisted in part of goods which were in transit from the Arabian markets (aromatic products, spices and similar luxuries), in part of agricultural products from Palestine itself (grain, olive oil, wine and so forth), and finally of imported products which the country itself was unable to produce.

Administrators at the court and central administration were also recruited from the more eminent families of the upper class. A ramified administration arose around the Hasmonean royal house, and this did not shrink during the Herodian epoch. Other members went into the service of the foreign potentates as tax-gatherers, an office which not only enabled its incumbent to collect taxes for the Romans, but also to garner considerable private income for himself. All things considered, this was a time which offered rich developmental potential to the upper class. At the same time, however, we see that this was a class which was obliged to wage war on several fronts in order to maintain its position within a society which was developing progressively.

In terms of numbers, the upper class—in theory, at least, the locus of social power—was modest. By way of contrast, the *middle class* was more extensive, and in the very developed society which Jewish society of these centuries was (or at least became), the middle class was highly differentiated. This was not so much the case out in the country, where most were farmers, many of them clients of the great landowners, whose upper-class existence took place in the cities. A village had its council of elders, and perhaps a town scribe, and, if there were royal lands in the vicinity, there was a royal official to administer them. But in the towns—and this applies as much to the hellenistic free cities as to the larger towns in the Jewish territories (above all Jaffa and Jerusalem)—we find many different occupations to have been characteristic of the middle class: merchants, artisans of all sorts, temple functionaries, court and central-adminstrative personnel, and finally, in the case of Jerusalem, the extensive group of priests.

As we have seen, only the leading priests belonged to the group which we have termed the priestly aristocracy; the remainder were ordinary priests and levites, whose numbers, however, were considerable. Scholars have attempted to calculate how many priests and functionaries, broadly construed, were attached to the Jerusalem temple, and the result was 18,000! Admittedly, they did not all live in the city, as many came from the provinces and served their turns by rota, according to a sophisticated system. Their various tasks were carefully allotted, and we may suppose that it all ran perfectly.

We have already seen that the middle class had no political influence. We also observed, however, that a new development was under way, which, in conjunction with the central position of the Pharisaic party later on in the period, eventually gave representatives of the middle class increased influence on both religious and political life. In the first centuries of antiquity there was only a single group from the middle class which had access to the Council of Elders and thus to a share

of power, namely the scribes, and their juridical and theological insight was indispensable to the Council. As, later on,
the scribes more or less merged with the Pharisaic party, they
paved the way for the ascent of the middle class to power and
influence.

Naturally the middle class profited from the general
prosperity. At the same time, however, the antique period was
characterized by a social unrest which had negative consequences for many members of the middle class. Noticeable
dislocations occured within the social pattern, and external
trade entailed a powerful concentration of capital into the
hands of the upper class, as we have seen. Extensive purchase
of land by the upper class, combined with harsh land policies
on the part of the royal house and the Romans, meant difficulties for the lesser landowners. This led to the
proletarization of the rural populace and their flight to the
cities, not least to the new hellenistic cities. The lack of political
stability in the country, the shifting forms of government, the
harsh taxation policy, the changing religious tendencies with
many foreign influences, all contributed to a climate of
imminent social dissolution. Groups of rootless citizens arose
who were relegated to the margins of society: militant
partisan movements, whose emergence was produced by
religious, social, and political forces; religious sectarians like
the Essenes and the Qumran sect, and, later, the young
Christian community. Such movements were collectors of the
dissatisfied, and most of their membership came from the
middle class.

Thus it is possible to see that there were contradictory
tendencies in both the upper and middle classes. The upper
class were experiencing powerful economic advancement,
but, by the same token, difficulty in retaining their power. The
middle class also got a share in the general prosperity and,
eventually, some share of power, but at the same time suffered
from social unrest and instability.

We have already perceived that the many problems in the
middle class entailed the growth of the *lower class*. In addition
to slaves, this group comprised those without property, rural
workers and the city proletariat. The difficulties of paying
taxes and meeting land-use contracts, plus, conceivably,

paying off loans, could quickly force a small farmer off his land, so that his only recourse was to take what work was available from the great landowners. Those who fled to the cities led a wretched existence; there was frequent unemployment, and they were often reduced to begging and charity, if they did not simply take the law into their own hands and steal the necessities of existence. The situation was worse for those who, having once led a reasonable existence in the middle class, were reduced by force of circumstance to the lower class. They were likely candidates for the above mentioned protest and rejuvenation movements.

Bibliographic Note to pp. 47-53
Information about social conditions is occasionally to be found in Josephus (the quotation on p. 47 from *Contra Ap.* 2.164-67), in the New Testament, and in Rabbinical sources. In addition to the works mentioned in the note on p. 33, several of which touch upon social problems, reference should be made to J. Jeremias, *Jerusalem in the Time of Jesus* (London, 1969); J. Leipoldt and W. Grundmann, *Umwelt des Urchristentums* I (Berlin, 1967); S. Safrai and M. Stern, *The Jewish People in the First Century* I-II (Assen/Amsterdam, 1974-76); W.W. Buehler, *The Pre-Herodian Civil War and Social Debate* (Basel, 1974); H.G. Kippenberg, *Religion und Klassenbildung im antiken Judäa* (Göttingen, 1978); G. Theissen, *Sociology of Early Palestinian Christianity* (London, 1978).

The Diaspora

The centre of gravity of this work is its account of the Jews' situation in Palestine. It would nevertheless be appropriate to comment, if at no great length, on the situation of Jewry in the diaspora, that is, of those Jews who dwelled outside of Palestine.

It is characteristic of the period after Alexander the Great, with which we are dealing, that there were lively interconnections between the various countries in the Mediterranean basin, more so than ever before. As we have seen, Alexander's conquests entailed that many non-Jews settled in Palestine, while at the same time many Jews abandoned Palestine and settled far from home. So many, in fact, that when we arrive at the era of Roman domination, more Jews dwelled outside of Palestine than in their mother country.

Now it was not only during the hellenistic-Roman period that emigration from Palestine was considerable. In our introductory sketch we (rather briefly) presented the events which took place in conjunction with the Babylonian exile. Already at that time—around 600 BCE—many Judeans were carried off to Babylon, while many others fled into Egypt. In this way, two of the diaspora communities were formed that were to become so important later; they survived throughout the Persian period, in the fifth and fourth centuries, and persisted throughout antiquity.

The acceleration of this movement away from Palestine in hellenistic-Roman times had many reasons; some of them have been discussed in the course of our study of the historical developments: political difficulties, religious persecution, conflicts between various groups within Jewish society, possible over-population in Palestine, and better economic possibilities abroad. At all events, the extant diaspora communities grew explosively in the centuries approaching the birth of Christ.

As we should expect, the largest concentrations of Jews outside of Palestine were located in the eastern end of the Mediterranean: in Babylonia, Egypt, Syria, and Asia Minor. Such cities as Alexandria in Egypt, Nehardea and Nisibis in Mesopotamia, Antioch in Syria, Sardis in Phrygia and Corinth in Greece, had large Jewish minorities. Later this was also true of Rome. The Jews in these countries and cities were distributed through all classes of society, but our fund of information concerning Ptolemaic Egypt indicates that many Jews there had military and administrative functions. In fact, in Egypt there were even specifically Jewish military encampments; a group of Jews might constitute a settlement in which they partly lived from agriculture and partly constituted a military reserve unit. Within such settlements— and there were several of them—the Jews were able to observe their religious regulations in peace. The most famous was Leontopolis in the Nile Delta. Its fame derives from the fact that it possessed one of the period's few Jewish temples outside Jerusalem, thought to have been founded by Onias IV, who was obliged to flee from Palestine in connection with the many conflicts centring on high-priestly office in early Maccabean times. In reality, a temple with a sacrificial cultus outside of Jerusalem contravened all laws, or at least those of the Jerusalemite priesthood. The temple in Leontopolis remains mysterious, not least because it does not seem to have had any significance for other Egyptian Jews.

If one really wishes to understand the situation of the Jews in the diaspora, one must examine their status in the great cities. In this connection we are probably best informed about conditions in Alexandria, whose Jewish population was greater than that in any other hellenistic city. Alexandria was a *polis*, a free city as described above, and its Jewish contingent formed a *politeuma*, that is, a recognized and distinct group of foreigners possessing the right to settle in a *polis*. They made up a semi-autonomous population element, a 'city within the city'. Each *politeuma* had its own constitution and regulated its internal affairs through leaders, who operated independently of the government of the *polis* in question. A system worthy of a 'free city'!

It was not only in Alexandria that such conditions obtained. In most of the hundreds of Greek *poleis* which arose in the hellenistic-Roman world, there eventually developed Jewish minorities of greater or lesser size, and the *politeuma* system is attested at numerous sites. It was even enacted in the Greek *poleis* in Palestine. Against this background it is possible to understand that these centuries witnessed the emergence of enterprising and prosperous Jewish populations throughout the Mediterranean region. The Jews enjoyed all the advantages, particularly as far as business was concerned, of the *polis* system. Moreover, their lively participation in the economic life of the various cities by no means entailed surrendering their cultural and religious uniqueness. On the contrary, it was in Alexandria that two beautiful monuments to Jewish spiritual life appeared: the Greek translation of the Old Testament (the so-called Septuagint), and the extensive works of the Jewish philosopher Philo, who made splendid efforts to reconcile Jewish faith with Greek philosophy.

A continuous influx of Jews to Rome characterized the first centuries before and after the birth of Christ. In Rome they appear to have had a different status from that which they enjoyed in the Greek free cities. This is not to say that they lacked privileges; the decisive difference lay in the fact that it was not the Jewish minority as such which achieved special status at Rome. Rather, an individual Jewish community, gathered around a synagogue, was regarded as a *collegium*: the Roman designation for the many 'lodges', most of them religious, which flourished in the city, and which had special permission to convene for purposes of worship. The privileges accorded to the Jews, however, were more extensive than those normally granted under the *collegium* system. The Jews were not only entitled to observe the Sabbath, but the leadership of the individual synagogue was responsible for the administration of the synagogue in question, in addition to the legal problems of the congregation. Even when other *collegia* were closed under both Caesar and Augustus, the Jews retained their rights.

Problems occurred in Egypt during the transition from Ptolemaic to Roman rule in 30 BCE. In the first place, the change of power meant that many Jews lost their positions in the Ptolemaic army and administration, declining to the lower social status of farmers. In the second place, conflicts of interest arose between the Greek *polis* citizens, who were not obliged to pay taxes to the Romans, and the Jewish *politeuma* citizens, who were not full citizens and so had to pay taxes. For their part, the Jews did what they could to attain citizenship equivalent to that of the Greek citizens of the city, and so to obtain tax relief. The Greeks however, held that the Jews already enjoyed considerable privileges from the Romans, and felt that the Jews exploited the special protection extended to them by the Romans at the expense of other Alexandrine population groups. This was at least one of the causes of incipient anti-Semitism and persecution of Jews in Alexandria, and elsewhere in the diaspora.

The most important issue for diaspora Jews was preservation of their religious rights. Under Roman rule they were dispensed from the obligation to perform military service, which could not be reconciled with keeping the Sabbath or with the laws regulating ritual purity; nor were they obliged to participate in the cult of the Emperor. The centre of their religious life was the synagogue, where they held services without sacrifices on the Sabbath. The institution of the synagogue no doubt had its origins in the diaspora, but it also became very important to the religious life of Palestinian Jewry, and we shall return to it later. It would be impossible to overestimate the importance of the synagogue as a central focus for Jews in foreign lands. The regular services controlled tendencies among Jews to allow themselves to be assimilated into their heathen milieux, and the priests and legal experts who were attached to a synagogue attained natural leadership positions among the Jews who gathered around them.

But in reality, it was the temple at Jerusalem which was the centre of Jewish religious consciousness. All pious Jews in the diaspora paid temple tax amounting to half a shekel (two or three days' pay for a worker) a year, while wealthier Jews tried to visit Jerusalem as often as possible. In principle, all adult male Jews were obliged to be present in the temple for the three pilgrimage festivals, Passover, Pentecost (the Feast of Weeks), and the Feast of Booths. Not even the Jews in Palestine were able to live up to this demand, not to mention those spread all over the Mediterranean world. Nevertheless, many diaspora Jews strove to visit the temple at least once in their lives, so that every pilgrimage festival saw many foreigners in Jerusalem. And more than a few diaspora Jews travelled in the autumn of their lives to Jerusalem in order to die in the vicinity of the temple and be buried on the Mount of Olives.

How did Greeks and Romans regard the Jewish religion? The tolerance of foreign religions which was characteristic of hellenistic-Roman culture was of benefit to the Jews. Moreover, the oriental religions often fascinated Westerners, so that more than a few became proselytes of the Jewish faith. Nevertheless, there were limits as to how far this understanding extended. In one of his decrees, Augustus said that the Jews were to be permitted to gather in their synagogues on the Sabbath 'in order to receive public instruction as to their national philosophy', incidentally revealing what is, undeniably, a somewhat inaccurate description of Jewish faith and worship! Similar ignorance allowed many Westerners to feel themselves repelled by the exclusiveness of the Jews and by their dismissive attitude towards others' religious faith and cult. Many regarded the Jews as 'strange', if not simply 'barbarian'. In this we may see yet another reason for the growth of anti-Semitism in the centuries after the birth of Christ, an anti-Semitism which was eventually enhanced by the antipathy of many Christians towards Jewry. The developmental lines run directly from these attitudes in antiquity up to the present.

Bibliographic Note to pp. 53-58
E. Schürer, *History*, III,1 (Edinburgh 1986); E.M. Smallwood, *The Jews under Roman Rule* (Leiden, 1976); A. Kasher, *Jews in Hellenistic and Roman Egypt* (Tübingen, 1985); S. Safrai and M. Stern, *The Jewish People in the First Century* I-II (Assen/Amsterdam, 1974-76).

PART II

JEWISH RELIGION IN ANTIQUITY

Hardly anyone would deny that there is a reciprocal relationship between political and social factors on the one hand, and religious currents and innovations on the other. But this relationship is hardly unambiguous; it is debatable in which direction the strongest influence is felt. If we look back on the political and social developments which we have tried to trace in the preceding section, and if we look forward to the religious movements and innovations which we are about to tackle, we find that the change in political and social relationships was, in many cases, the undeniable catalyst which initiated the development of new religious conceptions and ideas, as well as new religious constellations. The antique period was, as mentioned earlier, a time of new departures in every respect; there were violent upheavals in social and power structures, and religious forms of expression changed correspondingly in an attempt to relate to the new social forms and political signals.

At the same time one ought not to lose sight of the fact that religious reactions repeatedly initiated events which proved to be important, in the long run, for both political and social developments. This applies to the Maccabean revolt in the 160s BCE and to the anti-Roman revolt in the 60s CE; both were undeniably religious reactions whose consequences for Jewish society were, at the time, as incalculable as they were fateful.

All this is rather obvious. It is nevertheless tempting to try to reduce the entire development, political, social and religious, to a single formula. If we look back over the preceding sections, it seems appropriate to maintain that the tension in the period may be characterized by the paired conceptual terms *polis* and *ethnos*, the tension consisting of Greek influence on the one hand which emanated from the many Greek free cities in Palestine, and on the other the traditional Jewish faith and

understanding of society, as was present in the Jewish populace of the country. It is certain that this dualism was present
throughout the period, and that it proved time and again to be
determinative of the course of events. There is no doubt that
this tension between the two cultures was of greater significance than any of the external circumstances connected with,
respectively, Seleucid, Hasmonean, Herodian, or Roman rule.
It was not Antiochus Epiphanes, or the Hasmonean kings, or
Herod and his sons, or the Roman procurators who determined developments. Rather, all were imprisoned in the field
of tension between Eastern and Western culture, so that in
one or another way they all became tools of an inevitable
developmental process.

Having said this, it is nevertheless important to emphasize
that there is a very real distinction to be made between political and social developments in the period on one side and
religious developments on the other. In political terms, violent
things happened throughout the whole of the antique period,
and it ended in catastrophe and dissolution. From a social
point of view the evolution may be regarded positively.
Urbanization and international trade brought about an
improved standard of living, although the shadowy side of this
was the increased social stratification and proletarization of
certain parts of the populace. At all events, by the end of the
period, Jewish society was very different from what it had
been at the beginning.

However, if one were to maintain that after the fall of
Jerusalem a Jewish religion emerged which, under the
impress of these centennial developments, was something
completely new—perhaps representing a suitable mixture of
ancient Israelite religion and later philosophical and religious
currents from the West—one would be much deceived. It is
true that Jewish religion was subject to many influences
during the period, and that these influences were occasionally
so powerful, that Judaism was in danger of losing its unique
character. What is truly extraordinary is that when we come
to the end of the period, not so very much has actually happened to the Jewish religion. Yet, on reflection, this is perhaps
not so strange after all. Jewish religion had had to struggle to
survive. Some might say that it did so by encapsulating itself; it

might be more appropriate to say that it erected defensive works. During these centuries, the Jewish believer reflected on his inheritance from his fathers, in the sense that he attempted to clarify the question of what was central and indispensable to Jewish religion. He attempted to find a viewpoint from which he could determine, at any given time, just what was authentic in Jewish religion, and what was foreign to it.

This defence process took effect in several ways. In the first place, the Jews had to decide which of the many 'sacred' writings within the compass of Judaism, that had accrued over time, were authorative and normative. It became necessary to compose a 'canon': a collection of writings which could be used to decide questions concerning the central tenets of the faith. The Pentateuch was probably collected and completed by the third century BCE. After this time other books were incorporated so that around 100 CE; that is, after the fall of the temple, a precisely delimited Jewish Bible existed. The efforts maintained throughout the period in question, to define the teachings of Judaism in written form, were of decisive importance. They provided strength, in that it became more difficult for new ideas to force their way into Jewish religion, both from within and without. Every discussion of the content and nature of Jewish religion had necessarily to take place within the limits enforced by the canon; every view had to be supported by reference to scripture. This no doubt entailed the religion becoming somewhat more static; on the other hand, anyone wishing to defend the integrity of Jewish religion can point out, with the book in his hand, that the faith of the Jews is not a faith with arbitrary contents. At this time, the fact of a religion receiving its codex, its written norm, was by no means a matter of course. It was no accident that Mohammed characterized the Jews (and also the Christians), several hundred years later, as 'people of the Book'.

It is one thing to agree on the extent of a collection of writings; it is quite another to agree as to their interpretation. Disagreements of this kind may force a breach in the defensive works, re-opening the possibility of infiltration from foreign ideas. But in this connection the interpretative efforts of the Pharisees and the later rabbis may be seen as a further phase in the defensive project; or rather, it was a phase which ran parallel to the process of canonization and continued far beyond it into the Middle Ages, and, strictly speaking, to the present. The results of this continual process of interpretation and understanding were determinative for the Jews in all their relations. They influenced the decision procedures of the Council and thus its decisions in religious and juridical matters. They regulated the priestly work in the temple in conjunction with the sacrifices. They were expressed in the preaching of the synagogue, and, above all, they aided the individual Jew to understand what he was to 'believe and do'.

In the next section we shall return to the problems connected with the Law, Holy Scripture, and the teachings of the rabbis. It has been our aim here simply to show that it is not unwarranted, when, in connection with our ensuing treatment of the basic structure of Jewish religion, we maintain that its main lines in the antique period represent a genuine continuation of classical Israelite religion, as we know it from the Old Testament, and that this basic structure is preserved in spite of all outward changes. To that extent, the defensive works are effective.

But some change did take place—naturally, one might be tempted to say. Hellenistic culture may have been unable to influence Jewish culture fundamentally, especially if we make comparisons with other oriental religions which were totally transformed in their confrontation with western religious and cultural currents. Yet some concepts and complexes of ideas do appear in Jewish religion, which clearly took their origin from the hellenistic world. This is manifest in such later works in the Old Testament as, for example, Ecclesiastes; it is also true of the apocryphal book of Sirach, dating from the second century BCE, and the apocryphal book of Wisdom, of a somewhat later date. Not least, stoic philosophy and religion made their influence felt here. Stoicism was probably the phenomenon of hellenistic thought least foreign to the Jews, and towards which they in fact felt themselves attracted. In the stoic concept of God, and particularly in stoic ethics, it was possible for them to see features related to Jewish thought, and in the following we shall repeatedly meet concepts and formulations which derive from stoicism. Otherwise, it is in the apocalyptic writings of the antique period that foreign elements are especially evident. Yet it is also significant that apocalyptic speculations were kept at a safe distance from mainline Judaism, so that apocalyptic writings were not incorporated into the canon. Those Jews who cultivated apocalyptic were not centrally placed in Jewish society; indeed, some of them separated off from the temple congregation. We shall return to all this subsequently.

One might expect that the Jewish communities in the diaspora experienced some influence from their gentile surroundings. This was not the case, at least not to the extent that one would suppose. Precisely the fact that the Jewish congregations in Mesopotamia, Egypt, Asia Minor, Rome, and so on were surrounded by gentiles meant that those Jews who had not simply been assimilated were eminently conscious of their Jewishness. In principle they were subject to the temple and Council in Jerusalem, and this bond was intimate, as we have seen. The diaspora Jews paid their temple tax and—an important feature in this connection—all manner of cases were subject to appeal to the Council at Jerusalem. Many diaspora Jews were unable to read Hebrew, but the Old Testament was translated into Greek—the Pentateuch perhaps already in the third century BCE—so that they were able to hold worship services in the synagogues. In their daily life they were able to observe Jewish rules in ways hardly different from contemporary Palestinian practice.

But there was a small Jewish elite in the diaspora, above all in Alexandria, which was concerned with Greek philosophy. Philo, who was probably born around 20 BCE, was the writer belonging to this group whose works have been best preserved. Philo emphasized that the Jewish religion was his fulcrum and point of departure, but by means of the allegorical method he reinterpreted the Biblical narratives and laws into abstract ideas which he had found in philosophy. His thought is thoroughly permeated by a pronounced dualism, and both platonic and stoic ideas were among his presuppositions. But he was an isolated phenomenon, and his significance was greater for the early fathers of the church than it was for Judaism.

In the following sections we shall first attempt to penetrate to the basic structure of antique Jewish religion. We shall then adopt a sociological vantagepoint by examining some groupings, or 'parties', as they have also been termed, within Judaism. Each of these groupings had a religious character that was peculiarly its own; at the same time, however, they also represented particular social classes. Finally, we shall concern ourselves with apocalyptic, which represents the actual innovation within the Judaism of antiquity.

Chapter 3

THE BASIC RELIGIOUS STRUCTURE

The Jews have always possessed a religious genius. With its lush multiplicity of religious expressions and interpretations of life, the Old Testament bears witness to a concentration, in this numerically small people, of a special religious capacity. It is no accident that the Jewish religion was to be of decisive importance for the two world religions, Christianity and Islam.

Scholars have often attempted to show that the life and vitality which is evident in ancient Israelite religion from c. 1200 to c. 300 BCE, and which we encounter in the Old Testament, had disappeared by the time of Early Judaism, around the birth of Christ. In this epoch, it has been claimed, Jewish religion had become a barren and fossilized religion of law. This oversimplified account is in no way satisfactory.

It is certainly true that changes had occurred in Jewish religion by the antique period, but, as we have seen, they were not fundamental changes. In relation to the classical Israelite religion, these changes are primarily a matter of relocating the centre of gravity, a process of selection in which one of the lines running from the Old Testament religion was assigned more weight than others. One must recall that ancient Israelite religion was an extremely composite quantity, and that the component which points back to Moses and the giving of the law on Sinai was only one of many. Nevertheless, it was this part of the ancient Israelite religion which was cultivated in the antique period, so that the law recieved a central place in the Jewish consciousness. In reality, the Old Testament law had arisen over many centuries, and presumably only a very small part of it may be traced back to Moses around 1200 BCE. But the Old Testament received its final form in a highly edited and retouched Jerusalemite edition. Moreover, precisely in Jerusalem in the seventh to sixth centuries BCE a particular ideology, now called 'Deuteronomistic', placed heavy emphasis on the legislatory aspect of the tradition, and it was this emphasis which continued on into the antique period.

Of course, this does not mean that the other sides of Old Testament religion did not come into their own. It was probably the apostle Paul who was mainly responsible for our present, one-sided understanding of the Jewish religion of antiquity as a sterile religion of law. But Jewish piety has at all times received rich nourishment from, for example, the psalms and the prophetic writings. As we shall see later, the Old Testament Wisdom tradition also became especially important in the antique period.

Around 200 CE the *Mishnah*, the first of the great rabbinical works, was completed. It is a collection of laws which were originally transmitted orally, and which were developed in the centuries around the time of Christ. One of the tractates in the Mishnah, the *Pirqe Aboth* ('the traditions of the fathers'), contains statements deriving from Jewish scholars from early times, among which is the following: 'By three things is the world sustained: by the Law, by the (Temple-)service, and by deeds of loving-kindness'. The statement has often been regarded as a brilliant summary of the essence of Jewish religion. When, in what follows, we shall attempt to penetrate to the basic underlying structure of Jewish religious life in antiquity, we shall regard Jewish religion from these three points of view. First, we will examine the concept of the Law; then we will investigate Jewish anthropology and ethics; and finally, we will examine the temple and synagogue as the two institutions which provided Jewish piety a framework.

Law and Revelation

Since we have repeatedly stated above that 'the Law', that is, the Torah, was the central religious concept of ancient Judaism, it would be reasonable to attempt to clarify what the Jew understood the Law to be. The very expression leads our thoughts in a particular direction; we imagine something in the nature of a 'moral code' or 'collection of rules', or perhaps even a sort of 'etiquette primer', with religious overtones. Such a view is reinforced when we learn that the rabbis of antiquity undertook to count the laws and so arrived at the conclusion that the laws of the Pentateuch consist of 613 injunctions and prohibitions. And when we are additionally told that the rabbis concluded that, of these, the 248 injunctions correspond to the 248 joints of the human body, while the 365 prohibitions correspond to the body's 365 veins and arteries, then all of our prejudices about Judaism as a law-religion, and indeed as a religion which was oddly allied to Cabbalistic speculation, seem to be confirmed.

It is the easiest thing in the world to ridicule the Jews' relationship to the Law; innumerable examples may be found of the rabbis' quite curious reasonings about individual laws. There is practically an academic tradition in which the author of a book like this one lists some of the more comical examples of rabbinical attempts to circumvent, for example, the provisions regulating the Sabbath. But if one follows this course, one may be certain of one thing: that one prevents oneself from ever understanding what the Law is.

To a Jew the Law is more than mere injunction and prohibition. It is revelation. To an orthodox Jew the Pentateuch contains everything that it has pleased the Lord to reveal to his chosen people Israel about his nature and will, neither more nor less. In principle the *entire* revelation is contained in the Law, that is, in the Pentateuch. The rest of the Old Testament contains nothing which goes beyond the Law—and certainly nothing which contradicts it.

In classical Israelite times, that is, earlier in the first millennium before Christ, a different concept of revelation was operative. Revelation was not confined to a single book, for there was at that time no precisely delimited collection of writings possessing canonical status. In Ancient Israel, divine revelation was experienced in many and various ways. In Genesis the patriarchs Abraham, Isaac, and Jacob are described as recipients of revelation. Later, other selected persons appear through whom God makes his will known; these are the so-called 'men of God', such as Samuel, Elijah and, above all, Moses, the figure who became to later Judaism the revelation recipient *par excellence*. The same applies to the prophets down to the middle of the millennium, Amos,

Hosea, Isaiah, and so on, whose writings have been preserved
in the Old Testament. Revelation had many channels, and the
ordinary Israelite saw the finger of God, and thus his
revelation, in natural and historical events.

But this living concept of revelation underwent a transformation in the centuries following the Babylonian exile. This
was interconnected with the canonization of the Old Testament writings, mentioned above. The Pentateuch, which had
continually received changes and additions over the years,
was eventually 'closed', so that revelation was effectively
confined to its limits. Moses wrote what he wrote, one might
have said, and not a tittle was to be added to it. But the
rabbinical process of interpreting scripture, not least that part
of the Pentateuch which makes up the Law in a narrow
sense—that is, the many laws which regulate the Jew's daily
life—continued. This means that the living legal tradition
from which even the Pentateuch had derived its legal
material, lived on, even after it was encapsulated once again
in a book—namely in the great Talmudic works which were
not completed until the Middle Ages.

One can easily imagine a conflict within the Judaism of
antiquity between, on the one hand, the written Law of the
Pentateuch, which all agreed contained the whole of
revelation, and on the other hand the oral tradition of the
rabbis, whose endless series of new legal formulations
attempted to cover every conceivable situation in which a Jew
could legitimately expect guidance as to what he or she should
do. In short, a conflict between the static and the dynamic. But
the rabbis do not—or will not—acknowledge this problem. In
the first place, they claim that their legal formulations are not
'new', arguing that on Sinai Moses had received not only the
written law (the Pentateuch), but also the unwritten law,
which has since been transmitted by word of mouth down
through the generations. The written law is nevertheless the
higher, for which reason a rabbi will invariably argue that his
'new' formulation is either to be understood as an interpretation of one of the Pentateuchal laws, or as directly
derivable from a Mosaic formulation.

The problem appeared in a different guise in Early Judaism,
namely in the question as to the relationship between the

Pentateuch and the rest of the Old Testament. If the entire revelation was contained in the Pentateuch, then the rest of the biblical writings had necessarily to take a subordinate place, which is what actually happened. As has already been said, to a Jew in antiquity it was obvious that the other Old Testament writings cannot reveal anything about God's nature or will which goes beyond the revelation contained in the Pentateuch. At most, the other writings may be regarded as developments of the revelation that was vouchsafed to Moses. In the words of George Foot Moore: 'Thus all the rest of the sacred books, with no detraction from their divine inspiration and authority, are an authority of the second rank: they repeat, reinforce, amplify, and explain the Law, but are never independent of it'. This could not be more accurately put.

If we follow the definition according to which the Law is to the orthodox Jew the entire revelation of God's nature and will, we must acknowledge that the centre of gravity becomes displaced. The Law is then no longer simply the many commandments and prohibitions in the Pentateuch. Rather, it becomes in the widest sense the basis of Jewish existence, the source from which Jews derive their understanding of God, and from which comes their faith in God as the god of the world and of Israel. The many commandments and prohibitions remain, but they are not to be seen in isolation from the account of the God who is the creator and lord of the world— the God who chose Abraham to be Israel's ancestral father, who led the Israelites through the desert away from Egypt, who entered into a covenant with them on Sinai, and who finally gave them the land of Canaan to possess. It is within this salvation-historical framework that the Law, narrowly considered, with all its 613 commandments and prohibitions, is to be understood. The Law is indissolubly wedded to the concept of Israel's election. In the Old Testament, the election of Israel is uniquely bonded to the covenant and means that Yahweh leads his people through history, while his people in return acknowledge him as God and undertake to honour his demands: that is, 'keep the covenant'. This concept was also maintained in Early Judaism, with the difference that it was the Law which simultaneously revealed the election and its 'history' as well as the covenant and its demands.

If it was the case that to the Jew of antiquity the Law was the revelation of God's nature and will, in what follows we shall best understand the Law by studying it in the light of the early Judaic understanding of God, as distinct from the classical Israelite understanding.

It is admittedly difficult to get a grip on the specifics of the understanding of God in Early Judaism. Naturally, it was based on the Old Testament understanding of Yahweh, the God of Israel. What enables us to speak of the 'specifics' of the early Jewish view of God is once again the matter of the centre of gravity. The understanding of Yahweh changed from the days of Moses and over the centuries, so that in its final form the Old Testament contains a picture of Yahweh composed of quite disparate features: Yahweh as a tribal god or god of warfare; Yahweh as the god of the covenant and the divine regulations; Yahweh as creator and ruler of the world, and of the heavens; and, not least in the prophet proclamation, Yahweh as the judge of his people Israel and of the gentiles, who nevertheless remains true to his promises to Israel. These many different features reflect a development in which the Israelite understanding of Yahweh changed along with changes in Israel's social situation.

Naturally, the Judaism of antiquity took the Old Testament understanding of Yahweh to be a unity; the God of Israel was thought to have been one and the same from the dawn of time, so that all of the features mentioned above became part of the early Jewish understanding of God. But some features were emphasized more than others. It was taken for granted that God is the creator of heaven and earth, and that he dwells in heaven, as is often stated in prayers and psalms of praise—but nearly always *en passant*, as, for example, in the beginning of the *Eighteen Benedictions:*

> Great, mighty, and awesome God,
> God Most High, creator of heaven and earth,
> Our shield and shield of our fathers,
> Our refuge in every generation.
> (After J. Heinemann, *Literature of the Synagogue* [1975], pp. 33f.).

Here it is God as creator and protector who is praised, as in the prayer in 2 Macc. 1.24, 'O Lord God, creator of all things, thou the terrible, the mighty, the just and the merciful', and in many similar passages elsewhere. Also in the apocryphal book of Sirach from around 180 BCE we find a concept of God as creator in which the purposefulness of the creation are emphasized.

On the face of it, these kinds of statements do not go beyond anything we find in the Old Testament praises of the creator god. But a closer look at the book of Sirach clearly shows that here the thought of God as creator of heaven and earth has found a new dimension. In a very characteristic way, the concept of God as creator has been joined to the idea of God as representing all-encompassing and all-penetrating wisdom:

> All wisdom is from the Lord;
> wisdom is with him for ever.
> ....
> It is he who created her, surveyed and measured her,
> and infused her into all his works (Sir. 1.1, 9).

In the famous descriptions of wisdom in Sirach 24, a section which is heavily laden with mythological material from Egypt, but which has been transformed in a typically Jewish manner, Wisdom says of itself,

> I am the word which was spoken by the Most High;
> it was I who covered the earth like a mist.
> My dwelling-place was in high heaven;
> my throne was in a pillar of cloud.
> Alone I made a circuit of the sky
> and traversed the depth of the abyss.
> The waves of the sea, the whole earth,
> every people and nation were under my sway (Sir. 24.3-6).

Here divine wisdom is the principle of creation, and the order of the created world is an expression of the in-dwelling wisdom. The idea is rooted in the Old Testament (Prov. 8.22-31), and other passages in Sirach (e.g. 16.24-30; 39.16-35; 42–43) all stress the same idea, namely that God's work of creation is perfect and well ordered because it is interpenetrated by God's wisdom.

These ideas, however, receive a characteristic twist. In chapter 24, Wisdom goes on to depict how it wanders through all creation and at last takes up its abode in Israel:

> I took root among the people whom the Lord had honoured
> by choosing them to be his special possession.
> There I grew like a cedar of Lebanon,
> like a cypress on the slopes of Hermon,
> like a date-palm at Engedi,
> like roses at Jericho.
> I grew like a fair olive-tree in the vale,
> or like a plane-tree planted beside the water (Sir. 24.12-14).

The notion of election is here introduced: Israel has been elected to possess the wisdom which was deposed in the creation. But how? We are told at the end, as, surprisingly, or perhaps not so surprisingly after all, the long praise of Wisdom concludes with the following words:

> All this is the covenant-book of God Most High,
> the law which Moses enacted to be the heritage
> of the assemblies of Jacob (Sir. 24.23).

The same thought is present in the apocryphal book of Baruch, which is thought to be somewhat later than Sirach; here the conclusion of a praise of Wisdom reads,

> She is the book of the commandments of God,
> the law that stands for ever.
> All who hold fast to her shall live,
> but those who forsake her shall die (Bar. 4.1).

In short, we have returned to the Law! The connections between belief in creation, the idea of election, the notion of wisdom, and the Law are quite clear. The combination of ideas in and of itself is peculiar and presumably dependent on Greek, particularly stoic idea about the 'world reason' which has been part and parcel of everything since the creation. A pantheistic motive probably underlies the Greek concept, namely the idea that it is the deity which interpenetrates the created world, but such an idea was entirely foreign to Judaism. What is momentous in the Jewish version of the idea is the identification of the Law with the divine wisdom which was active in the creation, and which, in a manner of speaking, represents the principle of creation. This concept elevates the law to a cosmic quantity; it becomes a revelation of the world-reason or, perhaps better, world-order. The Jewish philosopher, Philo of Alexandria, mentioned above, went a step further and identified the Law with the *logos*, the 'word', the Greek concept which, in the introduction to the Gospel of John, is used of Christ. In doing so, Philo is expressing the idea that the Law is a revelation of the order of creation, a sort of cosmic principle. Similar ideas are found in later Gnostic writings.

It is important to note the connection established in the wisdom teaching of Sirach between election and the Law. It means that the Jew of antiquity saw the demand to keep all of the commandments of the Law in a special perspective. The demand was not seen as the unreasonable whims of an arbitrary god; rather, in the Law the God of Israel had given his people insight into the order of creation, and thus by keeping the Law the individual Jew was in a position to help maintain the order of the world. The early Jews did not understand the demand to keep the Law as a heavy yoke that was imposed upon them; instead, they saw it from the perspective of election. They had received the Law as a gift through which they were chosen, before any other people in the world, to achieve insight into the divinely established world order, thus giving them the further possibility to act in accordance with that order. This is really the import of the mishnaic statement quoted earlier, 'By three things is the world sustained: by the Law, by the (Temple-)service, and by deeds of loving-kindness'. Here the law is the domain-concept, the very principle of existence, while the last two clauses refer to the two most important aspects of the commandments in the Law: the cultic laws, and those which regulate relations among people (ethical laws, if you prefer).

The converse of this picture is that a trespass against the Law is a disturbance of the world order. A rabbi writing some time after the birth of Christ even found it possible to claim that if Israel did not keep the Law the world would subside into chaos. Another rabbi held that whoever removes a single letter from the Law, or adds to it, is to be regarded as one who destroys the whole world. This is radically stated, of course, but nevertheless expresses an authentic understanding of the Law. The rabbis' attempts to interpret the Law down to the

least and most insignificant detail—attempts which to us
might seem at best either futile or bizarre, and at worst
crazy—are to be seen in the same light. The endeavour itself is
both reasonable and logical: it was essential to ensure for the
Jewish believer in every conceivable situation the possibility of
knowing how to respond so as to be in accordance with the
divine will, so as to act in conformity with the world order.

We have attempted to deal with the early Jews'
fundamental understanding of the Law by introducing such
concepts as revelation, creation, election, wisdom and world
order; in so doing, it is possible that the discussion has become
too abstract. For is it not well known that the Jews have an
extremely practical, not to say pragmatic, relationship to the
Law? Is it completely out of court to claim instead that the
Jewish attitude to the Law is as a juridical relation, one in
which some sort of proportion exists between law-observance
and reward, on the one hand, and disobedience and punishment, on the other? Thus: if one keeps the ordinances of the
Law, one receives a reward, either in this life or elsewhere,
corresponding punishments being accorded to trespassers.

Such a view is not expressly wrong, and it would hardly be
difficult to find numerous Jewish quotations referring to
reward and punishment in quite concrete ways. But the
decisive factor is that the motive for keeping the Law is not to
achieve a reward or to avoid punishment. The Law is to be
fulfilled 'for love of God', since it is the expression of the divine
will and of the divinely established order of creation. The Jews'
relationship to the Law and to such concepts as reward and
punishment is more sophisticated than one might think on
first acquaintance. It must be understood in relation to the
Jews' understanding of God. It must also be understood in the
light of one of Early Judaism's classical problems: God as
simultaneously just and merciful. And, finally, there is the
question of the conflict which necessarily arises in Jewish
thought between the concept of election and the awareness
that there are, in fact, Jews who trespass against the Law in
such a way that they cannot be forgiven, and are lost.

Already ancient Israel knew something of reward and
punishment: keeping the covenant was rewarded, while
breaking it meant punishment. In ancient Israel the covenant

between Yahweh and Israel was a central concept. The relationship between Yahweh and his chosen people was, in a manner of speaking, manifest in the covenant into which Moses had entered on behalf of the people on Sinai. As we know, according to the covenant Yahweh was to be the God of Israel; he would make Israel into a great people as he had already promised the fathers Abraham, Isaac, and Jacob in the mists of time. In return, Israel had to refrain from worshipping other gods than Yahweh, and the people were to obey the cultic, legal, and ethical requirements which the Pentateuch represents as the law of Yahweh. The Old Testament books which follow the Pentateuch relate how Israel time and again failed to live up to her covenant with Yahweh; how the nation was punished again and again, yet each time restored, as Yahweh continued to stand by his promises.

In other words, it was not just a matter of jurisprudence. Ancient Israel knew that there was a decisive difference between reward and punishment. The Israelites maintained that Yahweh punishes the sins of fathers until the third and fourth generation, but that he also reveals his loyalty until the thousandth generation to those who love him and keep his commandments (Exod. 20.5-6, etc.). Superficially, it might appear as if there is a difference between Yahweh's justice and his mercy. The rabbis have grappled with this problem at great length. They explain that, for example, the election of Abraham and the promises to him and to Isaac and Jacob, and the realization of these promises in the miraculous liberation from Egypt, took place prior to the making of the covenant on Sinai, where the law was given to Israel through Moses. Therefore God's promises and his mercy take precedence over his punishing justice. This course of reasoning was also known to the apostle Paul (Gal. 3.15-18).

The covenant has to do with the relationship between Yahweh and the people of Israel. This entire complex of ideas was also incorporated into Early Judaism, and Jews still designated themselves—perhaps somewhat stereotypically— as 'Children of the Covenant'. But at this time the concept of the covenant was primarily seen in relation to the idea of election; the expression itself was mainly used of the twin institutions which, more than any others, emphasize Israel's status as the chosen people: circumcision and the Sabbath. Furthermore, since the Law was enhanced at the expense of the covenant, the emphasis came to reside on the relationship of the individual Jew to the keeping of the Law and its various regulations.

It is a fact that a people consists of individuals, and already in ancient Israel people were aware of the problem of the relationship between the collective and the individual, above all in the context of the relationship between reward and punishment. 'The fathers have eaten sour grapes, and the children's teeth are set on edge', was once the slogan. The prophet Jeremiah polemicized against this mechanical sort of collective thinking; he maintained that the individual is responsible for his own acts, a view which he shared with Ezekiel (cf. Jer. 31.29-30; Ezek. 18). And it is characteristic that Jeremiah also subjects the concept of the covenant to renewed consideration: days will come when the Lord will enter into a new covenant with Israel, when he will put his law in their inward parts and engrave it on their hearts.

Thus we see that the movement from covenant to law was accompanied by a movement from a collective understanding of the people's responsibility under the covenant, to private understanding of the duties of the individual with respect to the Law. But the problem of the relationship between reward and punishment still existed, for which reason its correlative problem did also, namely the question of the relationship between God's justice and his mercy.

If we read the book of Sirach and the somewhat later *Psalms of Solomon*—the two works which probably best express the ordinary and average understanding of the relationship in question—the problem looks quite simple. In the first place, Sirach voices an idea which was already present in the Old Testament wisdom literature, namely the notion that the divine world order is so regularly ordered that an evil deed bears its punishment in itself:

> Whoever throws a stone up in the air is throwing it at his
>   own head,
> and a treacherous blow means wounds all around.
> Dig a pit and you will fall into it,

> set a trap and you will be caught by it (Sir. 27.25-26; cf. Prov.
> 26.27; Eccl. 10.8).

But it is otherwise typical of both writings that they stress the idea of God as the just one who punishes sinners for their transgressions:

> To him belong both mercy and wrath,
> and sinners feel the weight of his retribution (Sir. 5.6).

Perhaps more interesting is the following section from the *Psalms of Solomon:*

> Bless God, you who fear the Lord with understanding,
> for the mercy of the Lord is on those who fear him in
>   judgment;
> so as to distinguish between righteous and sinner,
> to recompense sinners for ever according to their deeds;
> and to have mercy on the righteous, delivered him from the
>   affliction of the sinner,
> and to recompense the sinner for what he has done to the
>   righteous.
> For the Lord is good to those who call on him in patience,
> acting according to his mercy towards his holy ones,
> setting them continuously before him in strength (*Pss. Sol.*
>   2.33-36).

Here the matter is simple: the just God striking down the sinner with punishment, while the same merciful God rewards the righteous, which means that he forgives the sins which the righteous person commits. The distinction is made between hardened sinners, whom retribution strikes down 'eternally' and who are destined to destruction, and the righteous, who may decline into sin, but nevertheless encounter undeserved grace and forgiveness. If they are punished, their punishment has the character of a correction which will lead them to change their course. The following passage from the *Psalms of Solomon* very clearly describes how the matter was understood:

> The godly man was troubled on account of his errors,
> lest he should be taken away along with the sinners;
> for the overthrow of the sinner is terrible,
> but not one of these things shall touch the righteous.
> For the chastening of the righteous for sins done in
>   ignorance,

and the overthrow of the sinners are not alike.

...

For the Lord will spare his holy ones,
and will wipe out their errors by means of discipline.
For the life of the just is for ever,
but sinners shall be taken away into destruction,
and their memorial shall be found no more (*Pss. Sol.* 13.5-7,
      10-11).

In other words, the difference between the righteous who sin
and the unrighteous who sin is that the former repent and
turn away from their sin, while the latter remain in their sin,
and are therefore lost:

Thou shalt bless the righteous and not call them
to account for the sins they have committed;
and thy goodness is upon sinners when they repent (*Pss. Sol.*
      9.7).

This is straightforward pietistic religiosity of the sort we run
into in Christian pietistic circles even today. However, the
more sophisticated of the rabbis saw the problem as somewhat
more complicated and so discussed intensively the
relationship between God's 'quality of justice' and his 'quality
of mercy'. They attempted primarily to insist on the unity of
their concept of God. Thus they maintained that God is both
wholly and entirely just and wholly and entirely merciful,
whereas the quotations above from Sirach and the *Psalms of
Solomon* might lead one to suppose that he is either just or
merciful. But this sort of split in God's personality—or
however it is to be described—was unacceptable to the rabbis.
As one of them rather dramatically put it: if God departs by as
much as a footbreadth from his justice, the world will burn!
The rabbis attempted in one way or another to understand the
two aspects of justice and mercifulness as complementary
concepts. In so doing, their logic is not entirely unassailable, as
they simultaneously insist that the 'quality of mercy' was
stronger than the 'quality of justice', and that in the last
instance the human attitude determined whether justice or
mercy was to be dominant in the divine act.

But no matter how the question was analysed in early
Judaism—and there were many nuances among the various
views—one constant factor remained: the view that the

godless will be punished and the righteous will receive mercy. Should we inquire as to whether this divine repayment is to take place in this world or the next, and whether it is to be a present or future event, this leads into the vast complex of ideas of Jewish eschatology; that is, the many and various speculations as to the end of days, the Kingdom of God, the Messiah, Judgment Day, and so forth. We shall study these matters more closely in the final section on apocalyptic; here it is enough to acknowledge the notion of divine repayment taking place in this world, in the here and now, as well as in the world to come and in the future. The former view is an extension of the ancient Israelite understanding that they would achieve blessing and well-being by keeping the covenant, while they would be punished with famine or hostile attack if they broke it. In the period of Early Judaism, however, the tendency was more to emphasize the instantaneous rewards and punishments of the individual than the fortunes of the people. Indeed, Sirach says straightforwardly that it is worthwhile for the Jew to keep the Law and obey the dictates of Wisdom:

> She will promote him above his neighbours,
> and find words for him when he speaks in the assembly.
> He shall be crowned with joy and exultation;
> lasting honour shall be his heritage (Sir. 15.5-6).

In short, honour, prestige and fame were held to be the cash rewards of the righteous.

Conversely, the sinner was thought to be punished immediately. For example, the Old Testament relates that Jacob's son Reuben 'went and lay with his father's concubine Bilha' (Gen. 35.22). In the antique period a collection of legends about the sons of Jacob (the *Testaments of the Twelve Patriarchs*, 1st century BCE) emerged, which contains some reflections as to how Reuben was punished for his crime: 'He (the Lord) struck me with a foul disease in my loins for seven months; and had not my father Jacob prayed for me to the Lord, I would have died, for the Lord was minded to destroy me' (*T. Reuben* 1.7). We should note, as a further subtlety of this narrative, the fact that the punishment corresponds to the crime, as is expressed in the same collection of legends: 'By the very same things by which a man transgresses, by them is he punished' (*T. Gad* 5.10). Thus, whoever commits a sexual crime will be sexually affected by it. The rabbis expressed the same rule in a phrase which recurs in the Sermon on the Mount (Mt. 7.2), 'Whatever measure you deal out to others will be dealt back to you'. They also found lists of examples in the Old Testament which seem to suggest such a correspondence between crime and punishment (e.g., Absalom was proud of his long hair, and accordingly suffered death because his hair became caught in the branches of a tree).

The more pervasive idea, however, was that ultimate reward and punishment would be dealt out at the end of days. There were two ways to regard the last days, namely as a this-worldly kingdom of national glory, or as a supra-worldly kingdom of heaven. But no matter how one understood the matter, the general conviction was that the debt owed by every individual to his god was to be regulated in connection with the events of the last days. It is immediately clear that such a solution allowed various equations to balance out. Anyone could see that there is no balance present in this world; indeed, sinners often do well, while the righteous frequently experience suffering and misery. The Jew concluded that if God was just, then he had to ensure that equilibrium was ultimately maintained.

It was mentioned earlier that the early Jews had not quite abandoned the ancient Israelite idea that reward and punishment are apportioned already in this life. How, then, did they understand the relationship between the rewards and punishments which are dealt out in the here and now, and those which are to come in the final judgment? Numerous answers were proposed. Some rabbis maintained that lesser sins and lesser good works are summed up immediately, while the final balance have to await the ultimate accounting. Others proceeded on the basis of the fundamental distinction previously alluded to between the righteous and sinners, and so offered the following rule: the righteous are punished in this world for whatever sins they happen to commit, whereas their reward for their good deeds will first be accorded in the world to come. The opposite is the case with the sinners: in this world they are rewarded for their good deeds, while the reckoning for their sins will be presented in the world to come.

One question persists, namely, what distinguishes between the righteous who survive the judgment and enter into the Lord's pleasure and the unrighteous who do not survive it, and so cease to exist? After all, we have already noted that the righteous were held to commit sins and that the unrighteous were acknowledged to do good works! Some rabbis seem to have felt that it was a question of percentage—that if one's good works exceeded 50% of the total balance by just a little, then one would be acquitted at the judgment, the opposite being the case in the event of a lower percentage. Sometimes the ancient metaphor of the scales was used, which figures in other religions as well; thus, if the pan containing one's good works rises, then one has been weighed and found wanting.

There is admittedly a great deal of casuistic rule-obsession in the rabbis' tratment of these problems, but it is important to remember that these discussions took place very much on an academic plane, and that both the problems posed and their suggested solutions were at best only distantly connected with the religious ideas of the average Jew. If one asked an ordinary Jew as to the nature of the distinction between the righteous and the unrighteous, he (or she) would probably have answered that every Jew is subject to the covenant and hence embraced by election, so that he would also be able to receive forgiveness for his sins. But, he would have added, any Jew who does not acknowledge the Law, who refuses to bear the sign of the covenant (circumcision), and who will not attempt to keep even the simplest of the rules of the Law, has placed himself beyond election and so has forfeited any opportunity to receive forgiveness. The matter is quite simple; and, he might have continued, those who are subject to election are clearly instructed by the Law as to how they are to achieve forgiveness. This can occur through suffering, which was understood as punishment for past sins, and which thus lead to conversion and forgiveness. Of course, it was also possible to speculate as to which specific sufferings incurred the maximum of forgiveness—as the rabbis in fact did, producing in the process many and varied suggestions. One of the later rabbis maintained that there were three types of suffering which immediately freed one from the threat of eternal punishment. These were great poverty, pain in the nether regions, and political suppression; to which another rabbi added a fourth category: an evil wife!

Nevertheless, the way mainly recommended by the Law as a pathway to achieving forgiveness is the cult. Most of the sacrifices enshrined in the Law, above all in Leviticus, are atonement sacrifices. The daily sacrifices in the temple, as well as the sacrifice of the scapegoat on the Great Day of Atonement, provide atonement for Israel as such. But in addition to these it was possible for the individual Jew to offer sin, guilt, and purification sacrifices in the temple when he had trespassed against various provisions of the Law. In a later section we shall deal more extensively with the temple services and the sacrifices.

We have now attempted to comprehend the Law in a variety of ways. This has led us someway afield; we have concerned ourselves with the concept of revelation, the understanding of God, belief in Creation, and the concept of election. In the latter sections we have attempted to understand how the Jews saw their relationship to the Law and how they understood God as the just and punishing one as well as the merciful and forgiving one. We have also met both incisive and sophisticated arguments, in addition to the belief and conviction of the ordinary Jew that in the last instance the Law was given to Israel to lead it to the salvation that is reserved for the chosen people. In the next section we shall be concerned with the Jewish anthropology and with the question of the human potential for good; that is, with the question of Jewish ethics.

Bibliographic Note to pp. 59-82
The Appendix (pp. 225ff.) describes the Jewish writings which have been cited in this section. The rabbinical quotations, with the exception of those borrowed from the Mishna, have mainly been derived from the secondary literature which I have used here. The most important works are: W. Bousset, *Die Religion des Judentums im späthelleni-stischen Zeitalter* (3rd edn; Tübingen, 1926); G.F. Moore, *Judaism in the First Centuries of the Christian Era*, I-III (Cambridge, Mass., 1927-30); A. Büchler, *Sin and Atonement in the Rabbinic Literature* (Oxford, 1928); J. Bonsirven, *Le Judaïsme Palestinien*, I-II (Paris,

1934-35), E. Sjöberg, *Gott und die Sünder im palästinischen Judentum* (Stuttgart, 1939); M. Hengel, *Judaism and Hellenism* (London, 1973); J. Marböck, *Weisheit im Wandel. Untersuchungen zur Weisheits-theologie bei Ben Sira* (Bonn, 1971); M. Limbeck, *Die Ordnung des Heils. Untersuchungen zum Gesetzesverständnis des Frühjuden-tums* (Düsseldorf, 1971); B. Lee Mack, *Logos und Sophia* (Göttingen, 1973); E.P. Sanders, *Paul and Palestinian Judaism* (London, 1977). Extensive rabbinical material has been collected in Strack-Billerbeck, *Kommentar zum Neuen Testament aus Talmud und Midrasch,* I–IV (München, 1922-28) [in which a compendious index aids somewhat in charting a course through the realms of quotations]. The Mishnah quotations are taken from *The Mishnah*, translated by H. Danby (Oxford, 1933). Further literature in the bibliographical notes to the following sections.

Human Ethical Choice

In the previous section we were concerned with the funda-mental demand upon the Jew to deal in accord with the provisions of the Law. To some extent, we examined the Law as an abstract quantity, without studying the Law's concrete demands and without distinguishing between its cultic, social, and ethical demands. We were primarily concerned to arrive at an understanding of how the Jew, or rather, God, as the former would prefer to put it, regards those who keep the Law and those who trespass against it.

In this section we shall be more specific. We shall attempt to understand how the Jew understood the possibilities of doing good and avoiding evil; that is, the possibilities considered open to people for living in accordance with the Law. In so doing, we shall arrive at a Jewish anthropology and a Jewish ethics. Although we shall go into some detail, we shall at the same time be careful not to get lost in the jungle of individual regulations enshrined in the Law. It would, in any case, be a mammoth undertaking to attempt, first to order the Old Testament materials and systematize the 613 injunctions and prohibitions of the Pentateuch according to their kinds (cultic, social, and ethical), and subsequently to strain our powers in attempting to get a grip on the early rabbinical treatment of the Old Testament laws. Some delimitation is essential.

In earlier times, every serious account of Christian ethics was divided into two main sections entitled 'Duties towards God' and 'Duties towards one's Neighbour'. Although this distinction would be unintelligible to a Jew, it is nevertheless useful to revive it, if by 'duties towards God' in connection with Jewish ethics, we understand the many cultic obligations such as the rules governing sacrifice, the order of worship, the laws of purity, the food restrictions and so forth—matters we shall deal with in the next section. We are left with ethics as such, understood as those rules which deal with life among other people; that is, precisely, 'duties towards one's neighbour'.

In our subsequent study of apocalyptic we shall encounter the important concept of 'dualism'. However, it is not only apocalyptic which is deeply marked by dualistic thought; rather, dualism was implicit in the basic religious structure of Judaism. Already the fundamental ethical question—how can people do good and avoid doing evil—is dualistic in character. We shall subsequently see that dualistic ideas characterize in several ways the various Jewish attempts to determine the possibilities in the face of this choice. The basic view is that the individual is poised between two worlds, evil and good, and is obliged to choose between them. According to Jewish understanding, when people find themselves in this situation, what forces are operative on them? Further: is one's choice free?

We shall begin with an example drawn from the above-mentioned corpus of legends about Jacob's twelve sons (*Testaments of the Twelve Patriarchs*):

> For just as the potter knows how much the vessel he is making is to contain, and takes the right amount of clay for it, so too the Lord makes the body with a view to the spirit it is to contain, and he puts the spirit into it according to the body's capacity. And the proportions of the two correspond perfectly, for the whole creation of the Most High has been fashioned by weight and measure and rule. And just as the potter knows what the use of each vessel is, and what it is fit for, so also the Lord knows for how long the body will persist in goodness and when it will turn to evil (*T. Naphtali* 2.2-4).

It is clear that the text tries to say *something* about the nature of people as ethical beings, but what? One might be tempted to suppose that it operates with the traditional hellenistic body–

soul dualism, a concept with which we shall deal more closely in our section on apocalyptic; that is, that it regards the soul and the body as diametrically opposite entities. But this is not the case; in fact, quite the contrary. The fact that by 'body' and 'spirit' the notions of 'body' and 'soul' are intended is obvious enough. However, the text does not assume that there is an irremediable opposition between both; rather, it presupposes that soul and body were carefully attuned at their creation. Thus, if people attempt to live in accordance with the path determined for them, taking care to preserve the balance between soul and body, then they will live, as the text later has it, under the Law of the Lord and not that of Satan. But if they do not pay due heed to this balance, they will end up in darkness and be unable to perform the 'acts of light'. The idea seems to be that at their creation all people have received a certain measure of potential to live under the Law of the Lord. We note an element of predestination in this concept but with a typically Jewish development, in which predetermination is affirmed simultaneously with the individual's responsibility for their fate.

It is not an interest in the mysteries of psychology which underlies such concepts; rather, they centre on the problem of ethics. Their concern is that humankind has received the Law, so that its task is to realize the good. This fundamental ethical problem recurs in quite a number of early Jewish texts, which is hardly astonishing, when we consider the importance of the Law in this period, as emphasized in the preceding Chapter.

Another section of the *Testaments of the Twelve Patriarchs* seems to ignore the problem of the relationship between soul and body completely. It deals with people's relationship to good and evil in a different way, even though what might be termed 'psychological' insights form part of the account. First the text lists the seven 'spirits', senses, which an individual receives at his creation: the spirit of life, the spirit of vision, the spirit of hearing, the spirit of smelling, and so on. The text then goes on to say:

> With these spirits are mingled the spirits of error. The first, the spirit of fornication, is seated in the nature and the senses; the second, the spirit of insatiate desire, in the

> stomach; the third, the spirit of fighting, in the liver and
> gall. The fourth is the spirit of obsequiousness and chica-
> nery, so that by studied effort a man can make a good
> impression. The fifth is the spirit of arrogance, so that he
> can boast and have a good opinion of himself. The sixth is
> the spirit of lying...the seventh is the spirit of unrighteous-
> ness...And besides all these the spirit of sleep, the eighth
> spirit, is combined with error and phantasy. And so every
> young man perishes and plunges his mind into darkness
> away from the truth, inasmuch as he neither understands
> the law of God nor takes note of his father's warnings... (*T.
> Reuben* 3.2-8).

The introduction to this section characterizes these 'spirits'
more precisely; we learn that, 'Seven spirits were appointed by
Beliar (Belial, Satan) against man, and they are responsible
for the deeds of rebellion' (*T. Reuben* 2.2). In short, these
entities come to people from without; they do not 'indwell'
people, as we might say. This, however, is probably too sharp a
distinction. The idea is probably that these features are the
result of interaction between whatever is in people and
external forces. Humans dwell in a world which is dominated
by the struggle between God and Satan; thus the weak part of
human nature will inevitably be vulnerable to the attacks of
the evil powers. Humanity is itself part of the struggle, and so
is responsible for ensuring that Satan does not win control of it.
The following quotation from one of the other 'Testaments' is
characteristic:

> When the soul is stirred up continually, the Lord departs
> from it and Beliar has dominion over it. So keep, my
> children, the Lord's commands and observe his law; and
> turn from anger and hate falsehood, that the Lord may dwell
> in you and Beliar may flee from you (*T. Dan* 4.7–5.1).

These texts portray an extraordinary tension between a
view of humans as being in the power of the evil forces,
dominated by evil down to their very senses, and humans
under the Law, who thereby have received the possibility to
combat evil and 'do works of light'. It is entirely typical of the
anthropology of Early Judaism; humanity is the very battle-
ground for the good and evil forces in existence. The human
being stands between God and Satan, and is responsible for the

choice as to whether to belong to one or the other. There are many admonitions in the *Testaments of the Twelve Patriarchs;* they are to be seen in the light of this understanding of the human position between the two powers. It is no coincidence that the major ethical concept in the *Testaments* is represented by the Greek word *haplotēs*, which is perhaps best translated 'sincerity', and whose actual meaning is more like 'singleness'. Humanity is obliged to choose; it is to take God's part wholly and so no deal 'doubly'.

The previously cited text from the *Testament of Dan* merely refers to the Law and its commandments in general. The following text, however, shows us somewhat more explicitly what possibilities there were held to be, should humans attempt to guard themselves against Satan's attacks:

> Understand then, my children, that two spirits attend on man, the spirit of truth and the spirit of error. And in between is the spirit of rational understanding, to incline us whichever way it wills. And men's deeds of truth and deeds of error are written on their hearts (*T. Judah* 20.2-3).

Ultimately, it is simply a matter of reason; of 'rational understanding'. However, in reality we have once again to do with the Law since, as we have seen, wisdom and reasonableness are qualities which are only attainable through the Law. In addition, a number of manuscripts of the Greek text contain an interesting variant in which, instead of referring to the 'spirit of rational understanding', reference is made to the 'spirit of conscience', a concept which first entered into Judaism in the antique period.

In the last-cited text above, the dualistic idea of humanity in the forefront of the struggle between the two powers is hardly taken seriously; humanity's own contribution to the struggle between God and Satan looks modest indeed. A likewise harmonic view of humanity's relationship to existence is to be found in Sirach. It is probably no coincidence; Sirach lived in the years around 200 BCE, some decades before inner tensions became open conflict in the reign of Antiochus Epiphanes. Sirach knew about the contradictory tendencies inherent in existence, and we may suppose that he took them seriously.

But on Sirach's view there was no real problem, since this was simply how the good Lord had decided things were to be:

> As clay is in the potter's hands,
> to be moulded just as he chooses,
> so are men in the hands of their Maker,
> to be dealt with as he decides.
> God is the opposite of evil, and life of death;
> yes, and the sinner is the opposite of the godly.
> Look at all the works of the Most High:
> they go in pairs, one the opposite of the other (Sir. 33.13-15).

> He has set in order the masterpieces of his wisdom,
> he who is (or: they stay as they are) from eternity to eternity.
> ...
> All things go in pairs, one the opposite of the other;
> he has made nothing incomplete.
> One thing supplements the virtues of another (Sir. 42.21-25).

The contradictions within existence are part of the order of creation. Thus for Sirach there is no question of any battle between God and Satan; instead, individuals must subordinate themselves to the divine order, learn wisdom, and keep the Law. Then the contradictions will lose their contours. Elsewhere Sirach speaks of the gifts which humanity received at the creation: reason, knowledge, insight, the ability to distinguish between good and evil, and, not least, he received the 'Law of Life' as a possession (Sir. 17.5, 7). In short: whoever uses reason and insight to study the Law, and takes pains to keep it, will be able to control his or her existence.

There is nevertheless one important text in Sirach where the author penetrates deeper into the problems of existence, and where he reveals that the contradictions implicit in human existence are actually rather profound:

> When he (God) made man in the beginning,
> he left him free to take his own decisions;
> if you choose, you can keep the commandments;
> whether or not you keep faith is yours to decide.
> He has set before you fire and water;
> reach out and take which you choose;
> before man lie life and death,
> and whichever he prefers is his (Sir. 15.14-17).

Before we proceed to examine the concepts which Sirach introduces here, it would first be appropriate to cite yet another text from the *Testaments of the Twelve Patriarchs,* which in several respects is reminiscent of Sirach's ideas:

> Two ways has God appointed for mankind, and two inpulses, and two kinds of action, and two courses, and two ends. Thus, all things are in twos, one over against the other. There are two ways, of good and evil, and along with these are the two impulses in our breasts that make the distinctions between them. So, if the soul is well disposed to what is good, its every action is in righteousness, and, if it sins, it repents at once; for when a man's thoughts are set on things that are righteous and he rejects what is wicked, he upsets what is evil immediately and uproots what is sinful. But if the soul inclines the impulse to wickedness, its every action is in wickedness: having spurned what is good, such a man takes to himself what is evil, and under Beliar's control, even if he does anything good, he turns it to wickedness (*T. Asher* 1.3-8).

If we turn to the Greek texts underlying the English translations of the apocryphal book of Sirach and the *Testaments of the Twelve Patriarchs*, we discover that one and the same Greek word is translated in Sirach as 'free decision' and in the *Testament of Asher* as 'impulse'. The word in question is *diaboulion*, which actually means 'counsel' or 'decision', and which has received an idiomatic meaning in these Jewish writings. The word occurs about twenty times in the *Testaments*; most often it is used neutrally of the tendency of the mind in one or another direction. It is accordingly possible to speak of 'the good impulse' or 'the wicked inclination' (*T. Benjamin* 6.4; *T. Issachar* 6.2).

Now we are also fortunate in possessing certain portions of what is probably the original Hebrew text of Sirach, from which we can determine that 'the free decision' is represented by Hebrew *yeṣer*, a word meaning something like 'striving, will'. This leads us on to the conceptual world of the rabbis, since this very word plays a major part in rabbinical theology. They sometimes use it neutrally with reference to 'the good impulse' and 'the evil impulse' (*Aboth* 2.11; 4.1; *Berakoth* 9.5, etc.). But their primary use for the term is negative, as of a

striving or 'drive' which it is people's duty to contest: 'Who is
mighty? He that subdues his (evil) impulse' (*Aboth* 4.1).

The word *yeṣer* is used in the Qumran texts in almost the
same way. When they speak of the 'good impulse', they
usually employ a fixed expression which we would have to
render as 'a strong will' or 'steadfastness of heart' (1QS 4.5;
8.3; 1QH 1.35; 2.9). On the other hand, when they speak of the
'evil impulse', the word *yeṣer* always stands alone. Thus the
Community Rule opposes the one who walks 'in the stubbornness of his heart so that he strays after his heart and eyes and
evil inclination (*yeṣer*)' to the one who 'circumcises in the
Community the foreskin of evil inclination'. In a similar way,
1QH 5.6 finds it possible to speak of 'the designs of my inclination', while 6.32 refers to 'the guilty inclination'. In these and
similar contexts the word *yeṣer* has a negative significance in
its own right, one which is perhaps best rendered by English
'lust'.

It appears that the various texts cited above reveal a sliding
scale of meanings, ranging from the more or less neutral 'free
will' to the negatives 'drive' or 'lust'. Perhaps the matter could
be best expressed by saying that according to the Jewish
understanding the 'free will' or 'impulse' is the locus within
the human personality where the battle between good and evil
takes place. It is also the locus where people sometimes sur-
render in the face of evil; an idea not far removed from the
thought of the apostle Paul (Rom. 7, etc.).

The idea we find quite variously expressed in the texts is
that human beings are both free and, somehow, unfree; that
they will the good, but are in the clutches of their senses. This
is developed in the Qumran texts into the theological system,
whose clearest expression states that,

> He (God) has created man to govern the world, and has
> appointed for him two spirits in which to walk until the time
> of his visitation: the spirits of truth and falsehood... Until
> now the spirits of truth and falsehood struggle in the hearts
> of men and they walk in both wisdom and folly. According to
> his portion of truth so does a man hate falsehood, and
> according to his inheritance in the realm of falsehood is he
> wicked and so hates truth. For God has established the two

spirits in equal measure until the determined end, and until
the Renewal... (1QS 3.17-19; 4.23-25).

In many respects, this passage is on the same wavelength as
the others previously cited. Once again we find the odd
ambivalence of the two 'spirits', which at one and the same
time are something within people and something outside of
them. The 'spirit of truth' and the 'spirit of falsehood' seem at
first glance to be identical with 'the good impulse' and 'the evil
impulse' in the other texts. But the continuation establishes a
connection between these two spirits and, respectively, 'the
Angel of Darkness' and 'the Prince of Light'. There is no doubt
that the former is Satan or Belial; a little later we read of the
spirits of the Angel of darkness, whose task it is to 'lead the
Children of Light to fall'; they are, then, Belial's demons who
tempt the righteous. The 'Prince of Light' is presumably the
archangel Michael, to whom the text elsewhere refers as
'God's Angel of Truth' (3.24).

At the very least, it is obvious that the several texts studied
here deal in a variety of ways with the same essential problem:
humanity, poised between the two powers which determine its
existence. It is also clear that the concept of the good and evil
impulse or drive is combined with the notion that, opposed to
God, is the figure of Belial and his army of spirits, who
represent the evil in human existence. Some religions have
been based on the idea of an original antithesis between good
and evil, but a firmly monotheistic religion like Judaism insists
that God alone is the origin of everything. Satan and his spirits
are fallen angels; thus a number of Jewish texts from the
antique period take as their point of departure the strange
mini-story in Gen. 6.1-4, which relates how the 'sons of God'
went in to the 'daughters of men', who subsequently gave
birth to giants. This, according to the tradition, was the fall of
the angels, and it was assumed that the spirits of the fallen
angels have ever since been under the leadership of Satan,
Belial, Semyaza, and whatever else he may be called in the
various writings, and that together they attempt to lead
humankind away from God (see especially *1 Enoch* 6–11).

This recurrent idea of humanity caught between the two
powers is based on an integrated understanding of the world,

which is most clearly expressed in the apocalyptic speculations of Early Judaism. In the final section of this book, where we shall examine apocalyptic more closely, we shall deal with these ideas in more detail. Here we should note that they influenced Jewish anthropology in the antique period far outside of apocalyptic circles, so that it is reasonable to maintain, as we have done, that dualistic thought was the main constitutive element in the anthropology of Early Judaism, as such.

In short, people cannot do good without doing battle with the forces which desire them to do the opposite. This is the nature of things until 'the prince of this world' is removed from power at the end of time. Belial's spirits will continually exploit humans' evil impulse, so that even the most righteous will fail repeatedly. 'But the God of Israel and His Angel of Truth will succour all the Children of Light', according to the *Community Rule* (1QS 3.24-25); and the human being receives this divine assistance through the revelation, that is, the Law. The human is not alone in the struggle. 'Observe the whole of the law of the Lord, for there is hope for all who make straight their way', as the *Testament of Judah* (26.1) has it. And Sirach says, 'Whoever keeps the Law keeps his thoughts under control' (21.11).

Thus, the realization that the world is saturated in evil did not lead Jews to embrace ethical defeatism; they held instead that it *is* possible to do good. Accordingly, ancient Jewish writings abound with charges and admonitions to keep the Law, which enables us to work out the Jewish ethic that was characteristic of the period.

Naturally, this ethic was based on the Old Testament, and it is often emphasized, not least by the Jews themselves, that it is in the prophetic proclamation that this Jewish ethic reached its most beautiful and clearest expression. Reference is often made, for example, to the famous passage in Micah: 'God has told you what is good; and what is it that the Lord asks of you? Only to act justly, to love loyalty, to walk wisely before your God' (Mic. 6.8). But one could equally point to the following passage in Isaiah: 'Put away the evil of your deeds, away out of my sight. Cease to do evil and learn to do right, pursue justice and champion the oppressed; give the orphan his rights, plead the widow's cause' (Isa. 1.16-17). Here an ethic is expressed which has been valid for the Jews in every age—as it was for the Jews of the antique period. Indeed, its validity extends to all humanity.

This is no doubt correct. It is nevertheless characteristic that the ethical teaching of the prophets is formulated entirely in generalities; instead of detailed instruction some basic guidelines are offered which have a timeless character. Furthermore, when the prophets do speak of specifics, they do not address themselves to the individual, but to the people of Israel, or to particular groups within the people. What was important to the prophets was the relationship between Israel and Yahweh, its God, so if we read on in the book of Isaiah and further into the other prophetic writings we soon discover that the objects are invariably Israel, Jerusalem, kings, priests, prophets and the wealthy. There is virtually never an address to humanity as such.

In consequence, if one wants to find a developed moral teaching in the Old Testament, one should not turn to the prophets. An ethic containing guidelines for the multiplicity of human situations, a moral philosophy dealing with the elementary conditions of human social relations, is to be sought in the Pentateuch and the Wisdom literature. Proverbs is the most typical example of Old Testament Wisdom literature; the book contains rules of conduct either in the adhortatory thou form, or in the form of the proverb. The legal collections of the Pentateuch (e.g. Exod. 20–23, including the Ten Commandments; Lev. 18-19; Deut. 21–25 and so forth) contain a rich variety of rules regulating human intercourse. Here the individual is informed as to how he or she is to relate to his or her neighbour in the multiplicity of situations life offers.

It was characteristic of Early Judaism, in which it was very much the case that individualism gained ground at the expense of the collective understanding of existence, that these two particular types of literature were perpetuated. In many respects the book of Sirach belongs to the same genre as Proverbs, and their respective admonitions are closely related. The *Testaments of the Twelve Patriarchs* are characterized by a similar attitude, and each *Testament* deals with a particular ethical problem. Finally, the rabbinical tradition was a continuation of the particular type of ethical instruction contained in the Pentateuch.

'The fear of the Lord is the beginning of wisdom' is repeated several times in Proverbs (e.g. 1.7; 9.10). The idea is that those who acknowledge God as the Creator of the world and maintainer of world order have the possibility, via the Law, to achieve so much wisdom that they will be able to obtain insight into the world order and regulate their own existence in accordance with it. For this reason, 'wisdom' is the leading category throughout the whole of Proverbs; many of its proverbs describe the wise or the just in contradistinction to the godless or the fool. In other words, this concept of wisdom becomes a sort of life-wisdom, that wisdom or insight which it is necessary to possess if one is to be able to manage one's existence. There is practically no aspect of human existence which is not touched upon in the admonitions and sentences of Proverbs: exhortations to be diligent, modest, thrifty, meek, generous, righteous, true to one's word, and so on, are ranged together along with recommendations for good child-rearing principles and proper table manners. Conversely, the book also warns against all manner of vices, such as pride, duplicity, contentiousness, hatefulness, dishonesty and licentiousness. All these concerns witness to a healthy attitude toward life's problems, and many of the individual observations were borrowed from the cultures which surrounded Israel, including the Egyptian wisdom, tradition, and were eventually included in the Old Testament.

As mentioned previously, this line continues in the work of Sirach (and in the likewise apocryphal Wisdom of Solomon) within Early Judaism. Here we find exhortations and admonitions like those in the book of Proverbs, though with one significant difference: as we have seen, wisdom is straightforwardly identified with the Law, so that ultimate virtue consists in keeping the Law. There are, however, many specifications, and certain features are more strongly empha-sized than they are in Proverbs. These are such things as children's respect for their parents, mercy towards the poor, censures on licentiousness and inebriation and the like—

perhaps reflecting problems which emerged in the different social situation of a later age.

The Testaments of the Twelve Patriarchs are organized in such a way that each *Testament* concentrates on that virtue or vice with which the patriarch in question, according to Old Testament or early Jewish traditions, was associated. Thus *Reuben* speaks of fornication, *Simeon* of envy, *Levi* of arrogance, love of money and fornication, *Judah* of drunkenness and fornication, *Dan* of anger and falsehood and *Gad* of hatred. By way of contrast, *Issachar* urges sincerity, *Zebulon* advises compassion and mercy, *Naphtali* preaches goodness, *Joseph* recommends chastity, and *Benjamin* speaks in favour of 'a pure mind'. These vices and virtues are described in homiletic style, and the respective patriarchs are depicted as examples for either aversion or emulation. The general tenor of the work has been very neatly characterized as 'Jewish pietism'. In this connection it is probably not accidental that sexual trespasses play a notable role; thus an almost prurient interest centres on the story of Joseph and Potiphar's wife, as it does on Judah's relationship to his daugher-in-law and Reuben's to his stepmother.

In the Pentateuch, general life-conduct and ethical rules play a secondary role to the many cultic regulations. There are, however, some characteristic collections of such material: the Ten Commandments (Exod. 20; Deut. 5), the Book of the Covenant (Exod. 20–23), the beginning of the Holiness Code (Lev. 18–19), as well as a number of sections in Deuteronomy (esp. 21–25), which mainly consist of ethical injunctions and prohibitions. Such collections naturally formed the basis of a Jewish ethic in the antique period; and Pseudepigrapha for example, contain many allusions to the ethical teachings of the Pentateuch. But otherwise it was mainly in the rabbinical literature that the Pentateuchal law tradition was perpetuated. The Mishnah consists predominantly of cultic regulations, but the previously mentioned section, *Pirqe Aboth*, reveals a collection of ethical maxims of which many no doubt derive from our period. Once again we are told that the study of the Law is the virtue that surpasses all other virtues; accordingly, the following examples of general moral rules coupled with injunctions to study the Law are entirely typical:

'Hillel said: Be of the disciples of Aaron, loving peace and pursuing peace, loving mankind and bringing them nigh to the Law'. And in the same context: 'Shammai said: Make thy study of the Law a fixed habit; say little and do much, and receive all men with a cheerful countenance' (*Aboth* 1.12, 15). And when a rabbi warns against a number of sins, he does so primarily because they interfere with the study of the Law: 'Morning sleep and midday wine and children's talk and sitting in the meeting-houses of the ignorant people put a man out of the world' (*Aboth* 3.11). But we also find criticism of common moral weaknesses: 'Jealousy, lust and ambition put a man out of the world' (*Aboth* 4.21).

There is, then, ethical teaching in the *Pirqe Aboth* as well as a presentation of ethical ideals. These are by no means concrete, however; rather, a basic concept is stated, such as the well-known remark, 'By three things is the world sustained: by truth, by judgement, and by peace' (*Aboth* 1.18), or the following saying: 'A good eye and a humble spirit and a lowly soul—they in whom are these are of the disciples of Abraham our father. An evil eye, a haughty spirit, and a proud soul—they in whom are these are of the disciples of Balaam the wicked' (*Aboth* 5, 19). Such generalized virtues were as much recommended to early Jews by the Old Testament as by Stoicism, the popular moral philosophy of the antique period; and indeed, quite detailed ethical prescriptions was available in both traditions. But for early Jews the ethical centre of gravity lay in the cultic-ritual ambit: keeping the Sabbath and the sacrificial regulations, as well as observing the laws governing purity and eating. The main part of the Old Testament laws is concerned with cult and ritual; the same is also true of the Mishnah, where only a part of the six main sections is concerned with other matters (e.g. *Nezikin*, which has to do with social laws and laws of punishment, and in which the *Pirqe Aboth* is located).

In this section we have tried to say something about early Jewish ethics in conjunction with our study of Jewish anthropology. It is clear that we have only been able to deal with a very small segment of Jewish ethics. We have scarcely touched on that aspect of Jewish ethics which is most clearly expressed in the Old Testament, and which, accordingly, is not specific to early Judaism (the commandment to love one's neighbour, the understanding of woman, of the role of the weak in society, of the stranger, and so forth). In the following section we shall deal more extensively with the cultic and ritual laws.

Bibliographic Note to pp. 83-97
The Appendix (pp. 225ff.) accounts for the Jewish texts cited in this section. The mishnaic tract, *Pirqe Aboth*, is found in English translation in the *Jewish Prayer Book* and in H. Danby, *The Mishnah* (London, 1933). Most of the works mentioned in the bibliographical note on p. 82f. contain chapters dealing with anthropology and ethics. But see additionally R. Travers Herford, *Talmud and Apocrypha. A Comparative Study of the Jewish Ethical Teaching in the Rabbinical and Non-Rabbinical Sources in the Early Centuries* (London, 1933); E.J. Schnabel, *Law and Wisdom from Ben Sira to Paul* (Tübingen, 1985); A. Nissen, *Gott und der Nächste im antiken Judentum* (Tübingen, 1974); K. Berger, *Die Gesetzesauslegung Jesu. Ihr historischer Hintergrund im Judentum und im Alten Testament* (Neukirchen 1972); R. Eppel, *Le piétisme juif dans les Testaments des douze Patriarches* (Paris, 1930); H.W. Hollander, *Joseph as an Ethical Model in the Testaments of the Twelve Patriarchs* (Leiden, 1981); E. Schürer, *The History of the Jewish People*, II (Edinburgh, 1979), pp. 464-87, deals especially with the Sabbath and purity rules.

Temple and Synagogue

In classical Israelite times there were several temples in Palestine. In Judah, the temple of Solomon on Mount Zion was preeminent, while in the northern kingdom there were major temples in several of the more sizeable towns. The Jerusalem temple was destroyed during the Babylonian assault on Jerusalem in 587 BCE, but the second temple on Zion was finished around 520 and became the centre of the post-exilic Jewish temple congregation.

The second temple was completely rebuilt by Herod around the time of the birth of Christ. Extensive substructures enabled Herod and his architects to refashion the old temple area in the southeastern part of the city into a great platform (almost 500 × 300m) which exists to this very day. In the middle of this platform Herod situated the new temple, which was presumably partially built onto the old one; it must have been approximately where the Islamic Dome of the rock now stands. Herod's temple was hardly completed when the Romans destroyed it during the rebellion in 70 CE. Nevertheless, Jerusalem and Zion, the site where the temple might one day be built anew, retained special importance for the Jews, even when they had been expelled from the city after the second rebellion in the 130s CE.

The organization of the temple area and of the building itself was the same for all three structures. Only the system of external courts was probably extended in the case of Herod's temple, since the newly erected platform provided various possibilities which had been unavailable to the earlier environment. If it were possible to undertake archaeological excavation in the fill layers of the platform, we should no doubt find remnants of Herod's temple, and perhaps also of the previous temple structures. But respect for the Islamic sanctuaries forbids such archaeological works. On the other hand, we do possess extremely detailed descriptions of Herod's structure both in the Mishnah and in Josephus.

It was in the very nature of the temple that it should, as far as possible, be separate from the profane world. Holiness was concentrated in the temple, and the sacred and the profane are, of course, antithetical quantities. In the temple of Herod an attempt was made to attain this separation by means of a system of courtyards around and in front of the temple. The degree of holiness increased every time one passed through a courtyard, until at last one arrived at the inner one, where the temple itself was located. The Gentiles were kept furthest away; they were only allowed access to the platform, and to pass along the columned walks which defined it on all four sides, where those who dealt in sacrificial animals and money-changing resided. This entire area was termed the Court of the Gentiles. The middle section of the platform formed a terrace which probably measured a couple of hundred metres a side; it was here the temple complex proper was to be found. Gentiles were not allowed access, and inscriptions in Latin and Greek (scholars have found two of the Greek ones) warned them against trespass under pain of death. Only Jews were permitted to mount up to the enclosure, and of those who did so, any who failed to satisfy certain of the purity requirements were forbidden to come closer. Gates led into the Court of the Women, which measured about 80 × 80m; from there the Nicanor Gate led into the inmost court, which was divided into two forecourts: the Court of the Israelites and the Court of the Priests. The great altar of burnt offering was located in the latter, in front of the entrance to the temple building. Under normal conditions, only priests were allowed access here.

The temple structure, which measured approximately 50 × 35m, was divided into three chambers along the same plan as the Temple of Solomon. It consisted of a small outer hall to the east which gave access to the main chamber, the Holy, which contained the gilded incense altar, the shewbread table, and the great menorah. The western end of the chamber was curtained off; behind it was situated the Holy of Holies. In Solomon's temple, it was here the Ark of the covenant resided. It was no doubt destroyed in the fires of 587, when the temple was burnt; in the two later temples only the stone was present on which the Ark is supposed to have reposed.

No matter what were the religious feelings and attitudes of the individual Jew, the temple was the institution around which the religious life of the Jewish people was centred. Here the national religion was expressed in a highly rule-bound ritual. The same activities were repeated every day in the temple; only the Sabbath and the great festivals broke the monotony to some extent by requiring different rituals. The temple was above all the place where regular sacrifices were presented to the God of Israel according to the provisions of the Law of Moses. It would accordingly be appropriate to describe the various types and functions of the sacrifices, to account for the activities and tasks of the priests in connection with the ceremonies, and so forth. We shall return to these issues shortly.

For the present, however, it is more important that we try to understand what sort of ideology undergirded the extensive temple services, and, furthermore, that we make some effort to see the relation between this ideology and those early Jewish religious concepts and forms of self-expression with which we have so far been concerned. If one had asked the early Jews why temple services were maintained in Jerusalem, they would simply have replied that the demands of the Law have perforce to be obeyed. As we have seen, the Law was divine unto its very letter, therefore the temple cult was regarded as a matter of course, if a time-consuming and expensive one. By the same token, they would also have acknowledged their own difficulties in satisfying all the demands the Law made of daily existence; thus they would have found it comforting to know that 'society' took the greatest pains to fulfil its obligations in the Law, well knowing that most sacrifices served to atone for their own sins and those of their fellow Jews.

We have to move far back in time in order to understand just what went on in the temple. If we examine the associations which accrued to the sanctuaries and temples in ancient Israel, we note several common features: the temples were not built just anywhere, rather, a temple was built on a location where the ancient Israelites were convinced that Yahweh, the God of Israel, or one of his messengers, had revealed himself. The Old Testament contains a number of sanctuary legends which speak of such fundamental events. On the site where Yahweh showed himself on the heavenly stair to Jacob, the temple of Bethel was later erected. A Yahweh altar was built on the place where Gideon received his revelation. Finally, the temple in Jerusalem was built on the location where Abraham almost sacrificed his son Isaac, as is related in the presumably fairly late narrative in Genesis 22. The story about Jacob in Genesis 28 is typical, where the patriarch bursts out, 'How fearsome is this place! This is no other than the house of God, this is the gate of heaven!' The revelation expresses the idea that the sanctuary is God's dwelling-place on earth, a concept which is found in many of the religions of antiquity. On such a view, the temple is the place where one worships the god who has chosen the site as his abode. Further, depending on the character of the deity in question, the sacrifices are understood as food for the god, or as expressions of the believer's gratitude and dependence.

As the Jerusalem temple out-competed the other Israelite temples and achieved supremacy, it also acquired many legends which emphasize its particularly sacred quality; these are such narratives as those in 2 Samuel 24, Genesis 14 and Genesis 22, as already mentioned. The Jews could maintain that Yahweh dwelt simultaneously in heaven and in the temple on Zion, a conception which is expressed in many Old Testament psalms, many of which once had a function in the temple cult. For example, Ps. 11.4 notes that, 'The Lord is in his holy temple, the Lord's throne is in heaven'. The development of legends concerning Zion accelerated considerably in ancient Judaism especially after the fall of the temple. According to these legends, Zion was the navel of the world, the place where Paradise once was situated and where God's throne will be set up on Judgment Day, where the entrance to the underworld was, but also the entrance to heaven. Some rabbis even maintained that the sacred stone beneath the temple in reality belonged to heaven, and not to the earth. This brings us back to the idea of the temple as God's dwelling-place on earth; a continuation of the same concept is the early Jewish idea of 'the heavenly Jerusalem', which was adopted by the early Christians.

All of these ideas may be seen to be ramifications of the ancient Jewish concept of the temple in Jerusalem as a picture of heaven. It is primarily in the apocalyptic writings that we encounter descriptions of a heavenly topography including seven or even ten heavens. Just as these heavens increase in degree of holiness the higher up one comes, so, too, was the Jerusalem temple organized in several divisions, with correspondingly increasing degrees of sacrality. The concept is that of the macrocosm and the microcosm, the great and tiny worlds. On this understanding, heaven was the macrocosm, and the temple was its microcosm; it was heaven's correspondent on earth, an *imago coeli*, a picture of heaven. It was here that heaven and earth were thought to meet; indeed, in reality, the temple *was* heaven on earth.

This gives us some idea of how early Jews understood the temple in Jerusalem. It was the locus in which they made the closest contact with the forces which determined their life and being. Their own existence, their nation's, and, indeed, even that of the whole world, were dependent on the divine forces which entered the earthly sphere at precisely this spot. It was therefore of corresponding importance to ensure that the sacral rites, of inestimable origin and significance, be carried out with the greatest precision. The stability of the world-order was at stake. To the early Jew, God was not only the creator of the world, but also its maintainer; world-order and the laws of nature were at his command, and their persistence could only be enabled if the cult God had ordained were to be practised as intended. Fertility, and thereby life itself, depended on the cult.

But the continued survival of the nation was also so dependent. It was characteristic of Early Judaism, although the phenomenon dates back to Israelite times, that the earlier cultic forms which had withstood the test of time were to some extent refashioned. Or, to phrase it more accurately: the understanding of them changed in the light of Israel's special understanding of God. In many cases, aspects of the cult had been adopted from the Canaanites, among whom they had originally been closely associated with fertility and the progression of the seasons; their aim was to ensure 'fertility and good year-growth'. Already the Israelites had interpreted the cult on the basis of the notion of election and endowed it with salvation-historical content. Passover was originally a festival of the barley harvest and small-cattle breeding; the Israelites related it to their own fundamental experience of salvation: the liberation from Egypt. The Festival of Weeks had been an agricultural festival celebrating the wheat harvest; the Israelites transformed it into a commemorative celebration of the legislation on Sinai. Finally, the festival of Booths, associated with the autumnal fruit harvest, became a commemorative celebration of the desert wandering. In this fashion the central religious festivals of the year became festivals of remembrance of the Lord's great deeds on Israel's behalf in the past. The intention was, through sacrifices and ceremonies, to persuade him to continue holding his protective hand over his chosen people.

In other words, the temple cult was thought to maintain the proper relation between God and his people Israel. Sacrifices atoned for the sins of the people and of the individual (sin offerings, guilt offerings, atonement offerings); sacrifices also made it possible to demonstrate one's gratitude to the god who persistently showed himself to be the God of Israel and of every single Jew (sacrifices of thanksgiving and praise). Finally, it was also possible through sacrifice to attempt to win particular evidences of the divine favour (votive-sacrifices and freewill offerings). Every day two sacrifices were offered on the incense altar in the Holy, and two burnt offerings were made on the altar in the Court of the Priests. In addition to these, it was possible to make private sacrifices in the temple, with priestly assistance. Old Testament formulas of blessing and psalms were employed in conjunction with all sacrificial activities.

It has been repeatedly stated that in the antique period the sacrificial cult was confined to the Jerusalem temple. This meant that the Jews who were resident in remote parts of Palestine, not to mention the Diaspora, were excluded from participation in the temple cult, with the exception of the few times in their lives when they undertook a pilgrimage to Jerusalem, mainly in connection with the three pilgrimage festivals of Passover, Weeks, and Booths. Obviously, only a few could undertake such a journey, and there were no doubt many who never managed to do so. Already, however, in the centuries before the birth of Christ a different sort of religious service had arisen within Judaism. It was not intended to replace the temple service, although for many Jews who did not reside in Jerusalem that is what it eventually did. After the destruction of the temple it became the sole type of divine service of all Jews. We are speaking of the synagogal service.

When and where the institution of the synagogue arose is unclear. Most evidence points to the Egyptian diaspora, where we find reference to synagogues in existence as early as 225 BCE. At all events, as previously suggested, it would be reasonable to suppose that it was the Jews of the Diaspora who were most in need of a type of worship that was not dependent on the temple in Jerusalem. In the course of the succeeding centuries the synagogue seems to have become general in all Jewish communities, both within and without Palestine. Moreover, the fact that there were synagogues in Jerusalem itself—indeed, in the very temple enclosure—shows that synagogal worship was originally intended not to replace, but to supplement temple worship.

This development is both logical and intelligible. Synagogal worship met several of the needs of the early Jews. We have already described how individualism burgeoned in this period at the expense of collective thinking. The temple worship was in fact an expression of the collective impulse, for through it the Jewish nation worshipped the God of Israel through sacrifices and temple ceremonies. The priest was the active participant, while the individual Jew could only bring sacrificial gifts and was otherwise a passive observer. Matters were completely different in synagogal worship. The priest had no role to play; instead the individual worshipper shared in the entire procedure. One might read the text aloud and interpret it, or one might offer prayers and blessings. Synagogal worship allowed individual piety to express itself in ways that were impossible in temple worship. Moreover, the worship of the synagogue corresponded to another of the interests which had become actual in our period: the preoccupation with the Law. We have already dealt with the question of the relationship of the individual to God in Early Judaism, as expressed in the individual's relationship to the Law and its demands. Here we should note that whereas temple worship represented a more or less mechanical fulfilment of the sacrificial demands of the Law, the centre of synagogue worship was a continual concentration on the Law in an unending effort to determine what the demands of the Law might entail for the individual in his daily life.

It is immediately clear why the synagogue became a popular institution in antiquity, and also why it became a centripetal factor in Judaism, the influence of which has endured up to the present day. Every group of Jews, of whatever size, living in a foreign milieu, has had a synagogue as its spiritual home; and this has been of decisive importance as a protection against assimilation. Finally, the form of worship peculiar to the synagogue has endowed Jewish religion with an intellectualizing tendency which has probably been indirectly responsible for the role of the Jews in European cultural life. Centuries of honing of the Jewish intellect in the 'school' of the synagogue is the background of the central position of Jews in art and science for the last two centuries.

Archaeological excavations have laid bare some ancient synagogues, and we are familiar with the service of the synagogue through descriptions in the Mishnah and subsequent rabbinical writings. The New Testament, too, contains a couple of accounts which give quite a good picture of the course of this worship. The ruins of ancient synagogues have been found throughout the ancient world, although most have been unearthed in Palestine. With a couple of important exceptions, however, these all date from the time after the destruction of the temple. Most were rather stately structures, generally subdivided into several chambers by rows of columns. The Palestinian examples are normally oriented towards Jerusalem; thus, for example, the ones in Galilee point to the south. The ruins of the two synagogues which pre-date the destruction of the temple are the one in Masada by the Dead Sea, excavated in the 1960s, and the recently discovered one at Gamalah in the Golan Heights. Both of these also point towards Jerusalem. In other words, the orientation of the synagogues expressed a relationship to the temple of Jerusalem. This is also expressed by the internal architecture of the synagogue, which copied that of the temple. Corresponding to the Holy of Holies, every synagogue had (and has) a cabinet for the Torah concealed behind a curtain; in it are kept the scrolls containing the Pentateuch. It is quite characteristic that this cabinet is called the 'Ark'. Situated in front of it is an elevation on which the leaders of the synagogue sit, and from which the reading of the Scriptures takes place. This pretty much corresponds to the Holy in the temple. Finally, there is the main chamber itself, which must correspond to the inner court of the temple; it is also divided up, as we might expect, into men's and women's sections.

We do not know much about the financing and leadership of the ancient synagogue, although we may suppose that the communities either elected their leadership, or else that it comprised the oldest, most respected members of the communities in question. The scribes may also have held an important position in the institution of the synagogue, and there is reason to believe that the daily leader of the service, 'the ruler of the synagogue', was most often a scribe, with a synagogal 'minister' at his side to deal with practical matters.

The service of the synagogue was 'church and school under a single hat', as it has been put. One of its two main emphases was on praising God, confession of faith, prayer and blessing; the other consisted in the public reading of the Law and the Prophets, followed by a sermon-like interpretation. Various

Old Testament psalms were employed to praise God, not least the 'Hallelujah Psalms' at the close of the Psalter. Confession consisted of the so-called *Shema'* (after its first word, the Hebrew injunction, 'Hear...'), from Deut. 6.4-9, combined with 11.13-21 and Num. 15.37-41. Other texts from the Pentateuch may also have been included at a later date. Prayer included the *Eighteen Benedictions*. A variety of blessing formulas were employed in the first part of the service, and if a priest was present, he had the authority to pronounce the Aaronite Blessing. The fixed elements of the service were probably performed by the ruler of the synagogue, but it was possible for him to delegate them to others.

The public reading of the Scriptures consisted above all of readings in the Pentatuech. In practice, the books of Moses were read continuously, following either a one-year or three-year rota. For the benefit of those who had no Hebrew, a paraphrase or translation was provided in Aramaic (this orally supplied rendering was later written down as the *Targum*, the Aramaic translation of the Old Testament). After this, but only on the occasion of the morning service on the Sabbath or in the services accompanying the great festivals, certain sections of the prophetic corpus, which were connected on one way or another with the Pentateuchal reading of the day, were read aloud. Finally, there was the possibility of a sermon or an interpretation of what had been read.

In principle, both readings and sermon might be performed by any of those present, and the sermon offered particularly rich potential for individual self-expression. In the nature of things we have little information about this freely rendered sermon. There is no doubt that it may have differed widely, ranging from penetrating discussions of details in the Law to moralizing admonition. There is much to suggest that some of the texts which are now numbered among the Old Testament Pseudepigrapha may have derived from the sermons of the synagogue. Scholars have, for example, pointed to the admonitions in the *Testaments of the Twelve Patriarchs* in this connection, as they characteristically take their point of departure in the narratives of the Pentateuch. Here and elsewhere we also encounter a legendary tradition which elaborates on the biblical materials, and which probably also derives at least in part from the synagogue sermons.

The synagogue service was mainly appropriate on the Sabbath, when both afternoon and morning services were held, and in conjunction with the great festivals. On two weekdays, Monday and Thursday (originally the market days) there was an early morning service.

The early Jews also had a religious life outside of temple and synagogue, but it varied considerably according to such imponderables as the religious attitudes of the individuals in question, their ability and possibility to keep the many strictures imposed on them by the Law and, later, the rabbinical tradition. Most believers probably practised morning and evening prayer, and many of them will have participated in the ceremonies connected with the great festivals, Passover, Weeks, Booths, New Year, and the Great Day of Atonement. It must have been difficult for the average Jew to keep the many extremely detailed rules governing the Sabbath, purity, and eating. In reality it was only the Pharisees who were able to master these extensive complexes of rules and invest time and toil in their close observance. We shall return later to the role of the Pharisees as an élite within the people, whose daily life was determined by the Law from first to last.

Bibliographic Note to pp. 97-107

Josephus describes Solomon's temple at great length on the basis of the Old Testament accounts of its construction (*Ant.* 8.61-123; cf. 1 Kgs 5–8; 2 Chron. 2–7). His description of Herod's temple is less amply detailed (*Ant.* 15.380-425; cf. *Bell.* 5.184-237, and *Contra Ap.* 2.102-109). The mishnaic tract *Middoth* preserves the measurements of Herod's temple in detail. The reader will be able to find descriptions and plans of the temple system in most accounts of early Judaism, as well as in general reference works. Josephus describes the sacrificial worship in the temple, although he once again does so on the basis of the Old Testament materials (*Ant.* 3.224-257; cf. esp. Lev. 1–7. Sir. 50.1-21 contains a poetic description of temple worship). The mishnaic tract *Tamid* contains all of the later priestly rules governing daily sacrifice in the temple, and other tractates contain countless rules applying to daily temple worship and to worship in connection with the great festivals. The reader is advised to consult the general reference works. The most recent extensive account is in: S. Safrai and M. Stern, *The Jewish People in the First Century*, II (Assen/Amsterdam, 1974-76), pp. 865-907; E. Schürer, *The History of the Jewish People*, II (Edinburgh, 1979), pp. 237-313; and Johann Maier, *Temple und Tempelkult*, in: *Literatur und Religion des Frühjudentums* (Würzburg, 1973), pp. 371-90.

The worship of the synagogue is best known from later rabbinical works, but already the mishnaic tract *Megillah* 3–4 contains a good deal about the Sabbath service. In reality the New Testament is the earliest source which informs us about the structure of the worship service in the synagogue (cf. Luke 4; Acts 13.14-15). In addition to the general accounts, special reference should be made to Strack-Billerbeck, *Kommentar zum Neuen Testament aus Talmud und Midrasch*, IV, 1 (München, 1928), pp. 115-88; S. Safrai and M. Stern, *The Jewish People in the First Century*, II (Assen/Amsterdam, 1974-76), pp. 415-63; Peter Schäfer, *Der synagogale Gottesdienst,* in: *Literatur und Religion des Frühjudentums* (Würzburg, 1973), pp. 391-413.

Chapter 4

SOCIAL GROUPS AND
RELIGIOUS MOVEMENTS

In the previous sections we have attempted to regard early
Jewish religion as a unity and to lay bare its basic structure.
When Josephus tried to describe the religious aspect of
Judaism to his Roman public, he took the opposite course. He
maintained that from the dawn of time Judaism had been
subdivided into three 'philosophies', with a fourth being represented by the rebellious groups in Roman times. In Hellenistic
Greek the word 'philosophy' signifies philosophical-religious
schools, and what Josephus had in mind were the Sadducees,
the Pharisees, the Essenes, and the religious nationalists
alluded to above.

One might get the impression from Josephus' account that
all Jews were consignable to one or another of these four
groups. This was by no means his intention; nor was it by any
stretch of the imagination the case. However, as might be
expected, there were many nuances within the basic religious
structure we have described. And when we further consider
how great were the upheavals experienced by Jewish society
in this period, it is hardly surprising that the distinctions
between the various religious views to some extent followed
the distinctions separating the various social groups. Josephus
was already aware of this fact, when he noted that the
Sadducees enjoyed the confidence of the wealthy, but had no
adherents among the 'people', whereas the Pharisees enjoyed
popular support. It is accordingly not incorrect of Bo Reicke to
speak of the 'Aristocratic Party of the Sadducees' and the
'Popular Party of the Pharisees'. Josephus made no effort to
locate the Essenes sociologically, but at least in their origins
they seem to have been a priestly splinter party who tried to
distance themselves from the temple and the rest of the
priesthood. Finally, it is quite certain that the nationalistic

religious groups won many adherents among the dissatisfied members of the lower classes. Thus, in this section it is to some extent permissible to approach problems from the point of view of the sociology of religion, in an attempt to establish connections between the various social strata and the religious movements and party formations.

In the final section we shall devote our attention to the apocalyptic currents and movements. They enjoyed an independent position with respect to Josephus' four groups; to some degree they found adherents among all of the groups in question. It is significant that Josephus describes certain apocalyptic figures, 'false prophets' and *soi-disant* messiahs, but that he does not mention the apocalypticists directly, and in no sense as a delimited group. Nor can we speak of an 'apocalyptic party'; rather, the phenomenon was more in the nature of a strong religious undercurrent which on occasion troubled the surface of the waters. But this should not lead us to underestimate the importance of the movement; it exercised a pervasive influence, and those who were captivated by the spell of apocalyptic ideas underwent a complete change in their understanding of existence, God, the world, and the future.

Religious life in Early Judaism had, then, many facets. If we return briefly to the previously mentioned opposition within Early Judaism between western and eastern culture, to the struggle between *polis* and *ethnos*, we shall see that all of the many religious groupings related to this tension in one way or another. There were some who mainly accepted the influences emerging from the west (the Sadducees). Others, concerning whom we are best informed, were largely dismissive of such influence. Among the latter there were several nuances: some were aggressive (i.e. the militant religious nationalists); others were what sociologists term 'evasive', that is, they separated themselves from social life and isolated themselves (the Essenes and the people of Qumran), while at the same time rising above the actual problems of their day by embracing a theological, apocalyptic understanding of the world situation. Finally, there were the centrists (the Pharisees) who attempted pragmatically to ensure their religious rights, while at the same time adapting to the changing social situation.

The Upper Classes: The Sadducees

The Sadducees stand in a strange sort of *chiaroscuro*; were they as a party defined by certain special religious views, by social boundaries, or by political attitudes? Did they really make up a 'party' at all, or a 'philosophy', as Josephus suggests? One of the reasons why it is so difficult for us to get a grasp on the Sadducees today is that we only happen to know them through their opponents (the Pharisees, the rabbis, Josephus, and the New Testament). A secondary reason is that in any event the 'party' was associated with the upper classes, and among the Jews these classes underwent great transformations in the period from 200 BCE to 70 CE; accordingly, the Sadducean party was hardly the same at the period's beginning as at its end.

An additional obstacle to our describing the Sadducees is the fact that the party had a number of features so disparate that, at first glance, they appear to have been irreconcilable: religious conservatism and cultural liberalism were the strange bedfellows of the Sadducean attitude. The explanation of these inner tensions is no doubt to be sought in the party's social and political situation. In order to defend its eminence, while at the same time keeping pace with social developments, the party was obliged to take a pragmatic attitude to religious questions. The result is an impression of internal incoherence in Sadducee religious thought. Josephus and the rabbis, writing in later times, compared them to the Greek Epicureans, with whom they may indeed have had some common features. Nevertheless, Sadduceeism was by no means an integrated philosophical system like that of Epicurus.

The designation 'Sadducee' is ordinarily derived from the name 'Zadok', who some hold to have been a Pharisee of the second century BCE who left the Pharisees and founded his own party. However, the story of this Zadok is highly legendary, and most scholars prefer to see the origin of the name in that of David's high priest, who founded the Zadokite priesthood which was preeminent in Jerusalem for almost a millennium, until the Hasmoneans took the high priestly office for themselves. If this view is correct, then the Sadducees are in some way to be identified with the Jerusalemite priestly aristocracy, a thought which gains in appeal when we consider that at least some representatives of the higher priesthood were expressly designated 'Sadducees'.

Consequently, in earlier scholarship, many researchers were prepared without more ado to describe the Sadducee party as the Jerusalemite priestly party. But matters were hardly so straightforward. As the name 'Sadducee' seems to indicate, it is probably correct that the party was somehow connected with the Jerusalemite priestly aristocracy. However, the Sadducees first manifested themselves as a 'party' around 110 BCE, during the reign of the Hasmonean monarch, John Hyrcanus. According to Josephus, the king abandoned the Pharisees (who, with their Hasidic past, should have been the Hasmoneans' natural allies), in order to allign himself with the Sadducees. But does Josephus actually mean the Jerusalemite priestly aristocracy? It is hard to believe. A few years previously, the Hasmoneans had overturned all precedent by assuming the high-priestly office and the leadership of the priesthood. Is it, then, at all likely that the Zadokite priesthood would have forgiven the Hasmoneans so speedily? Admittedly, the Zadokite priesthood was divided over the issue, and those who simply could not find it in their hearts to acknowledge what they took to be illegitimate high priests migrated to Qumran under the name 'the Sons of Zadok'. We shall meet these figures again presently. Naturally, it is possible that the remaining priests eventually saw the advantages of supporting the Hasmoneans, so that it is not unthinkable that some parts of the priesthood made up the membership of the Sadducee party at the close of the century.

Nevertheless, this does not entail the Sadducees being a purely priestly party. Other elements of the upper classes were also included in it. The question is, which elements? It has been commonly assumed that the higher priesthood and the old hereditary aristocracy, that is, the elements which dominated the Council, taken together formed the Sadducee party. But a study by William Buehler has shown that the non-priestly segment of the Sadducee party consisted not so much of the old hereditary as of the new monied aristocracy. This accords well with the fact that the Council was weakened under Hasmonean rule, and that at this time the monied aristocracy was supplanting the old hereditary aristocracy—a development which intensified later under Herod.

If it is correct that the Sadducee party consisted of the liberal element of the higher priesthood together with the new upper class, then the fact that the Hasmoneans and the Sadducees got on so well together, at least for a time, becomes immediately intelligible. The new upper class was primarily motivated by its business interests, and a large and powerful Jewish state could only be to its advantage. Furthermore, the inclusion of the hellenistic free cities in the kingdom, which the Hasmoneans sought to bring about, would also have had as its natural result Jewish participation in the international trade which these cities represented. The new upper class probably did not think that the price for this was too high, namely the likelihood that closer relationships with the hellenistic cities would bring increased influence from the foreign cultural milieu in their train. The Sadducees recognized that if the Jewish state was to survive, it would be self-destructive to attempt to isolate itself out of fear of contact with non-Jews; one cannot, after all, conduct international trade with oneself. Thus the strongly nationalistic feelings of the Sadducees went hand in hand with their liberal attitude towards the foreign, hellenistic world.

However, the Sadducees were by no means hellenizers in any vulgar sense; they are not to be compared with the opportunistic hellenists who preceded the Maccabean revolt, and who were prepared to abandon their Jewish heritage. The nationalistic enthusiasm which the striking successes of the Maccabean wars had produced, and whose fruits the Hasmoneans still enjoyed, was also shared by the Sadducees. What they intended was a great and powerful *Jewish* state, and they felt, not without reason, that the Hasmoneans would be able to provide it. Admittedly, as we have seen, the new upper class owed its origins primarily to the hellenistic *poleis*. But it is not hard to conceive that the influence from these

towns, plus the general affluence which they had helped bring
to the country as a whole, probably also created a corresponding new upper class in Palestinian Jewish society, particularly
in Jerusalem. The alliance with the Hasmoneans made them
conscious of their responsibility towards this society, which
they felt they were helping to expand. They had in the course
of time come to represent the 'establishment', which presumably explains their religious conservatism.

On first consideration it might seem difficult to comprehend
how the cultural openness and liberalism of the Sadducees
could be reconciled with a religious conservatism, which in
reality brought them into opposition to the progressive
Pharisees. Both the new Testament and Josephus agree that
the Sadducees adhered rigorously to the Torah and declined to
acknowledge the new regulations which the Pharisees had
derived from their interpretation of the Torah. People who,
like the Sadducees, felt responsible for the maintenance of law
and order, regarded a freely evolving tradition like that
espoused by the Pharisees to be cumbersome. Against this,
they felt the precisely delimited Law of Moses to represent a
static codex of laws that was considerably more convenient.
Similar concerns also led them to turn against the wildly
flourishing apocalyptic speculations with which other circles
witin Judaism were then enamoured. It was felt that such
tendencies led to religious excesses, and might contain within
them the germ of odious popular movements, or even to direct
rebellion against those in authority. Thus the Sadducees
declined to acknowledge the 'modern' notion of the resurrection of the dead, which was gaining popularity among Jews in
the period. They further regarded speculations about angels
and demons as timewasting undertakings whose sole consequence could be to distract attention from the daily obligations to which all were committed under the Law of Moses. In
short, Sadducean liberality had its limits; as far as religious
matters were concerned they intended to maintain the *status
quo* and accordingly did what they could to discourage the
renewal of Judaism from within. Renewal came nevertheless
after the year 70 CE, for, with the fall of Jerusalem the role of
the Sadducees was exhausted.

But in barely 200 years between the days of John Hyrcanus and the year 70 Sadducean influence was great indeed. It is unclear whether they had managed already in Hyrcanus' time to displace the old aristocracy from the Council. But in any case, during the reigns of Hyrcanus and Alexander Jannaeus they achieved their central position by taking over certain important state offices. Herod, though, seems to have purged the old Council systematically; as mentioned above, he executed 45 members of the Council and thereby gave the Sadducees their chance. It was probably from this time that the Council mainly consisted of Sadducees and Pharisees. Conditions were more or less the same under the rule of the Roman procurators, although it is conceivable that the Sadducees had a harder time of it in their competition with the Pharisees, in both Jewish and Roman eyes. In reality, the Sadducee party was more a political than a religious quantity, so it cannot be thought surprising that the Sadducees disappeared with the Jewish national state in the year 70.

Bibliographic Note to pp. 109-115
The three passages where Josephus discusses the Sadducees fairly intensively are *Bell.* 2.164-166; *Ant.* 13.171-173, and *Ant.* 18.16-17. They are mentioned only rarely in the New Testament: we are above all informed as to their attitudes in Mk 12.18-27 (parr. Mt. 22.23-33; Lk. 20.27-40), and in the dramatic episode which is related in Acts 23.1-10. The passages in Josephus and the more important attestations in the rabbinical literature have been collected in E. Schürer, *History of the Jewish People*, II (Edinburgh, 1979), pp. 381-88; the Sadducees are dealt with on pp. 404-14. See also Strack-Billerbeck, *Kommentar zum NT*, IV, 1 (München, 1928), pp. 339-52. Modern treatments of the question of the Sadducees are those of J. Jeremias, *Jerusalem at the Time of Jesus* (London, 1969), pp. 228-32; R. Meyer, 'Sadducee', *TDNT*, VII (1971), pp. 35-54; Bo Reicke, *The New Testament Era* (London, 1968), pp. 152-56; and G. Baumbach, *Der sadduzäische Konservatismus*, in: *Literatur und Religion des Frühjudentums* (Würzburg, 1973), pp. 201-13. The most recent monograph on the Sadducees is J. Le Moyne, *Les Sadducéens* (Paris, 1972). The understanding of the Sadducees which has most influenced the account offered here is that of W.W. Buehler, *The Pre-Herodian Civil War and Social Debate* (Basel, 1974).

The Middle Class: The Pharisees

We have had numerous grounds for the supposition that the turbulent years after 170 BCE were decisive for the development of Early Judaism, and if we are to understand Pharisaism correctly it will be necessary to return to this important epoch. A thumbnail-sketch of Pharisaism would have to include the following observations: Pharisaism began as a national and religious revival movement among the laity of the middle class and parts of the priesthood. As a popular reaction to the general development, the movement contributed to the success of the Maccabean revolt; at the same time, it developed considerably and was itself changed by the struggle for freedom.

Early Pharisaism may be more or less directly identified with the Hasidic movement, 'the company of the pious', which formed the popular background of the Maccabean revolt in the 160s (cf. p. 31). This identification, however, is not entirely obvious. The sources bearing on the problem are not univocal; Josephus, for example, first mentions the Pharisees in connection with the events around the close of the second century BCE, that is, around fifty years after the Maccabean revolt. Conversely, later rabbinical texts refer to Pharisaic teachers of the law from the period shortly before 200 BCE and down to the middle of the second century. Thus the evolution which led up to the formation of the Pharisaic movement is not completely clear; but this evolution would be unintelligible if we did not suppose that there was a close connection between at least some parts of the Hasidic movement and the phenomenon which, later in the century, manifested itself as Pharisaism. In any event, it was the conflict between the hellenizing Jews and the old-fashioned orthodox Jews which formed the background of the emergence of the Pharisees.

What, then, was the mainspring of this 'revival'? In the first place, we should note that it was originally a movement among the laity. The Gospels in particular, where the Pharisees and the scribes are mentioned time and again in the same breath, create the impression that the Pharisees and the scribes were identical. It is correct that the Pharisees gathered around famous teachers of the Law, that there was eventually an alliance between 'scribes' and Pharisees, and that the scribes became, in a manner of speaking, the chief ideologues of the Pharisees. This was especially noticeable in the first century CE, when the scribes and Pharisees had achieved a position of power in the Council, but it was by no means the case earlier, during the rule of the upper class oligarchy. Things were certainly different when Pharisaism first arose, about 200 years earlier. Then it was a popular movement which had arisen spontaneously; or, perhaps better, it had developed in gradual reaction to the hellenizing tendencies, and then, when conflict became acute, Pharisaism broke through with great power.

Again: what was the distinguishing characteristic of the movement? If, for the present, we ignore the national-political and social aspects of the movement, and concentrate instead on its religious side, then it is permissible to characterize early Pharisaism as a revival and penitential movement. Its members intended to call the Jewish people to renewed awareness of their religious inheritance, to make them grasp the dangers to their religion which were inherent in hellenistic culture, and to attempt to adhere to what the membership regarded as the central line in Jewish religion: the Law as the norm for every detail of individual life. They sought furthermore to do penance for the people's failure to uphold the ancient religious ideals.

This was, so to speak, the programme of Pharisaism, for which reason it is often said that the Pharisees intensified the Law. As it stands, the statement is not wrong, but it is nevertheless inaccurate. It is insufficient to note that the Pharisees emphasized the rigorous observance of the Jewish law, since any serious Jew could have made the same claim. Rather, the Pharisees went beyond the general requirements and demanded instead the exceptional. They levied some quite specific demands which decisively exceeded the normal range of expectation as to keeping the Law: the Pharisees required that the purity regulations which had ordinarily to be observed only by priests in the course of their performance of their sacred duties in the temple should further apply to ordinary Jews in their everyday walks of life. On first consideration, perhaps this does not sound like so much to ask, but it is in fact a prodigious undertaking, so that whoever commits himself to it thereby obligates himself to an entirely new way of life.

In a manner of speaking, this requirement enacted the idea of the 'universal priesthood'. We read in the Old Testament (Exod. 19.6) that all of Israel was intended to be a priesthood before the Lord. The deeper significance of this idea was, as Exodus also explains, that Israel is to be a sacred people, and the more people who fulfil the most stringent demands of purity and sacrality, the closer Israel would come to this ideal. Furthermore, the fact that the laity undertook to live up to obligations otherwise only incumbent on the priests may be understood as a penitential act. After all, who was it who above all others had once failed the God of Israel? It was precisely the leading priesthood, who had been among those most receptive towards the new religious currents.

The innumerable priestly regulations concerning purity and holiness are quite technical by nature; in reality, they cannot be kept in all details in everyday life, not, that is, if one intends to lead anything approaching a normal everyday existence. The observance of the rigorous cultic purity laws outside of the temple simply had to interfere with the Pharisee's way of life at virtually every turn. Those who attempted to carry out the Pharisaic programme quickly discovered that their entire existence had to be ordered so as to enable them to keep the rules: they had to beware what they ate, whom they ate with, whom and what they touched; and they had to keep their distance from anything and everything which might conceivably sully their purity. Only the very few were able to live up to such demands, for which reason Pharisaism speedily became an elitist movement composed of strong-willed and principled men who were willing to sacrifice everything to realize their ideal. The true Pharisee was virtually compelled to dissociate himself from the common herd (in fact, the very name 'Pharisee' presumably means 'he who isolates himself'). The price he had to pay for this was very high, in that he was constrained hand and foot in his workaday life. The reward, however, was also high: he achieved status and acknowledgment as a Jew of the highest calibre. 'Purity leads to separation, separation to holiness', as the Mishnah has it; a statement which might be even more accurate had it said: 'separation leads to purity, purity to holiness'.

The demand for separateness from the profane realm which inevitably imposed itself on every Pharisee led quite naturally to the Pharisees' seeking to associate with one another. They established 'fraternities', exclusive clubs which made stringent demands on those who sought to join them. Within such closed fraternities one could be sure that only men of like mind, determined to uphold their purity, would be present. Here it was possible to dine together without running a risk of eating unclean food, or of sitting at table with someone who had not observed the dictates of cultic purity. Also, in such gatherings it was possible to discuss the many, detailed regulations of the Law and, not least, to work out new regulations designed to deal with the many situations which necessarily arose in everyday life for anyone who desired to fulfil the letter of the Law in its entirety.

In the course of time the fraternities developed into virtual 'schools', whose spiritual centre was some famous legal scholar. The best-known and most influential of the Pharisaic teachers of the Law were Hillel and Shammai, both of whom were active in Herod's day, but whose influence—via their 'schools'—extended long after the lifetime of Christ. Hillel advocated a mild interpretation of the Law, while Shammai endorsed a more rigorous form. Among the many sayings of Hillel, in particular, are examples reminiscent of Jesus' sayings in the Gospels. Characteristically enough, Hillel had his own version of the 'Golden Rule' of the Sermon on the Mount (negatively stated, as it is in fact to be found in other cultures as well). The brief anecdote which contains Hillel's version also helps to shed light on the psyche of the two figures:

> It happened that a certain heathen came before Shammai and said to him: 'Make me a proselyte, on condition that you teach me the whole Torah while I stand on one foot'. Thereupon he repulsed him with the builder's cubit which was in his hand. When he went before Hillel, he said to him: 'What is hateful to you, do not to your neighbour: that is the whole Torah, while the rest is commentary thereof; go and

learn it!' (*b.Shabb*. 31a; after E.P. Sanders, *Paul and Palestinian Judaism*, p. 113).

Of the later Pharisaic scholars, the more notable are mentioned in the Mishnah and other rabbinical writings. One of the most important was Gamaliel, the teacher of the apostle Paul (Acts 22.3). His moderate attitude towards the first Christians testifies to his wealth of sound common sense (Acts 5.34-39), and he received a beautiful obituary from his disciples:

> When Rabba Gamaliel the Elder died, the glory of the Law ceased and purity and abstinence died (*m.Sotah* 9.15).

Of decisive importance was Johanan ben Zakkai, who lived through the destruction of Jerusalem in 70 CE. It was largely owing to his efforts that the new centre for Pharisaic learning was established in Jabneh (Jamnia); much of his skill was devoted to the interpretation of the cultic laws in light of the new situation which had come about with the destruction of the temple and the cessation of the temple cult. When he was asked how it would in future be possible to live up to the basic statement, which we have met previously—that the world rests upon the Law, the temple cult, and the deeds of brotherly love—he answered that the deeds of love could assume the penitential function which the temple sacrifices had earlier enjoyed. In so saying, he pointed to the famous remark in Hosea, 'I desire mercy, and not sacrifice'. The Essenes of Qumran had already followed a similar argument when they had had to abandon their connection to the temple in Jerusalem.

Johanan ben Zakkai had numerous highly talented students who helped to consolidate and leave their mark on the rabbinical academy in Jabneh (Jamnia). Most of them belonged to the school of Hillel, but Shammai's school was also represented; the Mishnah cites many controversies between the two schools. Eliezer ben Hyrkanos and Josua ben Hanania were Johanan's most important students. The former was the most learned of all, and was gifted with a formidable memory ('he is like a well-plastered cistern that never loses a drop of water', as Johanan once said of him). He was an opponent of the authoritarian Gamaliel II, a grandchild of Gamaliel the

Elder, who led the academy for a time. The best-known of these later rabbis is probably Rabbi Akiba, who is remembered because he lent his authority to Bar Cochba's messianic claim in conjunction with the rebellion against Hadrian in the 130s. But he also seems to have been the first to undertake to collect and organize the many new legal formulations. He grouped them according to subject, which is how they appeared in the Mishnah when its editing was completed around the year 200.

These generations of rabbis were of vast importance for the subsequent development of Judaism. They introduced interpretive principles, so that the formulation of new rules on the basis of the Pentateuch is not a matter of happenstance. Already Hillel had proposed seven basic rules, and later, at the beginning of the second century CE, Rabbi Ishmael expanded the number to thirteen. It later rose to thirty-two. The rabbinical interpretation of Scripture may be composed as a *midrash*, that is, a running commentary on the books of the Law. Alternatively, one can take the opposite approach by posing a question which is not directly answered by the Torah; one then works towards a solution which is based on a statement in Scripture, frequently one which has no obvious relevance to the matter in hand. To take but a single example: Deut. 18.4 contains some rules for the offering of the first fruits, and in this connection we read that when one shears one's sheep, the first of the wool also belongs to the Lord. The wool from how many of the sheep?, the rabbis then ask. The mishnaic tractate *Hullim* 11.2 attempts to answer:

> The School of Shammai say: 'Two sheep; for it is written: A man shall nourish a young cow and two sheep' (Isa. 7.21). And the School of Hillel say: 'Five; for it is written: (Abigail brought David) five sheep ready dressed' (1 Sam. 25.18).

How typical this example is is open to discussion, and it may be unfair to use it to exemplify rabbinical exegesis. By contemporary exegetical standards, this form of argumentation seems to consist wholly of non-sequiturs. The point, however, is that to the rabbis it was a presupposition that Scripture contains words which in one way or another may be understood as providing answers to various questions.

This sort of judgment is called *halakah* (literally a rule to
guide one's wandering), and the Mishnah and the Talmud
contain thousands of them. Early *halakah* was concerned
mainly with the regulations governing purity and eating,
which fits well with what we have previously said about the
nature of early Pharisaism. As a natural continuation of such
matters, we also find rules concerned with sacrifice, with the
sale of comestibles, the tithe (according to the rules, only
agricultural products which have been tithed are 'clean' and
may be utilized for food), and the Sabbath (they are concerned
in particular with the preparation and preservation of food in
connection with the Sabbath). But also more ordinary social
laws (e.g. dealing with marriage, restitution and so forth)
were coined in *halakoth* at an early date.

In the process of working out *midrashim* to those parts of
the Pentateuch which do not contain legal material the rabbis
produced supplementary material called *haggadah*, 'story' or
'account'. Legendary in nature, these were morally improv-
ing or didactic interpretations of and additions to the biblical
narratives. Much of this sort of material is to be found outside
of the rabbinical literature, in the Pseudepigrapha; for example, *Jubilees* may be understood as a haggadic *midrash* on
Genesis. But *haggadah* is also to be found spread throughout
the entire rabbinic literature.

We have alluded previously to the Pharisee's tendency to
isolate himself. In order to act in harmony with his principles,
it was imperative that a Pharisee distance himself physically
from a society in which only a very few fulfilled the demands
of purity and holiness, which he saw as expressions of the
divine will. It seems likely that some segments of the original
Hasidic movement, who shared much of the basic attitude of
the later Pharisees, actually drew the consequences of their
principles and settled beyond the borders of their society.
There is much to suggest that these people were a wing of the
Hasidic movement, which represented the lower priesthood in
Jerusalem; they went into the desert and founded the Essene
society in Qumran. It is conceivable that non-priestly
Pharisees also joined the desert community, although self-
exile was not in general characteristic of the Pharisees.
Rather, the typical Pharisee remained true to his 'calling and

class', and attempted to maintain his cultic purity among the 'children of the world'. By the same token, since he was something of a missionary, he also attempted to win people who thought differently to his views. As we have seen, the Pharisees came from the middle class, and most of them had typical middle-class professions such as trade, manufacture, and so forth. There were also scribes and priests among their numbers, but there is no doubt that these represented a minority.

What all Pharisees had in common was, as we have seen, their attempt to keep the many rules of purity while as far as possible leading normal, middle-class lives. This meant that the Pharisee was by nature a pragmatist, in the sense that, on the one hand he intensified the demands of the Law to the extreme, while on the other he modified them so as to be able to live with them. In the later Pharisaic-rabbinical legal discussion there are many examples of rules which would appear to us to be attempts to circumvent the Law, or at the least to draw the sting from the more radical regulations. In fact these efforts represent an attitude of compromise which, quite often, drew criticism from the more radical groups on the right wing of Judaism, as well as from such an offshoot as the young Christian congregation, which had quite a different understanding of the Law.

There is something endearingly human in this zeal on behalf of the Law coupled with an insistence that the Law must, in the last instance, be fulfillable! There is great psychological depth in the view that any religion undermines itself which issues commandments and prohibitions which are ultimately impracticable. At the same time it is unquestionable that much true piety and sincerity characterized the Pharisaic ideology. The Gospel picture of the Pharisees as thorough-going hypocrites does not apply, as this understanding was polemically weighted and produced by an acute conflict situation. Within Judaism, the Pharisees were the only qualified opponents of the emergent church, for which reason the Gospels are concerned to portray them as exponents of a cold and calculating morality of self-interest. As we have seen, piety and deep religious feeling were prominent characteristics of the best Pharisees. On the basis of the presuppositions of Jewish religion, Pharisaism was a serious attempt to 'fulfill the whole of the Law' for the simple reason that 'the Law is holy and its commandment holy and just', to use the words of the apostle Paul, the former Pharisee.

One hopes it will be apparent that Pharisaism was not only a religious phenomenon. We have seen that the movement had its roots in the national-religious revival which occurred in the context of the Maccabean revolt. At that time it functioned in opposition to the hellenizing currents within the Jewish people. Later in the development of early Judaism it is still appropriate to understand Pharisaism as a religious phenomenon, but one which is also to be seen from a sociological and a political point of view. The entire course of development may be seen as a class struggle, that is, as the attempt of the middle class to encroach on the power of the upper classes. In reality, as we have seen, the ideology of Pharisaism was based on the assumption of priestly privileges, and the Pharisees eagerly strove to be the teachers of the people in the religious field. The fraternities and 'academies' became small spiritual centres of power within society. When the Pharisees turned against the Hasmonean priest-kings, which they initially did because of religious motives, they also came into conflict with the aristocratic groups and the Sadducean party, who supported the Hasmoneans. This led to persecution and martyrdom, not least in the reign of Alexander Jannaeus in the 90s and 80s BCE. But time and political evolution were on the side of the Pharisees. It has been pointed out that it was impossible for either Jannaeus' widowed queen, Alexandra, who ruled in the 70s and 60s, or for Herod the Great to take the high priestly office as the earlier Hasmoneans had done. Accordingly, they no doubt saw it as in their own interest to suppress the priestly-dominated Council and the aristocratic Sadducean party, and to favour the middle class party of the Pharisees. By the time the Roman procurators came into power, the position of the Pharisees was so firmly entrenched that the Romans were obliged to respect it.

The political catastrophe of 70 CE, when the Romans destroyed Jerusalem, brought about a radical transformation of Jewish Palestinian society which was decisive for

Pharisaism. The power which had once been in the hands of the Sadducees had been a function of wealth, land-ownership, office-holding, and a fair endowment of political opportunism. Such things no longer applied, and the Sadducees consequently disappeared as a social group. By way of contrast, Pharisaism had developed into a solidly established social quantity, predicated solely on the idea of an Israel consisting of the pure and holy. The Pharisees managed to adhere to this idea and to lead their people successfully through the catastrophe. The Pharisees were entirely dominant in the quasi-political Council which was established in Jabneh on the Mediterranean coast, and the Pharisaic interpretation of the Law and its perpetuation of the oral tradition continued well into the Middle ages, when they achieved written form in the great rabbinical works.

Bibliographic Note to pp. 116-125
Josephus discusses the peculiarities of the Pharisees at length in three passages: *Bell.* 2.162-63; *Ant.* 13.171-72, and *Ant.* 18.11-15. The sections in question are reprinted in E. Schürer's *History of the Jewish People*, II (Edinburgh, 1979), pp. 381-88, along with the more important rabbinical descriptions of the Pharisees; these materials are critically investigated on pp. 388-404. See further Strack-Billerbeck, *Kommentar zum Neuen Testament aus Talmud und Midrasch*, IV, 1 (München, 1928), pp. 334-52. The Gospels refer to the Pharisees innumerable times; the more important of the so-called 'conflict-discussions' between Jesus and the Pharisees are in Mt. 12; 15–16; 23; Mk 2; 7; 10; Lk. 6; 11; 14; 16; 18; Jn 3; 5 and a number of other passages. The problem of the Pharisees is dealt with in all sizeable works dealing with early Jewish religion. See especially G.F. Moore, *Judaism in the First Centuries of the Christian Era*, I (Cambridge Mass., 1927), pp. 56-92; J. Jeremias, *Jerusalem at the Time of Jesus* (London, 1969), pp. 246-67; E.P. Sanders, *Paul and Palestinian Judaism* (London, 1977); R. Meyer and H.F. Weiss, 'Pharisee', *TDNT* IX (1974), pp. 11-48; C. Thoma, *Der Pharisäismus*, in: *Literatur und Religion des Frühjudentums* (Würzburg, 1973), pp. 254-72; W.W. Buehler, *The Pre-Herodian Civil War* (Basel, 1974), pp. 70-94. The most recent major work on Pharisaism is J. Neusner, *The Rabbinic Traditions about the Pharisees before 70*, I-III (Leiden, 1971); Neusner's views are also available in popular form in: *From Politics to Piety* (Grand Rapids, 1973). On the later rabbis, see E. Schürer, *History of the Jewish People*, II (Edinburgh, 1979), pp. 314-80; G. Stemberger, *Das Klassische Judentum. Kultur und Geschichte der rabbinischen*

Zeit (München, 1979), and P. Schäfer, *Geschichte der Juden in der Antike* (Stuttgart–Neukirchen, 1983), pp. 145-85; E.E. Urbach, *The Sages. Their Concepts and Beliefs* (Jerusalem, 1975).

The National-Religious Revolutionary Movements of the Lower Class

The extent to which the above heading adequately describes so composite a quantity as the Jewish revolutionary movements of the Roman period, is admittedly debatable. It is at least certain that in spite of the fact that the incitements to revolt repeatedly came from persons who seem to have belonged to the higher social classes, the recruits who participated in the various revolts were mostly drawn from the lower classes— proletarized priests, unpropertied peasants, or the dregs of the new urban populations. It is also undeniable that the motives underlying these revolutionary efforts comprised a mixture of religious, national and social resentments in the Jewish part of the Palestinian populace, although it is not possible to delimit these forces with respect to one another.

The revolutionary impulse was present throughout most of the Roman period, or at least from the beginning of the reign of Herod the Great in the 30s BCE. Concrete provocations—as a rule consisting of either conflict with the Roman authorities or of conflicts between Jews and the populations of the Greek *poleis*—repeatedly fanned the flames of rebellion. The process culminated in the great revolt in the 60s CE, which ended with the destruction of Jerusalem.

If we examine the tragic final phase even cursorily, we get a clear impression as to how complex was the composition of the revolutionary movements, and how powerful the contradictions were which obtained between the various groups. While the Romans were besieging Jerusalem, several revolutionary Jewish groups in the city were combatting one another. Groups from the country fought with groups from the city, priestly groups opposed lay interests, the priestly aristocracy fought the lower priests, not to speak of the contradictions which may be discerned within any revolution: the moderates against the radicals, the faint-hearted against the uncompromising, those who still have something left to salvage versus those who have everything to win and nothing to lose.

The reason why it is difficult for us to get a proper grip on the various groupings is that Josephus, who is virtually our only source, lays down a smokescreen in this area. There is no question but that he was in a difficult situation, as he had participated for a time in the revolt, seen what it must inevitably lead to, and changed adroitly over to the Roman side. When he wrote his great historical works in the 70s and 90s CE it was important to Josephus to impress on his Roman readership the fact that there were courageous men among the Jews (including himself), who had admittedly participated in the revolt, but they had done so primarily to keep the wilder elements in check and in the hope of arriving at a solution by arbitration with the Romans. Conversely, Josephus had no desire to appear both turncoat and traitor to his Jewish readers, for which reason he depicted the left wing of the revolt as wild and barbaric hordes with whom no one could conceivably sympathize. In this balancing act Josephus is at least partially successful, but the price he pays for the achievement is a degree of obscurity in his narrative. However, if we read Josephus critically, we may still manage to get a reasonable picture of the course of events. In the historical prospect at the beginning of this work we touched only briefly on the revolutionary movements. Here it will be necessary to go into more detail; we shall do so by looking at the events themselves, following which we shall try to understand the various causes and motives underlying them.

It is significant that when the Maccabean revolt began in the 160s BCE, it took place under the leadership of a single family, the priestly Maccabean line. If we proceed to the Roman period, which began with Pompey's conquest of Palestine in 63 BCE, we note the same phenomenon once more. For much of the Roman period, or at any rate from the last years of Herod the Great and until the fall of Jerusalem, we find that it was still members of the same line who were leading the various attempted revolts. Perhaps this does not apply to Ezekias, who was already leading a Galilean uprising against Herod in the 30s BCE; it is at best uncertain whether this Ezekias was related by blood to the later revolutionaries.

At all events, Herod had problems enough with Ezekias, who is known to have belonged to important Galilean bloodlines. Josephus attempts to distance himself from this Ezekias, whom he terms the 'archrobber', that is, a leader of bands of brigands. However, Ezekias was not just anyone, as we see from the fact that when Herod had him caught and executed, a complaint against Herod was raised with the Council, although he naturally made sure that the case came to nought. Ezekias' adherents seem to have come from the lower classes, and they continued the struggle even after his death. They abandoned their towns and villages and retreated to caves in the wilderness and the mountains until they were untimately defeated.

After Herod's day the revolutionary movements—in Josephus' account—receive sharper contours. Immediately after Herod's death in 4 BCE, problems erupted again in Galilee under the leadership of a certain Judas, whom some historians have assumed was a son of Ezekias. The revolt eventually reached Jerusalem, but the Roman commander Varus was able to suppress it with the help of a couple of his legions. There is good reason to suppose that this same Judas reappeared ten years later as the leading figure in yet another revolt. At this time he was called Judas the Galilean. This took place when Herod Archelaus was deposed by the Romans, and his territories, Judea, Idumea, and Samaria, were made subject to the authority of a Roman procurator. On the occasion of this transition to a new form of government the Roman governor in Syria, Quirinius, ordered the undertaking of a census in Palestine to provide a secure basis for taxation. Interestingly, it was this census which the Gospel of Luke uses to date Jesus' birth, and which it also erroneously assigns to the time of Herod (Lk. 2.2). It seems to have been the new taxation proposal which directly occasioned the revolt in question, which cost Judas his life.

Judas the Galilean and his revolt were not forgotten. He was referred to several decades later in the Acts of the Apostles (5.37), and his efforts may have provided the spark which led to the formation of the Zealot revolutionary movement, about which we are first informed in the New Testament when we learn that one of Jesus' disciples was called Simon Zelotes (Lk.

6.15; Acts 1.13). It is possible that Barabbas, who was freed instead of Jesus, was one of the Zealots (in Mk 15.7 and Lk. 23.19 he is called a rebel, whereas Jn 18.40 calls him a 'robber', using the same Greek term as Josephus applies to Ezekias). The sons of Judas apparently helped to continue the impulse towards rebellion, as two of them, Jacob and Simon, were crucified by the Romans in the 40s.

When the great altercation with the Romans began in the year 66, the divisions in the ranks of the rebels were already apparent. Menachem, a third son, or perhaps a grandson, of Judas the Galilean, was one of the leaders of rebellious groups which were originally active in the country and then subsequently in Jerusalem. They were called *sicarii*, literally 'daggermen', since they had specialized in the assassination of Romans and Jewish collaborators. Together with Eleazar, who was either a cousin or a nephew, Menachem occupied the desert fortress of Masada, by the Dead Sea. Later, however, when parts of the Jerusalem priesthood turned against the Romans, Menachem and his men entered the city and took part in the siege of the Roman fortifications. A dispute arose between Menachem and the leader of the priestly rebellion concerning each other's relative competence; the latter figure was also called Eleazar, and he was, incidentally, the son of the high priest Ananias, whom we know thanks to the New Testament (Acts 23.2; 24.1). Menachem was ultimately killed by the priests, and his cousin Eleazar fled together with some of the *sicarii* back to Masada, where, some years later, they died by their own hands just as the Romans stormed the fortress.

The killing of Menachem took place in the year 66; after this event the rebellion became so extremely complicated that we can make no attempt here to untangle the various threads. It will nevertheless be useful to identify the main *dramatis personae*. With the aid of his adherents, who were mainly found among the lower ranks of the priesthood, plus that of the citizens of Jerusalem and the *sicarii* from the provinces, Eleazar, the son of the high priest, succeeded in expelling the Romans from the city. This was no mean feat, but Eleazar proceeded to rest on his laurels and even made peace with the high priest Ananus (not to be confused with the earlier

Ananias), who up to that point had supported the Romans.
Thus the high priests and the most elevated social strata once
again had control of the city.

Not everyone in Jerusalem was satisfied with this conclusion to the story. A priest who, confusingly enough, was also
called Eleazar (the son of Simeon), formed a rebel group
which consisted of the lower priesthood, citizens of Jerusalem,
and those *sicarii* who had remained in the city. Together they
seized the temple area and chose a high priest by casting lots.
It is this group which Josephus designates 'the zealots'. The
higher priesthood had the support of some of the populace of
the city and accordingly besieged the temple, but the zealots
then received help from the Idumeans, who killed the high
priest Ananus. Together the zealots and the Idumeans introduced a reign of terror, in which quite a number of prominent
Jerusalemites were executed.

The zealots' democratic attitude did not suit everyone, and
in the course of the year 68 the movement splintered. An
ambitious Galilean named John of Gischala, who had so far
attempted to play both ends against the middle, put his hand
in; as Josephus says, 'he carried in his breast a dire passion for
despotic power' (*Bell.* 4.208). After having been the high priest
Ananus' righthand man for a while, John joined the zealots
and then broke their ranks, too, winning the support of
Galileans, Idumeans and others, so that for a time his group
appeared to be the largest in Jerusalem.

John was mainly motivated by personal ambition, but
instead of having to contend with a weakened zealot party he
soon encountered an opponent who was both an abler military
strategist, and who happened to have a programme. This was
Simon the son of Gioras who had, for a time, waged guerrilla
war against the Romans in the provinces, and also against the
well-situated Jewish landowners who supported the Romans.
Simon's programme was social in nature, and his troops
consequently consisted in the main of runaway slaves. His
ultimate goal was the establishment of a new and righteous
society. His task, then, was to reduce the influence of the
zealots and John of Gischala. Ironically enough, he first
managed to enter Jerusalem with his army of slaves after
having allied himself with the high priests, the Jerusalemite

upper class, and the Idumeans, who abandoned John. He fought for quite some time against the zealots, and when it became necessary to mobilize all available resources against the Roman siege he was the natural leader. The Romans, too, regarded him as the head of the revolt, and subsequently executed him in the Forum Romanum.

But it is not only Josephus's picture of the last decisive war with the Romans that is unclear; his accounts of the earlier rebellions are likewise murky. And this situation does not improve when we attempt to penetrate behind the many revolts and to inquire as to motives and driving forces. In fact, if we follow the path back to the earliest revolt, that of Ezekias against Herod in the 30s BCE, we discover that we are insufficiently informed. It may have been the case that there was a general resentment in the Galilean rural population towards Herod's harsh policies, but religious motives may also have contributed to Herod's unpopularity. The conservative populace can hardly have been enthusiastic supporters of the half-Jew who occupied David's throne. Moreover, Herod's benevolent attitude towards the Greek *poleis* contrasted sharply with the attempts of the early Hasmoneans to 'Judaize' the non-Jewish part of Palestine.

As we have seen, Ezekias did not belong to the lower class, although many of his supporters are likely to have done so. The privileged situation of the Greek free cities directly contributed to the proletarization of the poorer elements in the populace, so that Ezekias' revolt doubtless had a social aspect. At all events, we read that after Herod's death in 4 BCE a deputation of prominent Jews approached the emperor Augustus, explained about Herod's having exploited the country, and requested that Palestine be brought under direct Roman administration rather than being subjected to a continuation of Herod's policies under one of his sons. This provides indirect evidence that social and economic problems played a part in the attempted revolts during Herod's reign.

We have repeatedly mentioned the lower classes and the proletariat in connection with the revolts. It has been suggested that the initiative was usually taken by individuals belonging to the upper classes, whereas the outbreaks themselves were peopled by members of the lower classes. This assertion ought probably to be modified slightly. Gerd Theissen emphasizes, no doubt correctly, that people generally tend to rebel 'against threatening rather than existing misery'. And this means, as he continues, that the 'social basis (of the Jewish revolutionary movements) was not so much the very lowest elements in society as the members of a marginal middle stratum which was especially sensitive towards social and economic changes'. This applies especially to the rural citizens, who in many cases were merely tenant farmers; the land-owners were the royal household and the capitalists in the cities. If the peasants were unable to pay their taxes and imposts, they lost their leases and subsided into the the ranks of the unpropertied. In Herod's time both the tax and land-use policies were harsh, so that many people came into this unfortunate situation or else perceived it as an impending danger. In other words, out in the country the spirit of rebellion was strongest among those elements which we would characterize as the lower middle class. In Jerusalem it was particularly the members of the lower priesthood who were in danger of losing the privileges which the priesthood had enjoyed from ancient times. Capital and privileges were at this time concentrated in the higher ranks of the priesthood.

All this means that a variety of groups played a part in the various revolutionary movements, each of which had its own particular interests to defend. It is with the revolt of Judas the Galilean in 6 CE that we are first told anything about the ideology of the rebels. As we have mentioned, it was Quirinius' census which provided the external occasion. Josephus says that Judas, 'incited his countrymen to revolt, upbraiding them as cowards for consenting to pay tribute to the Romans and tolerating mortal masters, after having God for their lord' (*Bell.* 22.118). Furthermore, Josephus maintains that Judas became the leader of a party, called by Josephus 'the fourth philosophy', which was unlike the parties of the Pharisees, the Sadducees, or the Essenes. He modified this view, however, in his work on the history of the Jews, where he says simply that the 'fourth philosophy' agreed in all particulars with the teachings of the Pharisees. To this he adds that the rebels have 'a passion for liberty that is almost unconquerable'. They felt that any weakness in the face of the Romans' financial demands would force the Jews into slavery. If they resisted the demands of the Roman taxmen they would at best secure wealth, at worst, honour (*Ant*. 18.4-10, 23-25).

Josephus' claim that the ideology of the rebels was in every respect identical to the Pharisaic teaching is very interesting. But can we make it meaningful? Josephus mentions that alongside Judas the Galilean was another leader, 'Saddok, the Pharisee', and it is of course possible to see a connection between the Pharisaic demand that the Law determine all aspects of the Jews' life and the slogan of the rebels: no one over the Jews except God. It is likewise clear that the Pharisees must have regarded the daily temple sacrifices on the emperor's behalf as irreconcilable with the Law. But from such views to open rebellion against the Romans was quite a leap. Perhaps Josephus' own situation was symptomatic. It was presumably the case that the average Pharisee was originally opposed to rebellion against the Romans, and that after the final war between Jews and Romans had broken out in 66 CE he also regarded the undertaking as suicidal. But when the war raged in earnest, the Pharisees had to choose sides, so they took the side of the Jews and attempted to save whatever might be preserved.

But there were other religious groups which found it possible to participate in the revolutionary movements for quite different reasons. In particular, there were the apocalyptists, who saw in the rejection of the Roman yoke the first decisive step towards the last days. This apocalyptic element in the revolutionary movements was especially expressed in the messianic figures who appeared around the time of the birth of Christ. Josephus maintains that Judas the Galilean had royal aspirations, and so behaved as a messianic pretender. About the same time two representatives of the lower classes appeared, both of whom claimed to be the Messiah. These were the slave Simeon and the shepherd Atrongaios. Later the Theudas who is mentioned in Acts 5.36 probably made a similar claim, and Menachem, whom we mentioned above, behaved like a royal Messiah during the war in the 60s; he was also killed by the other rebels. Finally, it is also well known that Bar Cochba (cf. p. 44) was hailed as the Messiah during the rebellion in the 130s. Some scholars have spoken of charismatic leadership in conjunction with the revolutionary movements, and there can be no doubt that these Messiahs provided the rebellions with a religious dimension which they did not have originally.

The social aspect continued to play a part in the history of the movements. The social problems which had arisen in Herod's day did not wane in the period of direct Roman rule. The crown properties which Herod and his sons had amassed became Roman property, so that the leasehold imposts remained a mighty weight on the shoulders of the rural populace, alongside taxes, which had to be paid to both the Romans and the temple. The reason why 'freedom' is so heavily emphasized in Josephus' characterization of Judas' movement, and the reason for Josephus' having accused the rebels of 'greed', is probably that the struggle was a socio-political battle for freedom, in which the hoped-for tangible result was probably freedom from taxation. At all events, we hear in connection with the attempted revolts in the provinces, that the rebels turned against the wealthy and their property. This is true, for example, of the messianic pretender, Simeon, whom we have mentioned previously; but it also applies to Judas the Galilean at the beginning of the century, as well as to several revolts in the 50s BCE, and, above all, to the guerrilla war of Simon, the son of Gioras in the 60s. Moreover, at the beginning of the great revolt in the 60s something similar occurred in Jerusalem itself, as we read that the rebel group which was led by the lower priesthood burned the city archives, 'eager to destroy the money-lenders' bonds and the prevent the recovery of debts, in order to win over a host of grateful debtors and to cause a rising of the poor against the rich...' (*Bell.* 2.427).

In short, the underlying motives were a mixture of religious, national and social impulses, and the lower classes saw their own opportunity to hasten a social upheaval which could only be to their advantage. It is conceivable that at the beginning, the revolutionary movements were predominantly motivated by religion. It is also possible that the more radical wing of the Pharisaic movement, led by the followers of Shammai, contributed to the formulation of a religious foundation for the revolt: the idea that any connection with the heathen Romans must be regarded as contradictory to God's law. But other motives made their appearance as well, and the process of disintegration which characterized the final phase of the rebellion was not caused by religious contradictions between the various groups of rebels, but by violent social contradictions within the Jewish population of Palestine.

Bibliographic Note to pp. 126-35
Many of the passages in which Jospehus discusses the revolutionary movements are referred to in the text, but it would be impossible to list the countless contexts in which Josephus, particularly in *Bellum*, touches on the various rebellions. However, the famous description of the suicide of the *sicarii* at Masada is to be found in *Bell.* 7.252-406. The main work on the revolutionary movements is M. Hengel, *Die Zeloten* (Leiden, 1961); ET *The Zealots* (Edinburgh, 1989). The historical section of the present work mentions a number of works dealing with the history of the period; to these should be added: David M. Rhoads, *Israel in Revolution: 6-74 CE* (Philadelphia, 1976); W.R. Farmer, *Maccabees, Zealots, and Josephus* (New York, 1956); H.G. Kippenberg, *Religion und Klassenbildung im antiken Judäa* (Göttingen, 1978); G. Baumbach, *Die antirömischen Aufstandgruppen,* in: *Literatur und Religion des Frühjudentums* (Würzburg, 1973), pp. 273-83; Y. Yadin, *Masada* (London, 1966). The quotation on pp. 131f. is from G. Theissen, *Sociology of Early Palestinian Christianity* (London, 1978), pp. 53f.

Breaking Out of the Priesthood:
The Essenes and the Qumran Community

Neither in social nor in religious terms was the Essene movement like anything else in ancient Judaism; in fact, on first acquaintaince the movement seems non-Jewish in character. A number of features are quite striking: the movement separated itself from the balance of the population; it had a hierarchical organization; it held all property in common and practised ascesis; finally—a feature which characterizes it as a sect—it not only separated itself physically from Jewish society, but also definitively from the temple and temple worship, the principal institution in Judaism. Admittedly, we have already encountered a tendency towards isolation in Jewish society in the form of Pharisaism, but the Pharisees remained within the framework of official Judaism, whereas the Essenes made their exit and settled in the desert, beyond the bounds of law and society.

In fact, it is reasonable to ask whether the Essene movement may be appropriately termed a truly Jewish phenomenon at all, if by that we infer a further development of tendencies inherent in the ancient Israelite and Jewish faith and way of life. It is plausible to suggest that the special character of the movement was owing to its status as a 'mixed phenomenon'; that is, it may in reality have been a typical hellenistic phenomenon resulting from the encounter between East and West. Already Josephus seems to have had something of the sort in mind when he holds that the Essene movement was reminiscent of and connected with such western philisophical and religious movements as Pythagoreanism and Neo-Pythagoreanism.

Intensive research into the Essene movement has always posed questions like these, and the answers provided have been quite various: scholars have either regarded the movement as the noblest product of Jewish religion, or they have held it to be a thoroughly syncretistic phenomenon, incorporating elements from Persian, Babylonian, Egyptian, and Greek religion, as well as from late Greek philosophy. Paradoxically, matters have not been simplified by the sizeable corpus of source material. Both Josephus and Philo tell us more about the Essenes than they do about the Sadducees and Pharisees. In addition, we have received abundant information about the Essenes, or at least about an Essene-like society, through the discovery of the Qumran texts near the Dead Sea around 1950. Our picture remains, however, shaky, not least as far as such important issues as the origins of the Essenes and their sociological placement within Jewish society are concerned.

As mentioned, both Josephus and Philo devote considerable attention to the Essenes. The movement, then, has been well known since antiquity, and it has always fascinated Josephus' and Philo's readers. Particularly Philo's description of the 'therapeutes', an Egyptian group of Essenes, led such early church fathers as Eusebius to understand the Essenes as the first Christian monks, an idea that has retained stubborn popularity, especially in Catholic circles. In the eighteenth century Enlightenment scholars knew, of course, that the Essenes were Jews and not Christians, but the notable hypothesis was then proposed that Jesus himself was originally an Essene, and that early Christianity was in fact a continuation of the Essene teachings and way of life. Both Voltaire and Frederick the Great of Prussia were warm adherents of this view.

It might be mentioned in passing that this notion was, perhaps characteristically, seized upon by the Freemasons, who have claimed that in reality, Freemasonry represents the most original form of Christianity, identical with 'pure Essenism'. On this view, Jesus and John the Baptist were the main figures of the Essenes, and it was Paul, the Pharisee, who led the church astray. People went so far as to claim that the term 'Essene' was a corruption of 'Jessene', that is, 'follower of Jesus'! Connection between Jesus and the Essenes recurs repeatedly in the nineteenth-century biographies of Jesus, or rather, Jesus-novels, as they may perhaps more accurately be termed. When the Qumran texts were discovered and it was presumed that the texts derived from the Essenes, a number of scholars attempted once more to establish some sort of connection between the Essenes and the earliest Christians.

For the present, however, we shall dwell on the Essenes as presented by Josephus and Philo, before the discovery of the new texts. Josephus offers an extensive description of them in his *Jewish War* (*Bellum*), and a shorter one in *The Antiquities of the Jews* (*Antiquitates*). Philo deals with the Essenes in general in one of his writings, and in another he describes a special Egyptian version of them, the above-mentioned *therapeutes*. There are a number of divergences between the various accounts, and in some points they supplement one another. In what follows we shall, in the main, follow the description in *Bellum*, after which we shall include some observations from the other accounts.

It is probably not accidental that the first thing Josephus mentions in connection with the Essenes is their asceticism: 'They shun pleasures as a vice', he tells us immediately, and goes on to add, 'Marriage they disdain', which bears the following explanation: 'They do not, indeed, on principle condemn wedlock and the propagation thereby of the race, but they wish to protect themselves against women's wantonness, being persuaded that none of the sex keeps her plighted troth to one man'. A little later, however, he adds that one brand of Essenes acknowledge that if all men pursued this understanding of marriage, 'the whole race would very quickly die out'. He relates that these Essenes did in fact marry, but after having first devoted three years to making sure of their brides' spiritual qualities.

Josephus' next point concerns the Essene concept of communal property: 'They have a law that new members on admission to the sect shall confiscate their property to the order, with the result that you will nowhere see either abject poverty or inordinate wealth; the individual's possessions join the common stock and all, like brothers, enjoy a single patrimony'. This feature was combined with frugality: 'In their dress and deportment they resemble children under rigorous discipline'. Josephus further relates that the concept of communal property meant that when journeying, the Essenes could invariably stop with members of the order and receive according to their needs at no expense, for 'there is no buying or selling among themselves'. The same context informs us that 'they settle in large numbers in every town', and that they have an arrangement according to which, 'in every city there is one of the order expressly appointed to attend to strangers, who provides them with raiment and other necessities'.

Their piety was considerable, according to Josephus, who says that they declined to discuss profane matters before sunrise, and instead offered prayers, 'as though entreating the sun to rise'. After this, 'their superiors' assigned them their daily tasks, and at noon they bathed and donned sacred garments before the meal; as Josephus has it, 'they repair to the refectory, as to some sacred shrine'. A priest offered prayer both before and after the meal, which took place in silence. The silence, though, was not an expression of 'some awful mystery', but the result of the fact that the Essenes remained sober and ate only sufficiently to satisfy their appetites. The same procedure was repeated in the evenings.

The severe purity regulations were not confined to meal-
times alone, but extended to the whole of the Essene existence,
since the membership was possessed of varying degrees of
holiness. They were divided into four orders on the basis of
seniority, and any elder member was obliged to bathe and
purify himself if he happened to come into contact with any
member of a class junior to his own.

The 'superiors' wielded comprehensive authority; indeed,
without their say-so it was only permitted to do two things: to
help others, and to deal mercifully (though not to one's own
kinfolk!). Josephus further adduces a list of virtues which the
Essenes valued highly: they were righteous, peace-loving and
truthful, the last-mentioned to such a degree that oaths were
forbidden to them as superfluous. Their way of life was supported by assiduous reading of 'the writings of the ancients',
which presumably refers to the bibilical writings. Especially
the Essene Sabbath regulations were more severe than those
honoured by Jewish society at large.

Josephus dedicates a special section to the Essene quali-
fications for membership. It was difficult to join the society; for
a whole year the neophyte had to live outside it, while
adhering to its many regulations. Then for two years he was
permitted to take the Essene purificatory baths, and if he
showed himself worthy after this lengthy period, it was
possible to achieve membership and so obtain permission to
'touch the common food'.

An oath *was* sworn in token of final entrance into the
community; the new member took upon himself to honour the
community's ethical ideals, promised to obey those in authority in the society (and not to misuse his authority in the event
he himself should achieve any), not to hide anything from his
brothers in the order, and, finally, not to betray the order's
secrets to others, even under pain of death.

Significant malfeasances were punishable with banish-
ment. In the event, judgment was pronounced by a legal
assembly of 100 members, and the expelled member was not
dispensed from his sworn obligation to uphold the rules of the
community. Thus he was unable to accept food which had not
been prepared according to the Essenes' purificatory strictures, so that he was condemned to die of starvation if he were

not readmitted to the community. On occasion, presumably in consideration of obligation to deal mercifully, expelled members were readmitted, but only when they were 'in the last stage of exhaustion'.

In attempting to describe the specific religious views of the Essenes, Josephus employs Greek concepts exclusively. Concerning the soul, for example, Josephus says that the Essenes had the same views as 'the sons of Greece'. The pre-existent and immortal souls are confined by perishable bodies as by prisons; 'but when once they are released from the bonds of the flesh, then, as though liberated from a long servitude, they rejoice and are borne aloft'. Good souls reside in a sort of Elysium, but evil souls are relegated 'to a murky and tempestuous dungeon, big with never-ending punishments'. In Josephus' view, such concepts are uniquely suited to 'promote virtue and deter from vice'.

With this last, somewhat philistine observation, Josephus' account of the Essenes comes to a close, and we cannot help but note that there is much we have not been told. Josephus dwells on the quaint and curious aspects of the Essene way of life, and when he approaches religious matters, he feels that a bit of the Greek-hellenistic teaching on the soul, some general moral concepts and the purity regulations will suffice. It is probably correct that the last-named was central to Essene thought; indeed, one gets the impression that the purpose of the remarkable, quasi-monastic lifestyle was to enable the maintenance of the most extreme purity in comparison with the Essenes' surroundings. Should we attempt to simplify Essene life in a sentence, it might not be incorrect to say that they took the Pharisaic concept of isolation from the masses in 'fraternities' to absurd lengths. Moreover, as we shall see shortly, there was probably some original connection between the Pharisees and the Essenes.

If we seek sociological information about the Essenes, it is not to be found in Josephus. He tells us nothing about the historical background of the emergence of the community, nor are we told from what sort of background in Jewish society the Essene recruits came. Josephus' second and briefer account of Essene life is not helpful in this regard, as it supplements our knowledge with only a few observations: that they had distanced themselves from the temple in Jerusalem; that they did not conduct sacrifices; and that there were 4,000 Essenes (a figure already recorded by Philo).

As we have mentioned, Philo's first account of the Essenes deals with those in Palestine and Syria. His picture of them agrees in many respects with that of Josephus, but he also adds that they avoided the large towns and mainly dwelled in the villages; that many were artisans, who, however, declined to produce products which could be used for warfare; that they took no part in trade or transportation by ship, as they held that such things only accentuate the desire for luxury; and that their ethics could be summarized by the commandments to love God, virtue and one's neighbour.

Of more immediate interest is Philo's second account, which deals specifically with 'the contemplative Essenes', the *therapeutes*, who were presumably so called because they were thought to bring healing to the soul for all its ills. Philo maintains that they were to be found throughout the world, which, of course, means those parts of the then-known world where Jews dwelled. They avoided great cities and settled for choice in groups in the vicinity of villages. The more prominent of them were gathered in a colony outside of Alexandria; here, each of them had a small hut plus a chapel. It was here that they spent most of the day in prayer, studies, and contemplation. They studied the sacred writings in a constant endeavour to penetrate behind the literal sense in search of the deeper, 'mystical' significance of the text (since, as Philo explains, Scripture is like a human being, possessing both body and soul). They also studied the Essene writings and composed 'songs and hymns in praise of God'. They gathered in their synagogues on the Sabbath, and every seventh Sabbath was a day of festival on which all gathered together for a common meal. They did not eat flesh, but only bread, salt and hyssop; they drank no wine, but only water, although they permitted those with weak stomachs the luxury of drinking warm water!

One other author of the first century CE refers to the Essenes, namely the Roman historian Pliny the Elder. His mention of them is brief, but nevertheless invaluable, as he remarks that the Essenes (whom he incidentally held to be

entirely admirable, as they lived without women or money
and ate only the fruits of the palmtree) dwelled on the west
coast of the Dead Sea. This brings us close to the text finds
made in this century, namely the discovery of the previously
mentioned Dead Sea or Qumran scrolls. It was precisely on
the west coast of the Dead Sea that the bedouins and
archaeologists made their great discovery, in the years after
1947, of texts and ruins, all of which date from the centuries
around the time of Christ. Comparison of the contents of the
texts with the results of the excavations of the ruins—called
'Qumran' by the Arabs since ancient times—quickly revealed
that scholars were on the trail of a congregation of Jewish
schismatics (the Qumran community, as it is called) which
was in some way related to the Essenes.

It would lead us very far afield if we were to rehearse the
dramatic history of the finds: the Ta'amire bedouins and the
Bethlehemite dealer in antiquities; the Syrian monks and the
American archeologists in Jerusalem; the Jewish scholars of
the Hebrew University and the Arabic scholars of the
Rockefeller Museum; the archbishop who smuggled scrolls to
America; the wealthy Jew who bought them and donated
them to the new Israel Museum; both the illegal and the
legitimate scientific excavations in the desert, as well as the
continued hunt by both bedouins and archaeologists for more
caves containing scrolls. The story has been told innumerable
times. Here we may simply note that parchment scrolls and
scoll fragments, inscribed in Hebrew, were found in eleven of
the countless caves in the slopes on the west coast of the Dead
Sea. In all, there were about ten well-preserved scrolls containing a couple of hundred pages of text, plus 20,000–30,000
fragments. The finds represent a library which must have
contained more than 500 book-lengths scrolls; of these,
approximately 100 contained Old Testament texts, while the
rest contained Jewish texts from the period in question. Many
of these were produced by the community itself and reflect, in
one way or another, the faith and life of the community.

Excavation of the ruins below the slopes revealed a large
complex of structures, which was apparently the centre of the
Qumran community. It included a refectory and auditorium,
a scriptorium where some of the texts were presumably

written, a kitchen, work-shops, etc., and finally, a water supply which provides water for daily use and also filled the basins for ritual bathing. The traditional archaeological analyses (style of construction, pottery, coins, carbon-14 tests, and a study of the types of writing employed in the scrolls) all point to a date in the centuries around the time of the birth of Christ.

So far, so good. The question is, however, was this site the dwelling place of the Essenes? Was the Qumran community identical with the society of the Essenes? Can we be certain that the non-biblical texts were original Essene works? It is insufficient to point out the fact that the location of Qumran corresponds to Pliny's description. Only by comparing Josephus' and Philo's descriptions of the Essenes with the newly discovered texts can we reach a definitive conclusion as to their derivation.

As we have mentioned, a large part of the texts in question are non-biblical, and several of them (especially the so-called *Community Rule*) contain detailed accounts of the organization and special religious views of the Qumran community. Moreover, there are other texts which contain dim allusions to the history of the congregation; these are the commentaries on the Old Testament prophetic books of Habakkuk and Nahum. To these should be added the *Damascus Document* (or *Rule*), a mediaeval copy of which was found in a synagogue in Cairo in the 1890s, and which has now proved to belong with the Dead Sea texts. It should be possible, then, to undertake the sort of comparison suggested above, and in the event of a positive result we shall have made some considerable progress. The new texts would then be able to provide us with some information about the Essenes' historical background and location within Jewish society, which was so sadly lacking in Josephus and Philo.

The comparison in question was speedily undertaken years ago, with the result that scholars have since divided into two camps: those who emphasize the obvious similarities between the description of the Essenes' organization and lifestyle, and the picture of the organization and lifestyle of the Qumran community which emerges from the new texts. These scholars have analysed the differences which are undeniably present in a variety of ways: Josephus and Philo were describing late Essenism, whereas the new texts derive from the time of the emergence of the movement; Josephus and Philo had accommodated their account to the interests of Greek and Roman readers; finally, it was pointed out that Josephus and Philo expressly describe several different types of Essene society, so that, in a manner of speaking, they present an 'average picture' which could not be expected to fit in all details the Essene society which we now know from Qumran.

The other group has placed more emphasis on the differences and has hesitated to make a simple identification of the two quantities. They insist that Josephus and Philo are to be taken literally; and they point out that the little the two authors have to say about Essene religious concepts rather gives the impression that Essenism was a strongly hellenized phenomenon. Against this, they maintain, the newly discovered texts show us a Jewish group which may have broken with the Jerusalem temple, but which nevertheless represents legitimate, ancient Jewish faith and tradition.

In order to judge between the two views, the following factors should be considered: striking similarities are to be found precisely where Josephus and Philo are communicative, that is, in the areas of organization and lifestyle. We encounter differences mainly when we consider the question of religious concepts; at this level Josephus and Philo make only peripheral comments and do not attempt to describe the actual content of Essene concepts. They emphasize the purifications, refer to a number of general ethical ideals, and both employ the Greek teaching of the separation of soul and body. When we consider these facts together with the additional observation that no doubt a considerable span of time separates the Essenism of the texts from the variety known to Josephus and Philo, then we can maintain that it is over-cautious to refrain from combining the two quantities, and so allow the various accounts to supplement one another. This becomes even more inviting when we consider that there is good reason to trust Josephus' and Philo's claim, that there were several different sorts of Essene society. Thus it would probably not be claiming too much to maintain that although we do not meet *the Essenes* in Qumran, we do happen to make the acquaintance of *an* Essene community there.

The variety of Jewish religion which we meet in the new texts has its own specific character, and we shall examine it within a wider context in the concluding chapter on apocalyptic. For the present we shall concentrate on the community's organization and way of life as described in the new texts, and we shall make comparisons with the existing descriptions of the Essenes. Next, we shall look closely at the information concerning the history of the Essenes contained in the new texts; in this connection it will be worthwhile to try to describe in more detail those circles within Jewish society from which the Essenes and the people of Qumran were recruited.

The most striking similarity is to be found in the rules for the initiation of a new member. According to Josephus, the Essene novitiate lasted three years. The Qumran *Community Rule* has a prolix and not entirely clear presentation; according to it the novitiate seems to have lasted only two years. During the first year the new member was admitted onto 'the Council of the Community', but he was not permitted to 'touch the purity of the Congregation', referring to either the communal meals or the ritual baths. Probably the former is intended, as this sense agrees well with Josephus' information; moreover, the *Community Rule* says expressly that even in the second year of his novitiate the novice may not 'touch the meal of the Congregation'. On the other hand, we are ultimately told that it was when both novitial years had elapsed that the novice was to be inscribed 'for the Law, and for justice and for the pure meal' (1QS 6.13-23). In other words, there are numerous unclear passages in the *Community Rule*, so that the complete identity of Josephus' version of the Essene rules and the rules of Qumran cannot be established. But the basic principle is nevertheless identical; the membership rules are intended to ensure that no unworthy candidate is inducted into the community.

The fact that the goal is to protect and preserve the purity of the Qumran community at all costs emerges from the initiation procedure itself. We are told that the prospective member was obliged three times, in the course of his novitiate, to submit to a sort of 'exam', in which all members of the congregation examined him 'concerning his understanding and his deeds', or, as we read elsewhere, 'with respect to his understanding and practice of the Law'. When all those attending had been asked about the candidate's record, lots were cast (the word in question might be better translated by 'ballot', which would be a more reasonable ending to the procedure) to determine whether he should be inducted or not.

It was not only new members of the community who were obliged to run this gauntlet; rather, every member had annually to submit to a similar procedure, the result of which determined his position in the hierarchy of the society (1QS 5.23-26). The hierarchy was, then, changeable; a member could be advanced or demoted depending on his 'understanding and deeds'; subordinates were expected to be entirely obedient to their hierarchical superiors. The system has an obvious paedagogical function, in that it prompts the membership to do their best. It urged on them a noble competition which, however, may not have been so noble after all; another passage in the *Community Rule* measures the punishment to be visited on anyone who opposes his superior in the hierarchy (1QS 6.25-27). It requires but little imagination to see that this arrangement could easily have made communal life in Qumran difficult. Josephus' version of the Essene hierarchy is in reality more reasonable, as the system he reports is apparently based on seniority alone.

According to Josephus, community of property played a great part among the Essenes, or at least among those of them who lived in colonies. This was also the case at Qumran. Whenever a new member was inducted after his two-year novitiate he was expected to contribute his wealth to the common treasury, which was administered by the priests and the council as a whole. However, a different passage has it that the priests alone had authority over the common funds (1QS 9.7-8).

The ritual baths mentioned by Josephus played a central part at Qumran, on the assumption that such obscure, or current phrases as 'purity', the 'purity of the men of holiness', or 'the purity of the Congregation', actually refer to this institution. When Josephus speaks of the Essenes' assiduous reading of 'the writings of the ancients', this no doubt corresponds to the studies by the people of Qumran of the Law of Moses, studies which were carried out 'night and day, always by turns, one after another' (1QS 6.6-7).

The common meal, which both Josephus and Philo mention in connection with the Essenes, was also a feature of life at Qumran; it took place under the supervision of a priest who blessed the bread and the must, the participants apparently seated according to their respective ranks in the hierarchy. This was also the case on the occasion of the general council, at which all the members of the society were present, and at which were dealt with 'any counsel or matter coming before the Congregation'. Here, too, the seating was by rank and degree; even taking the floor was determined by hierarchical order (1QS 6.8ff.).

The council was a sort of general assembly in which everyone was entitled to speak. One might be tempted to suppose that it was a democratically structured society; this, however, was by no means the case. In the first place, alongside the hierarchy based on 'understanding and deeds' there was also one based on calling and social position: 'The Priests shall enter first, ranked one after another according to the perfection of their spirit; then the Levites; and thirdly, all the people, one after another' (1QS 2.19-21). Priests, Levites, laity: a social pecking-order which corresponds exactly to that acknowledged in contemporary Jewish society as a whole. The further stipulation, that the priestly groups were individually subdivided 'according to the spirit', was probably an innovation which was specific to Qumran. At all events, the leading functionaries in the community were priests and Levites.

There is no doubt that the Qumran congregation was dominated by the priests, a feature nowhere mentioned by Josephus in connection with the Essenes. This brings us to the important question as to the origin of the congregation, a question which has two facets: (1) what historical circumstances conditioned the formation of the congregation? and (2) from which circles within contemporary Judaism were the members of the congregation recruited?

The question of the historical background of the Qumran community is immensely complicated; here we must deal

with it somewhat summarily. The problem is, above all, that
none of the texts gives a proper account of the matter. Many
of them touch on the question of the origin of the community,
but they do so in a strange code-like language, in which all of
the parties involved are referred to by cover-names. In brief,
we may fairly say that behind the codes and cover-names in
the texts we seem to glimpse events which took place in the
century between the Maccabean revolt and the Roman
conquest of Palestine, that is, in the period between the 160s
BCE and 63 BCE. As we have mentioned before, these
'historical' references are only to be found in the Damascus
Document and in a couple of commentaries on Old Testament
prophetic writings. The commentaries are peculiar, in that
they regard the old prophecies from the seventh century BCE
as predictions of the events which led to the emergence of the
Qumran community. Rather than being interpretations of
ancient texts which refer to events in the actual times of the
prophets in question, these Qumran commentaries are in the
nature of actualizing reinterpretations. They are on much the
same lines as the exegesis undertaken by the early Christians
when they found in the writings of Isaiah, a prophet of the
eighth century BCE, predictions of events in the life of Christ.

The texts reveal that the community collected around a
leader, whose cover-name is 'the Teacher of Righteousness'.
He knew the right interpretation of Scripture and the right
understanding of the Law, and he came into an oppositional
relationship to those at the head of affairs in Jerusalem, whose
ultimate leader was the high priest, known in the texts as 'the
Wicked Priest'. As a result, the Teacher of Righteousness and
his adherents more or less voluntarily abandoned Jerusalem
and entered into a 'New Covenant in the Land of Damascus'.
There they awaited better times—and the advent of the
Messiah. Presumably 'the Land of Damascus' was a code-
name for the desert colony at Qumran. The commentary on
Habakkuk offers us a particularly clear impression of the
later course of events. 'The Wicked Priest', who is also called
'the Liar' or 'the Speaker of Lies', was originally called by 'the
Name of Truth', but he subsequently failed his commission
and led the people astray. On the Great Day of Atonement he
followed 'the Teacher of Righteousness' and the congregation

all the way to 'the place to which he had fled'. But God punished the Wicked Priest by delivering him into the hands of his enemies. Later we read of 'the Last Priests of Jerusalem' who amass great wealth, which is, however, ultimately to fall into the hands of the 'Kittim'.

Most scholars have preferred to localize the many events referred to in the texts to a fairly narrow period of time which has resulted in a number of standard interpretations.

(1) In particular, the English scholar H.H. Rowley has repeatedly argued in favour of dating the whole course of events to the 170s and 160s BCE, that is, during the reign of Antiochus Epiphanes and the crisis which led to the Maccabean revolt. Against this background, the Teacher of Righteousness was Onias III, the deposed high priest, the Wicked Priest was his successor Menelaos, and the 'Kittim' were the Seleucids. Later in the century, after the death of Onias, the congregation emigrated to Qumran, where they remained for the succeeding two centuries.

(2) Others, including the Danish scholar Eduard Nielsen, displace the entire scheme to the first decades of the first pre-Christian century (from the 90s to the 60s BCE). It is no longer possible to identify the Teacher of Righteousness, but it is assumed that he was a leader of the pious circles among the Jews which were persecuted by the Hasmonean king, Alexander Jannaeus, who reigned and bore the high-priestly title from 103 to 76 BCE. He was the Wicked Priest, and the 'Kittim' would be the Romans, who were then approaching, menacingly, on the horizon.

(3) The last view I personally regard as the most probable, given the state of our present knowledge. It has been advocated by such scholars as England's Geza Vermes and the Swedish scholar Helmer Ringgren. This view has the advantage of assuming that the various historical allusions in the texts actually span a lengthy period in the early history of the community. Thus we are able to suggest plausible explanations for many isolated details in the

vague formulations of the texts. The roots of the congregation are to be sought right back in the days of the Maccabean revolt in the 160s BCE. The Qumran community was an emergent strain of the Hasidic movement, 'the assembly of the pious', which opposed the hellenizing tendencies of the leading priesthood in Jerusalem and Antiochus Epiphanes. But the conflict which culminated in the confrontation between the Teacher of Righteousness and the Wicked Priest took place in the time around 152 BCE, when Jonathan, as the first of the Hasmoneans, assumed the office of high priest. The Teacher of Righteousness cannot be identified, while the Wicked Priest is most certainly Jonathan, whose career in fact ended when he was captured by the Seleucids and ultimately executed. On this view, the 'Last Priests of Jerusalem' were presumably the later Hasmoneans, including Alexander Jannaeus, while the 'Kittim' were the Romans, who threatened from afar.

This provides a key for answering our second question: from which circles within Judaism were the people of Qumran, and presumably also the Essenes, recruited? Who were the main opponents of the Hasmonean assumption of the high-priestly office, an act which broke with all applicable rules and traditions? It would be remarkable if they were not members of the conservative and legalistic wing of the Jerusalem priesthood. The new texts expressly describe the Teacher of Righteousness as a priest, and the congregation was dominated by priests, even referring to itself as 'the Sons of Zadok'. It is conceivable that a schism arose within the Jerusalem priesthood when Jonathan took over the high-priestly office, and that some of the priests, unable to accept the new state of affairs, departed in a company of like-minded laymen who had submitted themselves to the severe priestly rules governing social intercourse.

The fact that the congregation in Qumran had its origins in priestly circles helps to explain a further feature of the movement. Several of the texts inform us that one of the points at issue between the Teacher of Righteousness and the

Wicked Priest had to do with the question of the calendar. This problem might seem slight to us, but it was of crucial importance to any ancient society. Disagreement as to the calendar meant disagreement as to the dates of the great religious festivals, which were thought to sustain the life of society and to ensure the connection between society and the higher powers. We happen to know that in hellenistic times the Jewish society changed its calendar repeatedly, to some extent as a result of western influence. If the conservative part of the priesthood felt that the high priest—who, of course, already possessed his office thanks only to illegal means—had changed the calendar, so that it was no longer in accord with the Law of Moses, then they would also have been unable to recognize the festivals, making a schism inevitable.

Thus it seems to have been the case that the original Hasidic movement of the 160s BCE split into two factions later in the century. One wing was Pharisaism, which we have already discussed; the other, priestly-dominated wing was reflected in Essenism and the Qumran congregation. On consideration, this view is attractive. As far as their basic attitudes are concerned, Pharisaism and Essenism have much in common, with the decisive difference that Essenism always represents the radical consequence of a chain of ideas. The Pharisees isolated themselves with respect to ordinary Jews; the Essenes went the whole distance and removed themselves to the desert. The Pharisees kept the priestly rules of purity; the Essenes went even further and insisted on a degree of purity which ruled out any kind of normal life in a normal society. The Pharisees were opposed to the Hasmonean high priests; the Essenes broke completely with the Hasmoneans and the temple congregation which they led. The Pharisees studied the Law intensively; the Essenes provided for the continuous study of the Law in Qumran 'in shifts'. One could go on. It is not wrong to claim, as some scholars have done, that Essenism was Pharisaism raised by the power of ten.

One might be tempted to suppose that by virtue of its radical character the Qumran congregation was far to the left of normative Judaism. This is not wrong, but at the same time one must recognize that the movement was a composite phenomenon, and that it was also placed in the central tradition of ancient Jewish religion. In many ways, the theology of Qumran expresses legitimate Jewish religious thought, carried to its logical conclusion and enacted. Thus it was possible to cite passages from the Qumran literature in our examination above of the basic structure of Jewish religion. It applied, for example, to the field of ethics, since at Qumran we encounter an 'ethic of the neighbour' in many ways reminiscent of the one we met in the *Testaments of the Twelve Patriarchs*. Both the *Hymns* (Hodayot) and the *Community Rule* contain lists of the characteristics which were valued at Qumran. The following is a typical example:

> They shall practise truth and humility in common, and justice and uprightness and charity and modesty in all their ways. No man shall walk in the stubbornness of his heart so that he strays after his heart and eyes and evil inclination, but he shall circumcise in the Community the foreskin of evil inclination and of stiffness of neck, that may lay a foundation of truth for Israel, for the Community of the everlasting Covenant (1QS 5.3-5).

But the same applies to that aspect of the Law known as the cultic-ritual rules, which governed purity, food, and the Sabbath. As we have seen, ritual purifications played a major part in the life of the congregation; the *Damascus Document* contains some regulations which appear to be identical with those embraced by the Pharisees (CD 10.10-13, etc.), and the laws governing the Sabbath in the *Damascus Document* are extensive (10.14ff.). There was nevertheless an important complex of materials in the Law with which the people of Qumran had their difficulties: the laws of sacrifice. Since the community had dropped every connection with Jerusalem, it was impossible to deal with the vast system of regulations governing the various temple sacrifices. A daring move was made instead, a reinterpretation of the laws of sacrifice in a 'spiritualizing' direction, following the basic premise that the community at Qumran had assumed the atonement function once assigned to the sacrificial cult. It is said directly that the congregation is identical with the temple, and that the life of the congregation in accordance with the dictates of the Law brings about atonement. One text even calls the congregation 'a human temple'. After an introductory section dealing with the duty of the congregation to keep the provisions of the Law, an important but difficult passage in the *Community Rule* informs us that

> when these are in Israel, the Council of the Community shall be established in truth. It shall be an Everlasting Plantation, a House of Holiness for Israel, an Assembly of Supreme Holiness for Aaron. They shall be witnesses to the truth at the Judgement, and shall be the elect of Goodwill who shall atone for the Land and pay to the wicked their reward. It shall be that tried wall, that precious corner-stone, whose foundations shall neither rock nor sway in their place (Isa. 28.16). It shall be a Most Holy Dwelling for Aaron, with everlasting knowledge of the Covenant of justice, and shall offer up sweet fragrance (1QS 8.4-9).

Israel's 'House of Holiness' and Aaron's 'Assembly of Supreme Holiness' are both designations of the temple. And what is meant by the 'sweet fragrance' emerges from the following passage, where we are told that the formation of the congregation is intended to

> atone for guilty rebellion and for sins of unfaithfulness that they may obtain lovingkindness for the Land without the flesh of holocausts and the fat of sacrifice. And prayer rightly offered shall be as an acceptable fragrance of righteousness, and perfection of way as a delectable free-will offering (1QS 9.4-5).

What we encounter here is a grandiose reinterpretation of the institution of temple sacrifice which had been constitutive of Israel's religious life for centuries. In embracing this line, the members of the congregation abandoned the central line of Jewish religion and characterized their movement as a sect; the word 'sect' is here used advisedly, as its literal meaning is 'something that has been cut out'. But this reinterpretation of the laws of sacrifice was of vital importance for the people of Qumran. It was essential to convince themselves that what they had done was correct, and that they remained on the firm ground of the Law even though they had abandoned the temple. They concluded it would only be at the end of time that a new temple, one completely in accord with God's will, would be constructed, and that a temple service would be reintroduced which would follow the Law in every particular. The

congregation developed these ideas in a work known as the
Temple Scroll.

This brings us to the apocalyptic element which is
ultimately the definitive characteristic of the congregation. As
was said previously, we shall deal with the apocalyptic
Qumran theology in the final section, in conjunction with the
other apocalyptic currents. It would nevertheless be appropriate to say a few words here. It is normally held that there
were two main lines in Early Judaism. One of these, the
official and normative line, is the one we attempted to describe
in the section dealing with the basic structure; it is represented
in the first instance by legalistic Pharisaism. Against this, the
other line moves on the periphery of Jewish tradition and ends
in the wild speculations of apocalyptic concerning the other-
worldly, the end of days and the coming kingdom of God.
These two lines or themes are thought to have been as opposed
to one another as can be imagined. However, the distinction
does not hold in the case of the congregation of Qumran. What
makes this community a unique quantity within Early
Judaism is precisely the fact that it manages to reconcile these
two themes. We have seen that in its origins the Qumran
movement was closely related to Pharisaism, and that at a
number of points it retained its Pharisaic orthodox character.
But in embracing the dualistic-apocalyptic doctrine about the
Children of Light and the Children of Darkness, as well as the
expectation of the imminent advent of the eschatological
events, the movement removed itself from the compass of
normative Judaism. For in fact, adherence to these doctrines
established an abyss between the movement and the other
Jews, and even the rest of humanity. The movement did not
hesitate to maintain that only the Children of Light, which is
to say, the members of the Qumran congregation, would be
saved at the end of days. The Children of Darkness—the rest
of the Jews along with the rest of humanity—would ultimately be lost. The congregation of Qumran considered itself
to be the true Israel. The divine promises which were vouchsafed in the dawn of time to Abraham, and which were
repeated by the prophets, and to which Israel had clung for
centuries, only really applied to this tiny band in the desert.
There is something pathetic about this attitude, which we

recognize only too well in modern sectarian phenomena on the periphery of Christian tradition.

For the 200 years of its existence the congregation was able to sustain the expectation that the end of days was just around the corner, together with the dream that the Children of Light alone would go into the eternal light. The dream collapsed sometime after the revolt in 66 CE, when Roman soldiers advanced and destroyed the centre in Qumran. Many of the members of the congregation were no doubt killed; others presumably fled, although we do not know where. They had burnt their bridges behind them and so could not return to the Jewish congregation in Jerusalem, even though much had changed in the city after the catastrophe of 70 CE. Some seem to have fled to Masada, where they presumably died by their own hands together with the *sicarii*. But who knows? Perhaps some of them joined the infant Christian church, which was likewise a breakaway sect of Judaism, and which by virtue of its critical attitude towards established Judaism, and its expectations towards the future, was in many ways reminiscent of the congregation of Qumran.

Bibliographic Note to pp. 135-55
The Appendix (pp. 225ff.) accounts for the Jewish texts quoted in this section. Josephus' description of the Essenes is in *Bell.* 2.119-161 and *Ant.* 18.18-22. Philo refers to them in *Quod omnis probus liber sit* 75-87, and in his *Hypothetica* (*Apology for the Jews*) 11.1-18; he describes the *therapeutes* in *De vita contemplativa.* Pliny's short reference is in his *Natural History* 5.17. Danish provides one of the classical accounts of what was known of Essenism prior to the Qumran discoveries: H. Mosbech, *Essæismen* (København, 1916). The research on the Essenes of the last few centuries has been reviewed by S. Wagner in *Die Essener in der wissenschaftlichen Diskussion vom Ausgang des 18. bis zum Beginn des 20. Jahrhunderts* (Berlin, 1960).

The Hebrew text of the Qumran writings is most easily accessible in Ed. Lohse, *Die Texte aus Qumran. Hebräisch und Deutsch* (München, 1964). English translations of the most important texts are numerous, and only a few of them can be mentioned here: M. Burrows, *The Dead Sea Scrolls*; idem, *More Light on the Dead Sea Scrolls* (New York, 1955-1958); T.H. Gaster, *The Dead Sea Scriptures in English Translation* (New York, 1956); G. Vermes, *The Dead Sea Scrolls in English* (Harmondsworth, 1962; Sheffield, 1987). Translations of individual texts, with commentary: P. Wernberg-Møller, *The Manual of Discipline* (Leiden, 1957); A.R.C. Leaney, *The Rule of Qumran and its Meaning* (London, 1966); P.R. Davies, *The Damascus Covenant: An Interpretation of the 'Damascus Document'* (Sheffield, 1983); S. Holm-Nielsen, *Hodayot. Psalms from Qumran*, (Aarhus, 1960); Y. Yadin, *The Scroll of the War of the Sons of Light against the Sons of Darkness* (Oxford, 1962); J. Maier, *The Temple Scroll: An Introduction, Translation and Commentary* (Sheffield, 1985). Extracts from important texts with introduction and commentary have been provided by M. Knibb, *The Qumran Community* (Cambridge, 1987).

The archaeological excavations at Qumran are dealt with in R. de Vaux, *Archaeology and the Dead Sea Scrolls* (Oxford, 1973), and P.R. Davies, *Qumran* (Guildford, 1982).

General treatments of the Qumran community, its history, life, and faith are given in works on Early Judaism which have appeared in recent years; important among them is E. Schürer *The History of the Jewish People in the Age of Jesus Christ*. New edition by G. Vermes et al. (Edinburgh, 1979-86), II, pp. 555-90, and III.1, pp. 380-469. Monographs: still valuable are the two volumes by M. Burrows mentioned above, as well as H.H. Rowley's pioneer work, *The Zadokite Fragments and the Dead Sea Scrolls* (Oxford, 1952). More recent works include: F.M. Cross, *The Ancient Library of Qumran and Modern Biblical Studies* (New York, 1961); H. Ringgren, *The Faith of Qumran* (Philadelphia, 1963); Eduard Nielsen, *Håndskriftfundene i Juda Ørken* (København, 1956); G. Vermes, *The Dead Sea Scrolls. Qumran in Perspective* (London, 1977); A.S. van der Woude, *Die messianischen Vorstellungen der Gemeinde von Qumran* (Assen, 1957); M. Black, *The Scrolls and Christian Origins* (New York, 1961). Most of the works mentioned have bibliographies.

Chapter 5

APOCALYPTIC—THE NEW RELIGIOUS MANIFESTATION

Description of Apocalyptic

The emergence of apocalyptic speculations and of apocalyptic literature is a sign of crisis. The crisis is the catalyst which sparks off the speculations, and apocalyptic literature performs its function in times of crisis: it exhorts its readers to bear their troubles. Jewish apocalyptic does so by making examples of historical figures of Israel's past, and it comforts by showing how the one who adheres to the God of Israel and to the Law always receives his reward in the end, no matter how many perils he is first obliged to suffer. But at the same time—and this is the essence of apocalyptic—it reveals the secrets of existence. It does not display these secrets to some 'cooly curious eye', but, once again, only to those who have begun to backslide and abandon hope because of their trials. Such people require to be convinced that the whole of existence has been organized in accordance with the divinely derived world order, that heaven and earth are governed by divinely appointed natural laws and that the course of history was settled once and for all by God at the beginning of time. This allows the weak-kneed to maintain their hope that at the end of history all devils and tyrants will be crushed, and that God will assume all power when he establishes his kingdom. Thus the notions of the end of time, that is, the Day of Judgment and the coming kingdom of God are central themes in apocalyptic.

It would be appropriate first to look closely at the word 'apocalyptic' and the concepts associated with it. The word derives from the Greek verb *apokalyptein*, which means, 'to uncover something that has been hidden'. In its Jewish context, the term is especially used with reference to the 'uncovering', that is, the revelation of the divine secrets. Among the Christians the noun 'apocalypse' became the designation for the Revelation of St. John in the New Testament (*Apocalypsis Ioannou*), which led to its transfer to the Jewish apocalyptic writings as well. In modern times theologians and historians of religion have coined the term 'apocalyptic' as a collective designation, encompasssing both the apocalyptic literature and the intellectual currents which produced it.

In other words, the apocalyptic literature contained revelations. But we saw in our section on the basic religious structure that ancient Judaism normally had a narrow understanding of revelation, which confined all revelation to the Pentateuch. How was this to be reconciled with the revelations in the apocalyptic books? After all, they go far beyond what is revealed in the Pentateuch, and even with the best will in the world (as, for example, when people were expected to accept the rabbis' new formulations of the Law as legitimate derivations of Old Testament law), the apocalyptic revelations could not be considered to be interpretations of or derivations of the materials in the Pentateuch. This makes it immediately intelligible why Early Judaism experienced difficulty in accepting this sort of revelation, and in point of fact with the exception of a single work they were excluded from the canon of the Old Testament. They would surely have been lost, had it not been for the fact that the Christians adopted them and so preserved them for posterity.

The authors of the apocalyptic writings did what they could to ensure that their new revelations would be acceptable to their public. Throughout the works, they attempted to create the impression that the writings were centuries older than they really were, and, indeed, that some of them even antedated the Pentateuch! It was claimed that certain figures from Israel's early history had been chosen to receive revelations concerning the hidden forces behind existence, the secrets of heaven, and what the future held in store. These revelations, so the illusion goes, were written down in documents which were hidden for centuries, only to appear by mysterious means at the present time, e.g. the time of Early Judaism.

To take but a single example: the group of apocalyptic writings known as the books of Enoch are notionally assigned to the Enoch who, according to the Biblical genealogies, was the great-great-great-great-grandchild of Adam and Eve. The Old Testament has little to relate about this Enoch except the remark that, 'having walked with God, Enoch was seen no more, because God had taken him away' (Gen. 5.24). This sounds cryptic, but in Early Judaism no one doubted what was meant: because of his righteousness, Enoch was taken up to God, allowed to see into the future and to be privy to the secrets of heaven, after which he returned to earth and wrote down his experiences. The people who produced the books of Enoch in antiquity will presumably have collected the Enoch narratives that happened to be in circulation; they may actually have believed that they were based on Enoch's own description of his experiences during his heavenly journey. But even if this was not the case, their object was to produce a pious fraud.

Works of varying degrees of apocalypticism appeared in a similar way in antiquity; they were ascribed to Abraham (the *Apocalypse of Abraham*), to Jacob's twelve sons (the *Testaments of the Twelve Patriarchs*), to Moses (*Jubilees,* the *Assumption of Moses*), to Jeremiah's scribe, Baruch (several books of Baruch), to Daniel (the book of Daniel), and to the learned Ezra (several books of Ezra). In reality, this literary fiction of the antique period represents a continuation of a tradition which had already left its traces in the Old Testament; for there, too, we find a number of works which cannot possibly derive from the persons to whom they are ascribed (Ecclesiastes is assigned to Solomon; the second half of Isaiah to the prophet himself, etc.).

As we have seen, ancient Judaism, or at least the official part of it represented by the Pharisees, declined to recognize these 'revealed writings'. To do so would have entailed breaking with the principle of revelation which had evolved in the course of time. It is not certain that the Pharisees knew that the works in question were by no means as old as they pretended to be. Their problem was, rather, that they had no idea what to do with them. This was presumably also a reflex of the fact that the apocalyptic writings had been produced in circles—to some extent sectarian circles—within Judaism which were quite remote from the Pharisaical-rabbinic line. However, several of the oriental Christian congregations regarded these writings as part of the Old Testament canon, for which reason they were translated (into Greek, Latin, Ethiopic, Syriac, and so on) and for a time were part of the canon of the churches in question. Later in the history of the church the nature of these writings was acknowledged, so that they came to be called Pseudepigraphical works, that is, works bearing false headings. However, the text group of the Pseudepigrapha also contains other things besides apocalyptic writings.

Before we go into the problems of apocalyptic in detail, it will be useful first to examine a single work so as to get some idea what apocalyptic is about. The book of Daniel will do in this context; it was the only really apocalyptic work which was included in the canon of the Old Testament. It was composed in the 160s BCE in conjunction with the Maccabean revolt. However, the work pretends to derive from the sixth century; the second half of the book, couched in the first person, presents itself as Daniel's own account of visions he had during the Babylonian captivity and the reign of the first Persian kings at the end of the sixth century. The first half of the work consists of narratives about Daniel and his friends and their experiences in Babylon.

In the first chapter we are told how Daniel and his three friends were kidnapped to Babylon around the year 600. Although captives in a heathen environment. Daniel and his friends manage to observe the Jewish dietary regulations; in return, God endows them with wisdom superior to that of all the Babylonian wisemen, and they receive high positions at court. The moral is amply clear, particularly when we consider the situation which obtained in the 160s: whoever keeps the Law and resists the temptations of the heathen milieu will be richly rewarded. In the second chapter, Daniel is the only one who is able to interpret the dream of Nebuchadnezzar. Here a typical apocalyptic historical revelation unfolds itself; the statue in the dream symbolizes the four world empires which were destined to succeed one another after the fall of Nebuchadnezzar's Babylonian empire. The last of them, which is, of course, the Greek or Seleucid empire, is to be crushed by a stone, 'though not by human hands', after which the stone will grow and fill the entire earth. These are words of consolation to the Jews enduring a reign of terror: the foreign kingdom will collapse and the kingdom of God will be established. The author of this apocalyptic tale claims that history was long ago established by God, and that it is now coming to an end, or so the reader is intended to think. In the fourth chapter, Daniel interprets a second dream; Nebuchadnezzar accepts the interpretation and acknowledges the God of Daniel and Israel. This, too, is a didactic story which proclaims that the God of Israel is 'the Ever-living One, whose sovereignty is never-ending, and whose rule endures through all generations' (4.34). The third and sixth chapters are like martyrologies, only they have happy endings; Daniel's three friends are saved from the fiery furnace, as is Daniel himself from the lions' den. Once again the moral is clear: those who keep to the Law and obey God are under his protection, a message which was no doubt comforting to the martyrs of the Maccabean period, at least until they were executed. Finally, the fifth chapter is once more a variety of historical revelation: Daniel interprets the writing on the wall and predicts the course of history.

The rest of the book is of a somewhat different nature, though its attitudes are the same. Daniel tells of his visions in chs. 7 and 8. A variety of different animals represent the four world empires from the days of Nebuchadnezzar down to the time the book was composed in the second century BCE. The seventh chapter contains the famous vision of 'one like a son of man', who comes on the clouds of heaven. He represents the kingdom of God which is to succeed the heathen world empires. In ch. 8 the ram and the goat symbolize the last two world empires. Antiochus Epiphanes ('the little horn') plays a major role in both; and numerical speculation plays a part in both chapters as well. Such speculations still play a part in ch. 9, in which the angel Gabriel interprets the seventy years mentioned in Jeremiah as seventy year-weeks, that is, periods of seven years each, making a total of 490 years. The author of this apocalyptic work held that it was precisely this span of time which ran from the days of Jeremiah around the year

600 down to the profaning of the temple, which took place in the reign of Antiochus Epiphanes. That this period is too long is probably due to the fact that the author did not possess a good chronology of the post-exilic period in the 160s; but this is of little importance. What was important was for him to be able to show that in naming the figure seventy, Jeremiah was not only thinking of the duration of the Babylonian exile; that he in fact saw even farther and so predicted events in the time of Antiochus Epiphanes. Chapters 10 and 11 provide a detailed account of the course of events from Cyrus in the sixth century down to Antiochus' time. The whole account is clothed in the garments of revelation, in that Daniel receives the narrative from an angel. Finally, ch. 12 concludes the work and also adjusts some of the previous numerological speculations in the light of the extraordinary developments which took place in Antiochus' reign.

What we have seen in Daniel are a number of characteristics which are typical of apocalyptic: 'revelations' concerning the course of history which are projected back into the past, although in reality they are seen from the point of view of the apocalyptic author (and his reader!); speculations about the 'period' of history, based on the assumption that history is predetermined by the hand of the Creator, so that it is possible to know when the end is coming; numerological speculations, which allow the apocalyptic author to calculate the time of the end with even greater accuracy. There is also the previously mentioned characteristic that the 'predictions' are placed in the mouth of one of the great figures of Israel's past. Admittedly, Daniel plays no part in Israel's early history; he is a more legendary figure, possibly deriving from Canaanite mythology.

Outside of the book of Daniel, there is a certain Daniel mentioned only a few times in the Old Testament (Ezek. 14.14, 20; 28.3) as a person possessing more wisdom than anyone else. It is presumably this figure we find employed in the book of Daniel in a very sophisticated way. He has been located temporally to the time of the Babylonian exile, which was a time of crisis. In this context, everything that he says and does points towards the 160s, which was likewise a time of crisis. In a manner of speaking, the divine words of consolation resound through the centuries to reach the tormented Jews in the days of Antiochus.

There is one particular element which is otherwise entirely typical of apocalyptic writings, but which is absent from the book of Daniel, namely heavenly visions. Although in ch. 7 Daniel sees a vision of the heavenly judge seated on his throne, the vision as such is no more than similar visions reported by Isaiah and Ezekiel (and we should note that Dan. 7 is in fact based on both Isa. 6 and Ezek. 1–3). Daniel is not escorted through the seven heavens, nor is he vouchsafed insight into the organization of the heavenly regions, the order of the world, or the secret forces of nature. Daniel is exclusively concerned with history, a concern which links the book with the works of the earlier prophets. Perhaps it was this fact which determined that Daniel, in contradistinction to so many other apocalyptic works of the period, could be assimilated into the canon of the Old Testament. The rabbis who, around 100 CE, were ultimately responsible for determining the final delimitation of the canon, were probably themselves given to speculations about the organization of the heavens and the like. But they regarded that sort of thing as *Geheimlehre*, which was not suitable for unprepared souls to behold. As the Mishnah has it, 'Whosoever gives his mind to four things, it were better for him if he had not come into the world—what is above? what is beneath? what was beforetime? and what will be hereafter?' (*m. Hag.* 2.1).

Research into apocalyptic

We have now gained a first, temporary impression of apocalyptic, and already at this juncture we may feel that in many ways it represents something different from what we have so far encountered in the Jewish religion of the antique period. But if we shall attempt to understand apocalyptic better still, it is insufficient to characterize it as a phenomenon of crisis. Apocalyptic is symptomatic of times of turmoil, and, as we have seen, it has an obvious function in such times. But this says nothing about its nature and origins. The scholarly disagreements about these issues are profound, which is no doubt because apocalyptic, both as an intellectual current and as a type of literature, is an extremely composite phenomenon.

It was suggested in the course of our examination of Daniel that the work seems to have points of contact with Old Testament prophetic literature. This observation enables us to understand earlier scholars' views of apocalyptic, which maintained that apocalyptic was the child of Old Testament prophecy—perhaps a late birth, as well as one that developed somewhat oddly, but all the same a child with recognizably inherited features. If we look to the standard works of scholarship from the turn of the century, we find many lists of points of similarity between prophecy and apocalyptic. Such things as ethical doctrine, interest in the future, messianic expectation, and the expectation of an imminent kingdom of God are mentioned. The matter is often represented in such a way that two lines descend from Old Testament prophecy: one representing the ethical proclamation of the prophets, which ends with the legalistic Pharisees and rabbis. The other emerges from what was once termed the 'fervent piety of the prophets' and their expectations of the future, which God was about to enact. It leads directly to apocalypticism.

This sort of very general description of apocalyptic as a continuation of prophecy was frequently repeated in the first half of this century; so often, in fact, that it was eventually accepted without further reflection. Symptomatic of this tradition is the work of H.H. Rowley, an English scholar of considerable influence who, in the apocalyptic year 1944 published a volume on Jewish and early Christian apocalyptic in which he said simply 'that apocalyptic is the child of prophecy, yet diverse from prophecy, can hardly be disputed' (p. 15). It was then possible to maintain such a simplistic view of the matter because the scholars of the day thought that apocalyptic and eschatology were identical, and, moreover, that eschatology was the substantive element in prophecy.

We have run into the concept of eschatology previously; the word itself is derived from the Greek *ta eschata*, 'the last things', and *logos*, 'word' or 'doctrine'; thus: 'the doctrine of the last things', meaning the Day of Judgment, the Messiah, the kingdom of God etc. As we shall see shortly, it is correct that eschatology is a central concept in both prophecy and apoca-

lyptic. However, apocalyptic is so much more than just eschatology, that to cite that derivation is far from proposing an
exhaustive definition.

It is interesting to note that by an early date scholars had
begun to see apocalyptic in a sociological context, an approach
to which we shall return later. Wilhelm Bousset, a German
theologian and historian of religion, wrote a handbook of the
religion of ancient Judaism around the turn of the century.
Like others, he had no doubt that apocalyptic was a continuation of prophecy. But he emphasized powerfully that apocalyptic gives expression to the popular faith and expectations of
pious but uneducated laypeople: they hoped for a better world
and embraced wild and naive speculations about the future.
This view has now surely had its day.

Considerably more sophistication has characterized recent
scholarly discussion. Otto Plöger, another German scholar,
has attempted to study Judaism from around the year 500
BCE down to the time of Christ—the period after the
Babylonian exile—from a distanced perspective, in order to be
able to fit apocalyptic into the scheme of things. He feels that
ancient Judaism was characterized by a chasm separating
two main groups. The more dominant group was represented
by the 'establishment', which consisted of the priestly aristocracy and the upper classes. Their understanding of society
and religion was essentially static, and they did whatever was
necessary to preserve a type of society in which the priesthood
possessed all power. It was a society whose centre was the
temple cult and its law-abiding congregation. Such circles had
little enthusiasm for visions of the future like those common to
prophetic eschatology and apocalyptic. Their members
already lived in a harmonious world and had little need to
peer into the future to find a better one.

Plöger finds that the well-established group who were in
charge of things were opposed by another group possessing
completely different characteristics. Ideologically and socially,
this group was excluded from the strong central group.
Rather than being concerned with the Law and the cult, it
was primarily interested in the ancient prophetic writings. In
particular, it was attracted by the eschatological sections
which depict a glorious future for the chosen people. Perhaps

they even went so far as to feel that it was they, in contra-distinction to the leaders of the society, who were to make up that 'remnant' of the people about which the prophets often spoke; that remnant which was destined to experience the coming kingdom of glory. They possessed neither power nor influence in the Jewish society which had evolved in these centuries, and chose instead to seek refuge in the ideal world of imagination and hope. They gathered in 'conventicles', which were small, closed assemblies on the periphery of society; they immersed themselves in the prophetic writings, attempting to understand them and to interpret them as a message addressed to their own situation. In this fashion, eschatology developed into apocalyptic.

Whereas the first-mentioned group in the post-exilic Jewish society represented a fundamentally static stance, the other group expressed a dynamic and progressive attitude. Unlike the 'establishment', the members of this group were receptive to foreign influences. Plöger holds, as already Bousset had done, that the influence of Persian religion was found especi-ally congenial, and that the transformation of Old Testament eschatology into apocalyptic was, to a considerable extent, the result of importing concepts from Persia. He maintains that cosmic dualism, which was characteristic of Persian religion, was interpreted as a reflex of the oppositional relationship which obtained between the leading Jewish circles and the 'eschatological' groups. He also says that much else besides foreign borrowings helped to characterize apocalyptic, evolv-ing as it did under the impress of the actualizing interpreta-tions of the Old Testament prophetic writing.

Plöger's entire understanding of the development from prophecy to apocalyptic is well balanced, and has much in its favour, particularly when we recall our previous observation that apocalyptic was very much a response to times of crisis. His view is nevertheless an oversimplification, and there are a number of questions for which it provides no ready answers. Plöger's point of departure is sociological, but his description of the second of the two groups is too vague, and he makes no attempt to identify its members within Jewish society.

The sociological analysis of religious phenomena is enthusi-astically pursued in America, which makes it appropriate to mention an American scholar who agrees with Plöger to a considerable extent. Harvard University's P.D. Hanson also regards post-exilic Judaism as a divided entity; he, too, sees classical Israelite prophecy as the decisive presupposition for the development of apocalyptic, and thinks he has discovered the beginnings of apocalyptic in certain of the post-exilic prophetic writings. Hanson calls Plöger's oppositional 'eschatological' group 'the visionaries'. In his view they were primarily disciples of Deutero-Isaiah. He finds it characteristic that, on the basis of their situation within Jewish society, they projected the eschatological events which the prophets had expected to occur within the framework of time and space, into a cosmic dimension. This elevated the events to a completely new plane, on which the world would totally perish, and from which a new and better one would arise. Unlike Plöger, Hanson does not think that Persian influence played any significant role in this context. Instead, he holds that old motifs from Canaanite-Israelite mythologies surfaced in this new interpretation of the prophetic eschatology. Such motifs include the idea of Yahweh as the divine warrior who, together with his legions, comes to liberate the enslaved, destroy the evil world and those who have power in it, and renew all things. Like Plöger, then, Hanson emphasizes that aspect of apocalyptic which conveniently served as an alternative ideology for the oppressed and alienated groups within Jewish society. They received a new identity through the comprehensive understanding of human existence offered by apocalyptic, with its interpretation of the world and its future. Thus Hanson regards the eschatological element as the main emphasis of Jewish apocalyptic. But he is also aware that there are different types of apocalyptic in which, for example, foreign influences were manifested more strongly, and in which both hellenistic and Persian ideas had gained a foothold.

In spite of all the various differences, it is clear that the study of apocalyptic from Bousset to Hanson insists on a connection leading back to Old Testament prophecy and its eschatology. It is completely clear that this connection is real; one does not have to read many apocalyptic writings before one senses that the prophetic linguistic tone and the world of prophetic concepts were determinative for the formulations involved. As a single example, one should consult *1 Enoch* 45–57, which is packed with both obvious allusions and more or less concealed quotations from the Old Testament prophetic literature. The question, then, has to do with the guiding viewpoints which allowed the authors of apocalyptic writings to make use of prophetic proclamations. Did they merely reproduce the ideas of the prophets, or did they somehow transform prophetic thought?

We may perhaps approach an answer to this question by investigating the most recent phase of research into apocalyptic, research which is indissolubly linked with the name of Gerhard von Rad. Around 1960, von Rad had arrived at an understanding of apocalyptic which surprised most scholars. He held that Jewish apocalyptic was not rooted in Old Testament prophecy, but in the Old Testament Wisdom literature instead. He claimed that the understanding of history which characterized the prophets is radically different from the apocalyptic view of history. The prophetic understanding of history was determined by the concepts of covenant and election, which led them to develop a sort of 'salvation history'. The prophets understood history as a series of divine events in which God leads his people towards the goal he had set for them when he chose them.

Von Rad held that we meet a different view of history in apocalyptic. The apocalyptic writer was not particularly interested in Israel's history. For him, history was a cosmic event, it was world-history; it had to do with the empires of the earth which must be felled so that the kingdom of God can be established, as we have seen to be the case in Daniel.

In von Rad's opinion, the apocalyptical concept of history originated in a notion fundamental to Wisdom literature; namely that there is a divinely ordained world order. The course of history was established once and for all, so that it, too, reflects this divine order. It is entirely characteristic of the Wisdom tradition that it unceasingly seeks to understand the world and human existence in the world; the Wisdom tradition is an intellectualistic current in ancient Israelite religion. And this very endeavour recurs in apocalyptic even more strongly, directed beyond the world of mankind. The apoc-

alyptic author is not content to understand human life in the
here and now; rather, he is concerned to arrive at total com-
prehension of heaven and earth, the world of angels and the
world of mankind, the natural laws and the heavenly powers,
as well as past and future history, since all of these are
encompassed by the divinely appointed world order.

Of course, Gerhard von Rad acknowledged that eschatological ideas play a prominent part in apocalyptic. He was also
fully aware that eschatology played no part in Wisdom teaching as it appears in Proverbs, Job and Sirach. But his feeling
was that eschatology entered apocalyptic at a late date, owing
to the influence of the highly eschatological Persian religion.
He also called attention to the fact that there are late works in
the Old Testament, particularly the so-called Priestly Work in
the Pentatuech, which make use of chronological periodization in conjunction with the observation of the course of history. But he maintained that the entire eschatological complex
in apocalyptic is primarily subordinated to the idea of world
order, the notion that history was preordained in the dawn of
time.

On the basis of this understanding of apocalyptic, von Rad
thought to discern two main purposes driving apocalyptic
literature. Like the Wisdom literature, it seeks to establish an
encyclopaedic understanding of man's world. The driving
force behind this impulse is not ordinary curiosity, but rather
the need to map out the world so that man can understand it
and make his way in it. It is entirely logical that both the
Wisdom literature and apocalyptic contain a wealth of ethical
teaching, as we have already noted in earlier sections of this
work. The man who understands his world, and the intentions
of the creator God in making his creation the way he has done,
is receptive to ethical instruction, if he is able to acknowledge
that it agrees with the world order and its laws.

The other main purpose, which, as far as von Rad was
concerned, applies mainly to later apocalyptic, is related to the
understanding of history. It is the acknowledgment, which
can be comforting in times of turmoil, that the way of all the
world has been established by God, and that it must have a
happy ending—a view of apocalyptic which we have
encountered previously. Von Rad's ultimate understanding of

apocalyptic is not really very different from the more traditional view. The views actually only differ on the question of
the origin of apocalyptic. At all events, it is of the greatest
importance that von Rad has called so much attention to the
element of Wisdom present in apocalyptic. It would be
incorrect to maintain, as some scholars have done, that it is a
question of an either/or, that is: either apocalyptic derived
from prophecy, or from Wisdom teachings. Like the
American scholar Frank Cross, I should prefer to see apocalyptic presented as a new interpretation of the prophetic
messsage, seen in the light of Wisdom and incorporating non-
Jewish materials. Thus there were actually several components in apocalyptic, although it was probably the Wisdom
teachings which added to it a new and fascinating dimension.

Up to this point we have examined a number of positions
with respect to apocalyptic. The reader will surely understand
that it is difficult to provide a comprehensive picture. Many
attempts have been made; they have usually ended in a
catalogue of motifs which one or another scholar has held to
be characteristic of apocalyptic. Many years ago, the Swedish
scholar Johannes Lindblom proposed the following list: trans-
cendentalism, mythologism, cosmological orientation, a pessimistic view of history, dualism, periodization of history, the
doctrine of the present age and the one to come, numerical
speculation, pseudo-ecstasy, a false concept of revelation,
pseudonymity, and the affectation of arcane lore! Others have
added to the list such phenomena as angelology, demonology
and messianism. It would present no problem to find yet more
topics. But such lists do not contribute to the clarity of the
picture; instead, one's view is confirmed, that disagreements
about the nature of apocalyptic are entirely well founded.

Should one, however, attempt to say something comprehensive about apocalyptic without doing violence to the materials,
one would be forced to choose some high-order concept, or
Leitmotiv, which applies to most of the possible contexts one
runs into when dealing with the highly composite phenomenon that apocalyptic undoubtedly is. Is there a sort of
'lowest common denominator' for most of the apocalyptic
concepts and ideas? In my opinion yes, and I would designate
this concept as *dualism*. My reason for regarding dualism as a

high-order concept with respect to apocalyptic, has to do with the fact that dualism can be traced back to many of the religious currents which meet in apocalyptic. There are dualistic features in prophetic eschatology, there is some sort of dualism in the ethics of the Wisdom tradition, there is a concrete dualism in Persian religion, in pre-Christian gnosis and in Greek-hellenistic popular philosophy. All of the above components meet in apocalyptic, where dualism is one of the substantive elements of most of the complexes of idea. Various approaches to this fact are possible; here, however, we shall attempt to view apocalyptic dualism under three aspects: cosmic dualism, anthropological-ethical dualism, and eschatological dualism. This may sound a little cryptic at present, but it will be further developed below.

We have, of course, encountered dualism previously, in the section dealing with ethics. The basic problem of Jewish ethics, the notion of humanity confronted with the need to choose between good and evil, is unmistakably dualistic in character. In other words, dualistic thought is not the exclusive property of apocalyptic, and we must be very careful not to draw too sharp distinctions between the basic religious structure and apocalyptic. Apocalyptic was so powerful a spiritual current that it could not avoid influencing even those who were not caught in its web.

Cosmic Dualism

Initially, we shall concentrate on cosmic dualism, which is the dualism expressed in definitive distinctions between God and man and between heaven and earth. We shall observe that this dualism is a striking feature in apocalyptic, but we shall also have occasion to see how it is broken, in a remarkable way, through the insight of the apocalyptic visionary into heavenly things and through his revelation of his insight to his readers. We shall also meet cosmic dualism in the great complex of ideas surrounding Satan, the demons and the angels.

The first word Johannes Lindblom included, in his long list of characteristics of apocalyptic, was 'trascendentalism'. By this he meant the way heaven and the divine world are

infinitely removed from man and man's world. Throughout
Israel's history a gradual development occurred in the
concept of God as distant and transcendent. In ancient Israel,
God addressed himself directly to selected individuals and
announced his will to them. He was the protector of the tribe
and its god of war. It was after his transfer to Jerusalem
that—under the influence of Canaanite conceptions—he
began more frequently to be seen as creator God and God of
heaven. During the Babylonian exile, when the Jews were
compelled by circumstance to worship Yahweh away from
the temple, it was strongly emphasized that God is in heaven
and is therefore simultaneously remote and omnipresent. It
was this development which determined the emphasis of
Early Judaism and, not least, of apocalyptic, on the understanding of God as the distant god of heaven.

Many reflexes of this manifested themselves in Early
Judaism: it was forbidden to name the divine name, except in
the temple cult; on reading the Law, even in synagogal
practice, one avoided the name by saying 'the Lord' instead, as
was also done in the Greek translation of the Law and the
other biblical writings. Alternatively, such circumlocutions
were employed as 'the Lord of Spirits', 'the Highest', 'the Holy
One', and so forth. Continuing this tradition, it was only
natural that both the Pseudepigrapha and the Greek
translation of the biblical writings avoided mention of the all-
too-human features which earlier Israelite tradition had
assigned to God. This was most commonly done by discreetly
changing the texts, so that an angel appeared in accounts
where God himself originally figured.

This tendency is stringently expressed in the *Hymns* from
Qumran. These psalms arose in the apocalyptic enthusiasm of
the desert congregation; thus they repeatedly emphasize the
abyss separating God and his 'creation of clay':

> What then is man that is earth,
> that is shaped from clay and returns to the dust?
>
> Clay and dust that I am,
> what can I devise unless Thou wish it,
> and what contrive unless Thou desire it?
> What strength shall I have
> unless Thou keep me upright,

and how shall I understand
unless by the spirit which Thou hast shaped for me?
What can I say unless Thou open my mouth,
and how can I answer unless Thou enlighten me?
Behold, Thou art Prince of gods
and King of majesties,
Lord of all spirits,
and Ruler of all creatures;
nothing is done without thee,
and nothing is known without thy will.
Beside Thee there is nothing,
and nothing can compare with Thee in strength;
in the presence of Thy glory there is nothing,
and Thy might is without price (1QH 10.3-10).

The human being is nothing, and God is everything! Or, more accurately: humans can do nothing except through the power of God; they are totally dependent on the distant and transcendent God of heaven. In other religions the transcendence of the heavenly god means that humans have been left to their own devices. This thought, however, is foreign to Judaism. No matter how remote and elevated God is to the individual Jew, he nevertheless remains the God of creation and providence, and the righteous and merciful judge of the individual. For the ordinary Jew, this distant God is present in his temple, and it is possible for humans to establish contact with him via the cult. For the apocalyptic visionary, however, the centre of gravity of religious life is located elsewhere than in the cult. God is above all the elevated one who created the world and who rules it through the world order and its natural laws. At the same time, as Judge, he is the God who has the power to destroy his work of creation and to build a new and better world.

Thus the cosmic dualism comes to expression in the transcendence of the remote God of heaven. But it was in the apocalyptic writings that this transcendence was broken. There is a fundamental ambivalence in apocalyptic: on the one hand it emphasizes, with all its power, the infinite distance separating God and humanity. On the other hand, however, the apocalyptic writings emphasize revelations which occurred to selected persons in the past, and these few chosen individuals received insight into the heavenly world and the nature of God and were instructed to reveal their insights to their readers. The apocalyptic authors themselves were probably aware of this ambivalence; indeed, in one of the late apocalyptic writings we are told directly that

> men on earth can understand earthly things and nothing else; only he who lives above the skies can understand the things above the skies (2 Esdras 4.21)

Thus it must have seemed marvellous indeed to the apocalyptic writer, that a journey through the heavenly regions could be vouchsafed to a mere human being.

It was mentioned earlier that the reference to Enoch in Genesis, as the one who was taken up to God, led to the production in the antique period of an entire Enoch literature. Enoch undertakes a heavenly journey on behalf of the fallen angels, who have asked him to intercede for them with God himself. He tells us about his sojourn, one moment as though it took place in vision, the next as if he really was led before the throne of God—an ambiguity which is also present in some of the accounts by the Old Testament prophets of their visions.

> And the vision appeared to me as follows: Behold clouds called me in the vision, and mist called me, and the path of the stars and flashes of lightning hastened me and drove me, and in the vision winds caused me to fly and hastened me and lifted me up into heaven. And I proceeded until I came near to a wall which was built of hailstones and a tongue of fire surrounded it, and it began to make me afraid. And I went into the tongue of fire and came near to a large house.... (*1 Enoch* 14.8-10).

Enoch then describes the house, which is built of crystal and surrounded by flames, 'and it was hot as fire and cold as snow'. He throws himself down and then sees yet another house:

> And I looked and saw in it a high throne, and its appearance was like ice and its surrounds like the shining sun and the sound of Cherubim. And from underneath the high throne there flowed out rivers of burning fire so that it was impossible to look at it. And He who is great in glory sat on it, and his raiment was brighter than the sun, and whiter than any snow (*1 Enoch* 14.18-20).

Enoch continues his journey in the succeeding chapters (*1 Enoch* 17–36). There are many unclear things in the text; one moment Enoch seems to be in heaven, the next on earth, or, rather, on the borders of the earth, 'at the place of the end of heaven and earth' (18.14). Here the forces of nature are anchored. He sees the places where thunder and lightning are stored, and then is led 'to the fire of the west, which receives every setting of the sun', and to 'the mountains of the darkness of winter', and sees 'the storehouses of all the winds'.

> And I saw the cornerstone of the earth, and I saw the four winds which support the earth and the firament of heaven. And I saw how the winds stretch out the height of heaven and how they position themselves between heaven and earth; they are the pillars of heaven. And I saw the winds which turn heaven and cause the disk of the sun and all the stars to set. And I saw the winds on the earth which support the clouds, and I saw the paths of the angels. I saw at the end of the earth the firmament of heaven above (*1 Enoch* 18.2-5).

In addition to these things, Enoch sees the place where the fallen angels are to be held prisoner for all eternity. He also sees the Kingdom of Death, with its separate chambers for the righteous and the wicked, in which they will remain until the Day of Judgment. He sees the mountain which is to be God's throne after the judgment; the sourrounding land, which is obviously Palestine, is described as a new Garden of Paradise, with the Tree of Life and Tree of Knowledge. And he returns to the ends of the earth, where he counts the heavenly gates through which the heavenly bodies and the winds wander. The reason why Enoch is allowed to glimpse the secrets of heaven and the forces of nature is stated at the end of ch. 36:

> And when I saw, I blessed, and I will always bless the Lord of Glory who has made great and glorious wonders that he might show the greatness of his work to his angels and to the souls of men, that they might praise his work, and that all his creatures might see the work of his power and praise the great work of his hands and bless him for ever (*1 Enoch* 36.4).

The idea is typical of apocalyptic: Enoch is allowed to see the secrets of existence, that he may acknowledge God as creator and lord and pass his knowledge on to mankind, that is, to those who have ears to hear. The same motifs recur later in *1 Enoch*: in ch. 71 Enoch once again relates his heavenly journey, while in 72–82 he expatiates about the forces of nature in a learned and complicated account of astronomic phenomena and the computations underlying the calendar.

Another Enoch work, the *2 Enoch*, which apparently dates from the first century CE, seems to be dependent on *1 Enoch* and further develops some of its ideas. But whereas *1 Enoch* is really an apocalyptic anthology containing all manner of materials, *2 Enoch* speaks, apart from an addition on the origin of the priesthood, solely of Enoch's heavenly journey. On the other hand, it is thoroughly descriptive: Enoch is led into the first heaven, in which 200 angels stand watch over the stars and the chambers containing snow, ice, dew, and clouds. The fallen angels are imprisoned in the second heaven. The third heaven contains two departments: to the south is Paradise, with its four rivers and Three of Life, where the righteous dead dwell. To the north he finds the place where all wicked and godless persons are kept,

> a very terrible place: every kind of torment and torture is in that place, and darkness and mist; and there is no light there, but a dark fire flaming up eternally in that place, and a river of fire rising up against all that place. And there are cold and ice and prisons in that place, and fierce and cruel angels who carry weapons and inflict torments without mercy (*2 Enoch* 5.11-13).

The movements of the sun and the moon proceed from the fourth heaven; the movements are described in astronomical formulas. In the fifth heaven he again finds the fallen angels, and in the sixth he sees the seven angels who supervise the world order; the movements of sun and moon, the times, the years, the rivers, seas, herbs, and so forth. In the seventh heaven, Enoch is led before the Lord, who is seated on his throne and surrounded by his archangels. He tells Enoch all about the mysteries of creation, including things he has not even revealed to the angels. Enoch is to write it all down in books which he is to pass on to his sons:

> And give them the books which your hand has written, and they will read them and recognize the creator, and they will

also understand that there is no other creator but me; and they will pass on the books your hand has written to their children, and their children to their children, and next-of-kin to next-of-kin, from one generation to another (2 *Enoch* 11.27).

A longer version of the work contains an addition in which Enoch is allowed to pass on into the eighth heaven, where the changing of the seasons is regulated. From there he proceeds to the ninth heaven, which contains the heavenly dwelling for the twelve signs of the zodiac. Finally, in the tenth heaven, he beholds

the appearance of the Lord's face, like iron made to glow in fire, and brought out, emitting sparks, and it burns. Thus I saw the Lord's face, but the Lord's face is ineffable, marvellous and very awful, and very, very terrible (2 *Enoch* 22.1 [Charles' edn.])

Two other heavenly visions are worthy of mention. In the *Testament of Levi* (yet another of the *Testaments of the Twelve Patriarchs*), Levi experiences a dream-vision in which he is led through the seven heavens. The text is disordered; some versions include only three heavens, and their sequence has been reversed. But the work is generally reminiscent of 2 *Enoch*: the first heaven is dark 'because it witnesses all the unrighteous deeds of men'. Fire, snow and ice are stored in the second heaven for later use as punishments for the godless. The third heaven contains those angels whose task it will be to execute the punishment; the sacred 'thrones and powers' are kept in the fourth, while the fifth heaven contains those angels who bear messages to the archangels. The sixth heaven contains the angels who stand before the face of the Lord and make sacrifice to him in order to atone for man's sin. In the seventh heaven, the Most High sits on the throne of glory in his holy temple (*T. Levi* 2.6–5.2).

Finally, there is the *Greek Apocalypse of Baruch* (3 *Baruch*), which is a fairly late work, perhaps deriving from the second century CE. The main content of the apocalypse is once again a heavenly journey. Baruch, who is the scribe of the prophet Jeremiah, and who experienced the destruction of Jerusalem in 587 BCE, is led by an angel through five heavens.

The description of the various heavens is so packed with motifs that it would be impossible here to account for them in detail. While the general run of apocalyptic heavenly visions verges on the grotesque, the vision here is bizarre, and such foreign motifs as, for example, the Phoenix, have made an entrance. At all events, *3 Baruch* is by no means boring, though I shall leave it up to the reader to make closer acquaintance with it.

There are many problems connected with this particular genre of apocalyptic, that is, the heavenly journey or heavenly vision. In the first place, there is the question of the conceptual source of a plurality of heavens. The rabbis held that such an Old Testament expression as 'heaven and the heaven of heavens' (1 Kgs 8.17) implies that there was in reality more than one heaven. However, it is probable that this was a question of influence from Babylonian religion. As is well known, the Babylonians had achieved much in the way of astronomical observation; they knew of five planets, and they had divided the heavens up into seven spheres on the basis of the courses of the planets, the sun, and the moon. It was no doubt such speculative ideas which the Jews transformed into the idea of the seven heavens.

A more interesting question has to do with the function of the heavenly visions. In this connection, the account in the *Testament of Levi* is of central importance. The angel announces to Levi (who is, after all, the grandfather of the Israelite priesthood) just why he is to see the various heavens:

> You will stand close to the Lord and be his minister,
> and you will declare his mysteries to men (*T. Levi* 2.10).

Later, speaking from his throne, the Lord himself says to Levi:

> To you I have given the blessings of the priesthood
> until I come and dwell in the midst of Israel (*T. Levi* 5.2).

Finally, in ch. 8 Levi is consecrated as a priest. Here we are clearly concerned with specifically priestly traditions, as insight into the heavenly mysteries is presupposed a priestly privilege. This accords well with the fact that the seventh heaven in the *Testament of Levi* is described as a temple, a notion we touched on in conjunction with our study of temple ideology.

The function of the other heavenly visions is, however, clearly different and more characteristic of apocalyptic. They convey the aforementioned idea of the need to convince humanity that the forces of nature are under divine control. The various elements of nature are located in different heavens, and the angels are charged with ensuring that they function in accordance with the divine will. In the last instance we also catch a glimpse of the eschatological motif of judgment; in several heavens the angles are ready to punish the godless, while the righteous reside in a new Paradise. We shall return to all this shortly.

The fact that, as we have seen, humans are allowed to obtain some insight into divinity does not eliminate the fundamental aspect of cosmic dualism, namely the infinite distance between God and humanity and between heaven and earth. In the hevenly visions, this is emphasized by the prominent role played by the angels. For the very reason that the distinction between humanity and God is absolute, the angels have an important function as mediatory figures which enable communication between the heavenly and the earthly. Angels are sent to Enoch to lead him up through the heavens; an angel comes on a similar mission to Baruch; an angel explains to Levi the details that he observes in his heavenly vision; angels have been appointed to execute the sentence on the Day of Judgment; and, characteristically, human prayers cannot reach God directly: instead they are borne by the archangel Michael to the throne of God (the *Greek Apocalypse of Baruch* 11.4). Indeed, there is a virtual hierarchy of angels in the apocalyptic writings. We have already seen how, in *2 Enoch*, the various sectors of the human world are subordinated to particular angels, who are thus co-responsible for the maintenance of world order. The archangels Michael, Gabriel, Uriel, Raphael and so on are at the apex of the hierarchy. Their numbers range from work to work between six and ten.

The angels have no well-defined role in the Old Testament religion. On some occasions they serve as Yahweh's messengers, and the frequent references to heavenly hosts are probably reminiscences of earlier conceptions of Yahweh which presuppose him, as God of war, surrounded by his armies. There can scarcely be any doubt that the prominent position of the angels in early Jewish religion was to some extent a function of the development of dualistic thought, as suggested previously. But there were certainly also external influences. The Jews were subject to Persian rule for more than 200 years, and the Persian influence on Jewish religion has already been mentioned. The Persian creator-god, Ahura Mazda, represents the good in existence. By his side are six 'immortal holy ones', some sort of superior angels, each of whom represents such qualities as 'good temperament', 'the truth', 'piety', 'health' and so forth. Beneath them, in turn, are countless angels who are charged with the supervision of every conceivable aspect of human life. This corresponds rather well to the Jewish system of arch- and lower-class angels who figure in the apocalypses and who were later adopted by the rabbis.

Thus in apocalyptic, both the heavenly visions and the concept of angels as mediatory figures constitute bridges over the abyss separating heaven and earth, God and humanity. However, the cosmic dualism of apocalyptic is also expressed through an opposition of even greater significance than these, namely the opposition between God and Satan. Once again, it is probably the case that Persian religion, the most thorough-going dualistic religion of all those with which the Jews came into contact, exercised some influence. The creator god, Ahura Mazda, was confronted by the deity Ahriman, who repre-sented all the evil of existence. He was an 'anti-god', if you will, a sort of devil, and he commanded an army of devils or demons who ceaselessly attempted to breach the power of goodness and light. This was a truly cosmic dualism, and it had its equivalent in early Jewish religion.

However, while it may not have been difficult for the Jew to adopt the angelology of Persian religion, since the good creator-god, Ahurza Mazda, was in many respects similar to Israel's god, Yahweh, it was more problematical for him to accept the notion of an anti-god like Ahriman. Jewish religion is, after all, fundamentally monistic, that is, based on faith in the one God as creator and lord. But the question of evil is bound to manifest itself in any monistic religion sooner or later. The Old Testament itself has an extremely realistic understanding of evil: it exists and manifests itself as sin, suffering, and death. But ultimately the Old Testament gives up the attempt to answer the question as to the origin of evil. From the creation narrative in Genesis, where the serpent represents evil, and on into the later writings, no serious attempt is made to confront this question. We meet Satan in the book of Job, but this figure is hardly a demonic figure like the Ahriman of Persian religion. He belongs instead to Yahweh's court and has the function of accuser (which is what the word *satan* means) in divine judicial proceedings.

It is probably in early Jewish literature that we first encounter a demonic figure, arising, perhaps, under the influence of the Persian Ahriman. He goes by a number of names in the various writings, Satan and Belial (or Beliar) being the most common designations. Nevertheless, he is not simply Ahriman translated into Jewish surroundings. No matter how strong the dualistic impulses which enter into Judaism, it is impossible for the Jew to conceive of an autonomous, divine figure possessing parallel status with Yahweh from the beginning. Instead, the Jews seized on the explanation described above in the section on ethics, according to which Belial and his devils were simply fallen angels. They originally belonged to Yahweh's creatures and his court, but they opposed Yahweh and his will, so that they stood outside of the sphere of Yahweh's power. Or, as an early Jew would perhaps have expressed the matter: Yahweh allows them their depredations as long as it pleases him to do so. Whatever day he chooses, he can make an end to evil and its power. In other words, the Jews retained the monistic view in unabbrieviated form. The fact that Yahweh actually does allow evil was explained by a conception of Early Judaism which we have also mentioned previously, namely the idea of human freedom to choose between good and evil.

In the section on ethics (see above, pp. 83ff.), we considered several texts dealing with ethical problems which indicate the belief that humanity in a situation of choice was poised between God and Satan. We shall not here investigate the many passages in apocalyptic literature in which Satan is characterized as the seducer. There are, however, some characteristic expressions which it would be wise to note. A legend dating from the first century CE, which describes the matyrdom of the prophet Isaiah (*Ascens. Isa* .1.3), refers to Satan as 'the prince of this world'; another passage tells us that 'the angel of lawlessness, who is the ruler of this world, is Beliar' (*Ascens. Isa.* 2.4). The latter expression recurs in the Christian additions to the legend (4.2; 10.29), and is also attested in the New Testament (Jn. 12.31; 14.30; 16.11). One of the *Testaments of the Twelve Patriarchs* refers explicitly to 'the kingdom of the enemy' (*T. Dan* 6.2, 4), a phrase which corresponds closely to a formulation which occurs frequently in the Qumran texts: 'the dominion of Belial' (1QS 1.18, 23; 2.19). All these expressions have in common the idea that the world is in the grip of evil, or, as the *Damascus Document* has it, 'during all those years Belial shall be unleashed against Israel' (4.12f.), where the expression 'all those years' means 'until the end of time'.

Thus the idea of the lordship of Belial means that the battle between good and evil will endure as long as this world exists. As we have seen, the battle takes place within individuals, but it also takes place between the two groups within humankind, namely between those who manage to resist Belial's attack, and those who succumb to it. And so we come to another aspect of cosmic dualism: the twofold division of humanity. There are some who, in a manner of speaking, have already withdrawn themselves from this world and rejected the mastery of Belial; they belong to God, while their opponents are in the sway of evil. This idea is not merely an import from the realms of Persian religion or Hellenistic-gnostic dualism. Already Old Testament Wisdom teaching, particularly as expressed in Proverbs, is actually based on a dualistic understanding of reality, as it divides humanity into two groups: the wise or righteous on the one side and the foolish or godless on the other. Furthermore, all conceivable human activities and attitudes are ordered in corresponding catalogues of virtues and vices and in long series of proverb-like utterances. Through Sirach and the Wisdom of Solomon this understanding of humanity gained ground in the antique period, when it also proved capable of combination with the new ideas of a dualistic nature, such as the doctrine of demons and devils.

In apocalyptic, it was primarily the Qumran texts which arrived at a consistent distinction between 'the Children of Light' and 'the Children of Darkness', or, as they are called elsewhere, 'the Children of Righteousness' and 'the Children of Falsehood' (1QS 1.9f. and 3.20f. respectively). When we consider our observations in the section on the Law, where we saw how difficult it was in Judaism to draw the line of demarcation between 'the righteous' and 'the sinners' (see above, pp. 81f.), we should expect the members of the Qumran community to have experienced similar difficulties with the oppositions mentioned above. But in fact, they found the matter quite simple: whoever was inducted into the congregation of Qumran belonged to the Children of Light, and so belonged to God, while whoever did not join them—meaning the other Jews and the rest of humanity—was among the Children of Darkness and belonged to Belial.

We shall not review here the many passages in which this demarcation figures in the Qumran texts. Already the liturgy in the first pages of the *Community Rule* highlights it sharply: first the priests bless 'the men of the lot of God', that is, the Children of Light, using a formula which is a paraphrase of the Aaronite Blessing. Then the Levites take over; they represent the lower order of the priesthood, so that one can reasonably delegate the task of cursing 'the men of the lot of Belial', that is, the Children of Darkness, to them:

> Be cursed because of all your guilty wickedness! May He deliver you up for torture at the hands of the vengeful Avengers! May he visit you with destruction by the hand of all the Wreakers of Revenge! Be cursed without mercy because of the darkness of your deeds! Be damned in the shadowy place of everlasting fire! May God not heed when you call on Him, nor pardon you by blotting out your sin! May he raise His angry face towards you for vengeance! May there be no 'Peace' for you in the mouth of those who hold fast to the Fathers! (1QS 2.5-9).

There is no doubt whatsoever as to the absolute distance between these two groups! Later in the *Community Rule* we find a more or less theoretical account of 'the two natures of man', an account which is, however, somewhat confusingly woven together with the piece dealing with the two tendencies within the same individual, which was cited earlier (pp. 90f.). The decisive passage informs us that

> those born of truth spring from a fountain of light, but those born of falsehood spring from a source of darkness. All the children of righteousness are ruled by the Prince of Light and walk in the ways of light, but all the children of falsehood are ruled by the Angel of Darkness and walk in the ways of darkness. The Angel of Darkness leads all the children of righteousness astray, and until his end, all their sin, iniquities, wickedness, and all their unlawful deeds are caused by his dominion in accordance with the mysteries of God (1 QS 3.19-23).

One almost gets the impression that people are predestined to belong to either the Children of Light or the Children of Darkness. In fact, there is a short passage among the Qumran texts which expresses what we might call a doctrine of predestination:

> From the God of Knowledge comes all that is and shall be. Before ever they existed He established their whole design, and when, as ordained for them, they come into being, it is in accord with His glorious design that they accomplish their task without change (1QS 3.15-16).

The thought expressed here is really a logical extension of a system like the theology cultivated in Qumran, where an attempt was made to think through the dualistic idea consistently, and to reconcile it with the fundamental Jewish understanding of God, man, and the Law. If, however, true dualism is ultimately irreconcilable with the Jewish belief in God, then a radical doctrine of predestination is likewise irreconcilable with Jewish ethics. It is nevertheless not coincidental if, in the course of reading this section on cosmic dualism as an aspect of the realm of apocalyptic thought, the reader has found himself repeatedly reminded of gnosticism. There are in fact numerous connections between Jewish apocalyptic and later gnosis. Some scholars would even go so far as to maintain that some of the roots of gnosticism lay in Judaism.

Anthropological-ethical Dualism

We have dwelt at some length on the subject of cosmic dualism and have seen that, in Qumran, this concept was taken to its ultimate consequence. At the same time, however, we have noted how close dualism actually is to what we, by way of anticipation, termed anthropological-ethical dualism. We can allow ourselves to be brief now on our review of this type of dualism, since we have already touched on this sort of concept in our examination of Jewish ethics. But there is reason to discuss one side of the early Jewish understanding of man which was influenced by a variety of dualism which enjoyed considerable popularity under hellenism, namely that view of the relationship between soul and body which was later to be fully developed in gnosticism. It is a typical result of the meeting between western philosophy and the eastern religions. Briefly, the concept asserts that God and the world are irreconcilable opposites; that humanity is situated between both quantities, in that the soul represents God, the good, while the body represents the world, that is, evil. The soul is bound to the body, and salvation consists in the liberation of the soul through knowledge, purification, or ascesis. These basic ideas were developed in a variety of ways, and it should be said at once that they never won significant support among the Jews.

In the creation narrative in Genesis Judaism found the basic elements of an anthropology: humanity was created by God; it was created from dust and spirit; it was made in God's image; and at the creation it was accorded lordship over the creation. Humanity is the crown of creation, an idea that the later rabbis expressed by means of the twin concepts microcosm and macrocosm, already encountered in a different connection. A human being is a microcosm, 'a little world' which contains everything that is to be found in the macrocosm, 'the great world', that is, the entire created world. The human being is a sort of reflection of the creation in its entirety; indeed, one might say that the whole of creation is represented in each person. Such ideas had already put in an appearance in the work of Aristotle and in the realm of Persian thought, so there is no doubt that the Jews derived them from some external source.

On the other hand, the idea of people being created 'in the image of God' was a naturalized Jewish concept, even though the ultimate parentage of the idea probably lay in Egypt or Mesopotamia. The phrase itself was understood variously in Early Judaism: in the apocryphal Wisdom of Solomon, which was assuredly composed in Alexandria around the time of Christ, human likeness to God meant that peope were originally created immortal, but forfeited immortality as a result of the Fall (Wisdom of Solomon 2.23). According to Sirach the idea means that humankind received authority over the creation (17.1-3), and some rabbis suggested that it signified that external human form is like that of the angels, the sons of God.

Philo, however, interpreted the idea of creation in the image of God quite differently. He found God's likeness to reside in the human soul, a view he substantiated by referring to the second creation narrative (Gen. 2), where we read that man was made from dust, representing the body, after which the divine spirit, which forms the soul, was blown into him. From this interpretation it was possible for Philo to arrive at the traditional hellenistic teaching about the soul in the prison of the body, like a mussel enclosed within its hard shell. He held that if the body gets the upper hand, the soul dies, and the body becomes its grave. But the soul which manages to suppress the demands of the body, its desires, may free itself of the power of the body; it will be able to do this if it attains to insight, virtue and the fear of God. The same understanding of the relationship between soul and body is probably present in the Wisdom of Solomon, which remarks that 'a perishable body weighs down the soul, and its frame of clay burdens the mind so full of thoughts' (9.15).

This sort of understanding of the creation narrative is thoroughly non-Jewish and was wholly foreign to the ancient Israelites who originally recounted the story. For them, the soul and the body formed a unity, and the notion that humanity was created from dust or clay meant only that humans—in both soul and body—are weak, and all too easily give in to sin. This was well understood in Early Judaism, so that, for example, the Qumran *Hymns* found it possible to use such strong words about the human being as a 'creature of clay' who stands 'in the realm of wickedness' (1QH 3.23f; cf. the quotation on pp. 172f.).

Without going as far as Philo had done, the apocalyptic authors nevertheless had their own ideas about the creation of humanity. Their primary reason for getting involved in such speculation was the need to follow their compulsion to plot out the human world, to comprehend the intentionality underlying the work of creation, and thereby to reinforce their faith in a good and reasonable God. Just as the heavenly visions served to convince readers that God had established the world order and the natural laws, so, too, they could take comfort in the knowledge that the human being was created, down to the slightest detail in accordance with the divine will. Admittedly, the remote God was in his heaven, while the human resided on earth, but even so this distant God took care of every single one of his creatures and equipped each of them with the same qualities which, once upon a far-away time, Adam had possessed. Thus Sirach, who knows so much about the reasonable and serviceable order of creation, relates that

> he gave men tongue and eyes and ears,
> the power of choice and a mind for thinking.
> He filled them with discernment
> and showed them good and evil (Sir. 17.6-7).

This is typical of Sirach; we have previously encountered his harmonic understanding of existence, and in the following we see how that pious man concludes his list of the excellent qualities of humanity:

> He gave them knowledge as well
> and endowed them with the life-giving law.
> He established a perpetual covenant with them
> and revealed to them his decrees (Sir. 17.11-12).

Here there is no suggestion of dualism. But if we proceed to a text which is more highly characterized by apocalyptic ideas, namely the *Testaments of the Twelve Patriarchs,* we find the following account of created humanity:

> Seven spirits were given him at the creation to be the means of his doing everything. The first is the spirit of life, with which man's substance is created. The second is the spirit of sight, with which comes desire. The third is the spirit of

> hearing, with which is given teaching. The fourth is the spirit of smell, with which taste is given to draw in air and breath. The fifth is the spirit of speech, with which comes knowledge. The sixth is the spirit of taste, with which comes eating and drinking; and by them man's strength is built up (for food is the foundation of strength). The seventh is the spirit of pro-creation and sexual intercourse, with which sin enters through love of pleasure. For this reason it is last in the order of creation and first among the desires of youth, because the truth about it goes unrecognized, and it leads the young man like a blind man to a pit, and like a beast over a precipice. Besides all these there is an eighth spirit of sleep, with which were brought into being the deep sleep of nature and the image of death (*T.Reuben* 2.3–3.1).

The above passage is connected with the text dealing with Belial's seven spirits quoted earlier (cf. pp. 85f.). At the same time, however, it also attempts to offer a picture of humanity and the senses. The Jews will surely have adopted this doctrine of the senses from the Stoics, who likewise listed the five senses, plus the ability to reproduce and the faculty of speech. The Jewish system lacks the sense of touch and adds instead the 'spirit of sleep'. But what is interesting is the fact that where the Stoics list reason as the eighth, supra-ordinate sense, the Jewish text lists the 'spirit of life', as constitutive of human essence. The idea is no doubt that of the divine spirit of life which is blown into the creature of clay. It is furthermore clear that there is an oppositional relationship between the spirit of life and the other spirits, all of which satisfy merely material demands, and some of which are spoken of condescendingly. There is, perhaps, a suggestion here of a body–soul dualism, but no more than a suggestion. By way of contrast, Philo adopts the entire Stoic system, in which the reason, represented by the Soul, is the dominant faculty. He says, with reference to the five senses plus the faculties of speech and reproduction:

> All these, as in marionette shows, are drawn with strings by the understanding, now resting, now moving, each in the attitudes and with the movements appropriate to it (*On the Creation, 117*).

Against this, Enoch seems not to have understood the point of it all when, in a similar effort to connect the senses with various human organs, he concludes by assigning the soul to the sense of smell (*2 Enoch* 30.8-9).

Once again we have to examine the texts from Qumran in order to find a truly anthropological dualism which goes far beyond what is said in other early Jewish works. We have to do with a fragment from Cave 4, the content of which is clearly related to the sections in the *Community Rule* which we touched on in our section on ethics (pp. 90ff.). It is the one which describes the warring of the spirits of truth and falsehood within the individual soul, and each individual's 'possession' of either truth and righteousness, or else wrongness. These thoughts are developed in the fragment in a very strange manner:

> a man...and his thighs are long and thin, and his toes are thin and long, and he is of the Second Vault. He has six (parts) spirit in the House of Light, and three in the Pit of Darkness. And this is the time of birth on which he is brought forth—on the fesival of Taurus. He will be poor; and this is his beast—Taurus.
>
> And his head... and his teeth are... and the fingers of his hands are thick, and his thighs are thick and each covered with hair; and his toes are thick and short. He has eight (parts) spirits in the House of Darkness and one (part) from the House of Light. And a man... (*4QCry*; after *Journal of Semitic Studies* 9 [1964], pp. 293-94).

In a way, the two dualistic systems in Qumran theology collide in the above text: the anthropological-ethical dualism, teaching that the spirits of truth and falsity are at war in the individual, and cosmic dualism, teaching that everyone belongs to either the Children of Light or the Children of Darkness. The text attempts to solve how one can determine whether a given person belongs to one group or the other. We seem to be arriving at the sort of percentage calculations employed by certain rabbis in their attempts to decide whether a man belongs to the righteous or to the lost sinners (see above, p. 81). The fragment from Qumran claims that an individual consists of nine 'parts'. Whoever belongs to the powers of darkness to the extent of eight ninths is presented as being virtually a freak, belonging to the Children of Darkness. On the other hand, whoever belongs by six ninths to the powers of light is described as quite well formed, even though such a person is still, apparently, only awarded second-class honours with respect to the Children of Light. It is a pity that the text is so fragmentary, but it would probably not be too venturesome to suggest that the watershed lies around the figures four and five (ninths), that is, that one has to possess at least five parts of the House of Light in order to belong to the Children of Light. But the whole is made no simpler by the rôle apparently played by astrological speculation in assigning a person's placement.

Eschatological Dualism

The last-cited text brought us into the realm of eccentric exaggeration characteristic of some apocalyptic works. We shall now turn to the third aspect of apocalypticism: eschatological dualism. We have here to do with a dualism on the temporal plane, a contradiction between that which has been and that which is to come. In other words, we shall touch on the question of the apocalyptic understanding of history, and on the vast complex of eschatological ideas, which is the term used for notions of the last times, the Day of Judgment, the Messiah, and so on. These bring us to the same difficulties we encountered in the previous chapter, since eschatological ideas are by no means confined to apocalyptic literature. When we encountered them in connection with the basic religious structure we put off dealing with them until the section dealing with apocalyptic, because one thing, at least, is certain: even though eschatological ideas are already present in Old Testament religion, it was with apocalyptic that eschatology first reached its fullest development.

Incidentally, this fact provides a good illustration of a feature discussed in our review of the most recent debate on the origins of apocalyptic, in either Old Testament prophetism or the Old Testament Wisdom teachings. I preferred to understand the matter in such a way that apocalyptic can be seen as a reinterpretation of prophecy in the light of the Wisdom tradition. It should be evident here that it was above all the prophetic eschatology which was reinterpreted. Eschatology's restatement as apocalyptic gave it a new dimension, combining it with Wisdom ideas about world order and with the new understanding of history which occurred in antiquity, whose origin was also in the Wisdom tradition.

In other words, some of the ideas that will be discussed in the following pages are valid for Early Judaism as such, while others are specific to apocalyptic. There can be no question of a sharp division, but we shall nevertheless attempt to distinguish where it is obviously appropriate to do so.

Eschatology is indissolubly linked with the understanding of history. Depending on one's interpretation, eschatological events signify either the end or the midpoint of history. In our review of Gerhard von Rad's position on apocalyptic we met the concept of 'salvation history'. This concept provides an appropriate summary of the prophets' understanding of history, and thus of eschatological events. The prophets understood history to be a series of events through which Yahweh, the God of Israel, demonstrated his will to stand by the covenant he had once concluded with his chosen people. The events themselves might be such things as happenings which were taken to be expressions of Yahweh's punishments for the people's apostasy, or events which showed that Yahweh would, in spite of everything, continue to hold his hand shelteringly over his people, and that he would restore them after they had been chastised. In this series of events, which was thought to comprise Israel's history, the eschatological events were understood more as a turning-point than as a final end. The following two quotations from the book of Jeremiah are typical. Having been asked why the catastrophe will come, the prophet answers:

> Because your forefathers forsook me, says the Lord, and followed other gods, serving them and bowing down to them. They forsook me and did not keep my law. And you yourselves have done worse than your forefathers; for each of you follows the promptings of his wicked and stubborn heart instead of obeying me. So I will fling you headlong out of this land into a country unknown to you and to your forefathers; there you can serve other gods day and night, for I will show you no favour (Jer. 16.11-13).

There are many such threats in the prophetic corpus. But immediately after the above-cited words of Jeremiah, we find an assurance that the people will be brought home again, 'to the soil which I gave to their forefathers'. There are likewise many such assurances among the prophets. To take another characteristic passage in Jeremiah:

> The time is coming when I will restore the fortunes of my people Israel and Judah, says the Lord, and bring them back to the land which I gave to their forefathers; and it shall be their possession...In that day, says the Lord of Hosts, I will break their yoke off their necks and snap their cords; foreigners shall no longer use them as they please; they shall serve the Lord their God and David their king, whom I will raise up for them (Jer. 30.3, 8-9).

These quotations give us the eschatological proclamation of the pre-exilic prophets in a nutshell: the threat of judgment and exile, and the promise of homecoming and national restoration. In the prophetic message there is a violent tension between these two poles, and, indeed, threat and promise are often placed starkly side by side. This is a function of the fact that, for the prophets, there was no shortcut to the glorious future that awaited the people. The path to salvation was through judgment and destruction. The people had broken their relationship to Yahweh, so that punishment had to be experienced before foreigiveness could come and restoration be experienced. The prophets of the eighth century BCE, Amos, Hosea, Isaiah, and Micah, quite naturally understood the Assyrians, the great power of their day, as the instrument of the judgment. However, this only proved to be the case as far as the northern kingdom was concerned, which, as we have seen, fell and was dissolved in 722 BCE. The southern kingdom, Judah, whose capital was Jerusalem, survived another 130 years and preserved its independence to some extent the whole time. The prophets who were active around 600 BCE, mainly Jeremiah and Ezekiel, had perforce to regard Babylon, the new great power, as the instrument of Yahweh's wrath towards Judah. And, as is well known, Jerusalem did fall in 587 BCE.

However, these prophets agreed that a new and brighter future awaited the people after their punishment. Incidentally, it is worth mentioning that both the eschatological predictions of judgment and the eschatological predictions of the time of glory are quite stereotyped in the prophetic works. As a rule, judgment was expected in the form of an enemy attack, while the time of glory was characterised as a time when the relationship between Yahweh and his people would be re-established, when the heathen oppressors would be crushed, when peace and harmony reigned in Israel, fertility abounded, and an heir of David's line occupied the throne. Further examples are legion in the prophetic works.*

In speaking of the understanding of history which underlies the eschatological proclamation of the prophets, scholars have often characterized the prophetic understanding of history as linear. Indeed, it has been held that this was characteristic of the classical Israelite understanding of history, in contradistinction to that of the cultures around Israel, which embraced a cyclical concept of history. The pan-oriental cyclical concept of the course of history was entirely determined by observation of the course of nature and was, in short, closely related to the fertility religions of these cultures. The cyclical view of history was rooted in cultic experience which attached to the recurrent cultic festivals, themselves determined by the yearly course of rain and drought, sowing and harvesting and so on.

The linear understanding of history as it developed in Israel was expressed in a number of ways. It had something to do with Israel's understanding of Yahweh, and so also with the salvation-historical view of history described above. In Israel, Yahweh was understood as a god who mainly manifested himself in historical events. We have already mentioned how such agricultural festivals as Passover, Pentecost, and so forth were transformed in Israel to festivals commemorating the great events of salvation history (above, p. 102). In addition to

---

* One will find the elements in question in the prophetic eschatological proclamation in the following—somewhat randomly chosen—passages: Isa. 5.25-29; Jer. 5.15-17; 6.22-26 (hostile attack); Isa. 10.12-19; 13-23; Jer. 46–51; Ezek. 25–32; 38–39; Joel 3.6-22; Zeph. 2 (on the destruction of the heathen); Jer. 31.31-34; Ezek. 11.19-20; Hos. 2.14-20 (on the new relationship to God); Isa. 32.15-20; 35; Ezek. 36.22-32; Hos. 14; Zeph. 3.12-20 (on peace and fertility); Isa. 9.1-7; 11.1-10; Jer. 23.5-6; 33.14-22; Ezek. 34.23-24; 37.24-25; Hos. 3.5; Mic. 5.1-5; Zech. 9.9-10 (on the Davidic Messiah).

this, history for the Israelite, consisted of a long series of events through which Yahweh led his people, including times when he had to punish them for their apostasy as well as times when the people were loyal to their god and enjoyed his protection. The late theological school in Israel, which we have called the Deuteronomists, even saw a pattern in Israel's history consisting of alternation between times of weal and times of woe, which approaches cyclical conception in a different way.

It was this pattern which the prophets continued with their expectation of decisive eschatological events. They, too, had a decidedly linear understanding of history, and it is conceivable that they regarded this expected course of events yet another example of Yahweh's intervention in Israel's history in the form of punishment and restoration. But the prophets held an even more radical view, and so regarded all that was fated to occur as something final: now is the last time! This time the punishment would be complete and the degradation total, but the resoration would be likewise absolute and unqualified. To this extent the coming events were seen by the prophets as final; yet it would probably be more accurate to characterize their understanding of eschatological events as a turning-point. It is characteristic of most of the prophets that they saw eschatological judgment and restoration as heralding a new beginning of salvation history. Thus Hosea looked forward to a new Exodus and Conquest (2.14ff.), Isaiah and Micah expected a new David and a new Zion (Isa. 11.1-10; 2.2-4; Mic. 5.1-3; 4.1-7), Jeremiah could go so far as to speak of a new covenant destined to replace the Sinai covenant (31.31-34), and both he and Ezekiel conceived of the relationship between God and Israel in a new way (Jer. 31.33; 24.7; Ezek. 36.26-28; 11.19).

The prophets were radical thinkers, but no more radical than that they imagined that all these things would be realized within the framework of history. Jeremiah expresses this very concisely when he has Yahweh declare that, 'I will restore their fortunes and build them again as once they were' (33.7). It is a matter of a return to an ideal state which in reality never existed. Indeed, Jeremiah might have said that the ideal was fulfilled when Yahweh led Israel safely out of

Egypt: 'I remember the unfailing devotion of your youth, the love of your bridal days, when you followed me in the wilderness, through a land unsown' (2.2). But in Palestine, this ideal state belonged to the future.

We have concentrated on prophetic eschatology at some length, and in the course of our study it has become clear that the phenomenon belongs under the heading of this section: eschatological dualism. The prophets' view of history and their eschatological proclamation is thoroughly determined by the opposition between past and present, eschatological events marking the turning-point. When we now proceed to apocalyptic eschatology, we are immediately confronted by one of the main distinctions between prophetic and apocalyptic eschatology. For the apocalyptic writers, the eschatological events were not merely a turning-point, but rather the end of history. Whatever is subsequently to come is of a completely different nature than what has gone before, so that it would be meaningless to say that history continues or begins anew. For the apocalyptic writers, both the eschatological events and the renewal to come were unearthly. In brief: for the apocalyptic authors, the eschatological events signified the end of the world, and what was to come was the Kingdom of God.

This thoroughly dualistic understanding of history, or, perhaps better, of the course of world events, was expressed by the apocalyptic writers with the concepts of 'this world' and 'the world to come'. The expressions in question occur in both Hebrew (but, characteristically enough, not in the Old Testament) and in Greek. The Greek expression is the more interesting of the two: *ho aiōn houtos*, ranged against *ho aiōn mellōn*. The word *aiōn* recurs in the English *aeon,* meanig 'age' or 'world-age'. The passage in which this view is classically formulated is in the late apocalyptic work 2 Esdras, where the angel says in the context of a discussion with Esdras concerning the fate of sinners and righteous men, 'The Highest has created not one, but two aeons' (7.50). Later we read:

> The present world is not the end, and the glory of God does not stay in it continually...But the day of judgment will be the end of the present world and the beginning of the eternal world to come, a world in which corruption will be over, all excess abolished, and unbelief uprooted, in which justice

will be full-grown, and truth will have risen like the sun (2 Esdras 7.112-114).

Another apocalypse, from the first century CE, gives us a more detailed account of the nature of the coming aeon with respect to the present one:

> When the whole creation which the Lord has made comes to an end, and every man goes to the Lord's great judgement, then the seasons will perish, and there will be no years any more, nor will the months nor the days and hours be reckoned any more, but there will be a single age. And all the righteous who escape the Lord's great judgement will be united with the great age, and the age will be united with the righteous, and they shall live eternally. And they shall have no more labour nor suffering nor sorrow nor fear....(2 Enoch 17.3-5).

The concept of time which dominates in this age will be dispelled in the one to come, just as the conditions of eternal life which the righteous will enjoy will be likewise different. A third text gives some impression of this:

> They shall behold the world which is now invisible to them
> and realms now hidden from them,
> and time shall no longer age them.
> For in the heights of that world shall they dwell,
> and they shall be made like angels,
> and be made equal to the stars;
> and they shall be changed into whatever form they will,
> from beauty into loveliness,
> and from light into the splendour of glory.
> For the extent of Paradise will be spread before them... (2 Bar. 51.8-11).

Even these few quotations give us some idea of the radical difference between the prophets' expectation of a new and better world within the framework of historical time and space and the visions of the apocalyptic authors of a future existence in a supra-terrestrial Kingdom of God. The questions which then present themselves are whether we can determine what conditions may have brought about this radical transformation, and what understanding of history and what total conception of the world and worldly existence underlie the new notion.

In the first instance, it is probably once again Persian influence that makes itself felt here. The cosmic universe of Persian religion with its strongly dualistic features is reminiscent, on quite a number of points, of the world-view of apocalyptic Judaism. It is difficult to conceive that Persian eschatology did not influence Judaism in its apocalyptic formation. We cannot go into detail here, but there are an astonishing number of points of agreement on such matters as the division of history into periods, messianic travails, the struggle against evil powers, judgment and punishment, the resurrection of the dead, the messianic Savior, and a Kingdom of God on earth.

But alongside this foreign influence there was certainly internal evolution. A more detailed description of transformation of prophetic eschatology under the influence of Wisdom teaching is useful. It is a matter of a transformation of the prophets' view of history. The concept of world-order, characteristic of Wisdom, importantly influenced the apocalyptic view of history, and hence its understanding of eschatology. In this view, history and eschatological events were predetermined at the dawn of time. This sort of determinism, a concept of predetermination in history, established the special character of apocalyptic eschatology and distinguished it from prophetic eschatology.

Some scholars have from time to time attempted to characterize the apocalyptic understanding of history as pessimistic with respect to the prophetic view, which regards history as a long series of saving actions by Yahweh on behalf of his people, and hence may be termed optimistic. The pessimistic aspect reveals itself particularly in the recurrently mentioned dualistic notion that the world, 'this age', is subject to Satan's lordship. For the apocalyptic author, history is not 'salvation history', but a long series of sad illustrations of the way evil invariably wins out. If the apocalyptic writer spoke of 'salvation history' at all, he saw it as reserved for the future. In short, for the apocalyptic writer, there were only two saving actions: the creation of the world and the establishment of the Kingdom of God after its destruction. Might this not be appropriately termed a pessimistic view of history?

The apocalyptic writings contain several reviews of Israel's history and world history. As we saw in the case of the book of Daniel, past history is seen from the vantagepoint of the time of composition. In the work, however, it is couched as a vision of the future, usually seen from the temporal viewpoint of the putative visionary protagonist: Enoch before the Flood, Baruch during the first destruction of Jerusalem, Daniel during the Babylonain exile, and so on. Such historical surveys are often formulated in obscure metaphorical language; thus Daniel sees the four world empires between 600 and 150 BCE as four metals making up a statue, and as four animals (Dan. 2; 7); Enoch offers a wide-ranging animal allegory, which reproduces the histories of Israel and the world from the creation until the Day of Judgment (*1 Enoch* 85–90); Baruch sees a cloud which covers the entire world and which alternately rains 'black waters' and 'light waters', which is interpreted as depicting the twelve phases of world history (*2 Bar.* 53–74; cf. *Apoc. Abraham* 29–30); and in a vision Esdras sees an eagle with twelve wings and twelve heads whose fortunes represent the history of Rome; the eagle faces its destruction when it is confronted with the lion, that is, the Messiah (2 Esdras 11–12). Other historical surveys are not visually conceived: on the basis of his reading (presumably in *1 Enoch*), Levi is able to account for the history and fortunes of the priesthood until the last times (*T. Levi* 14–18); Moses tells Joshua about Israel's history from the Conquest until the Day of Judgment (*Ass. Moses* 2–10), and the *Apocalypse of Weeks* subdivides history into ten periods, so-called 'weeks', describing the time from the Flood to the Day of Judgment (*1 Enoch* 92–93).

What is the intention underlying all these historical surveys? The prophets both expected and proclaimed God's intervention in history. The writer of apocalyptic did so as well, although there was a remarkable ambivalence in his attitude. On the one hand, no one could possibly claim that God is the sovereign lord of history more fervently than he did, since the God of apocalyptic created the world, established the world order and led history towards its assured final end and the Kingdom of God. On the other hand, the writer of apocalyptic asserted that history was determined once and for all at creation; thus Enoch, only a few generations after Adam and Eve, was already able to perceive the whole course of subsequent events through revelation. Such a view effectively expels God from history, as scholars have remarked. In a manner of speaking, the apocalyptic writer binds God hand and foot; the writer is unable to imagine a God who acts freely in history, since such a God might act against the very will which he revealed back in the beginning of time! Walter Schmithals puts the matter sharply when he says that 'The apocalyptic writer puts history behind him like a mechanism which runs without friction, but also without function'.

On the basis of this understanding of history, the interest of the apocalyptic writer was concentrated entirely on discovering the point in time at which history would end and the Kingdom of God would accordingly be established. And this is really the sole purpose underlying the many historical surveys in the apocalyptic literature. History as such had no interest for them; and in this connection it is to be noted that the historical surveys in question are quite stereotyped and schematic. What the deterministic understanding of history of the apocalyptic writer was concerned to make possible, through the putative historical revelations, was the calculations of the time of the final events. We should also observe that many of these surveys figure as answers to questions about the Day of Judgment (*2 Bar.* 55; *Apoc. Abraham* 23.1; 24.2, 4; 2 Esdras 12.9, etc.). The depiction of history moves forward to the time of the author and his readers, and in every case we discover that the present of author and reader is invariably the very last phase in the events leading up to the Day of Judgment. The crisis which dominates this particular present is always understood as signalling the imminence of the Day of Judgment.

This sort of 'imminent expectation' must have sparked the desire to know ever more precisely the details about when the final events would begin. It was no doubt comforting for the readers of Daniel to be told that the fourth empire, which they had no difficulty identifying with Antiochus Epiphanes' reign of terror, was to be the last, and that it would be vanquished and replaced by the Kingdom of God. But they surely also felt that it would be reassuring to know just when all this was going to take place. This concern was satisfied through the various calculations of periods and the numerological speculations. This topic, it should be noted, is one of the more curious aspects of the apocalyptic universe. One might be tempted to regard the apocalyptic writers' number-juggling as cabbalisticism, or numerological mysticism. But it is more accurately seen as an absurd consequence of the concept of order which the apocalypticists inherited from the Wisdom tradition. History is structured, and periods and numbers provide yet further instances of that world-order which the apocalyptic writers so highly valued.

Admittedly, the Old Testament itself has room for the notion of a history organized into periods of weal and woe. But a developed speculation about time periods such as that employed in apocalyptic no doubt arose under the influence of Persian religion, which taught that the world will endure for 12,000 years, that this span is divisible into four periods of 3,000 years, and that evil, represented by Ahriman, grows in force throughout the various periods, only to be vanquished at its culmination, after which the end of the world will occur and a new world will be created.

The Jewish apocalyptic writers also had some figures in mind as to the collective length of world history (7,000 years, 6,000 years, 4,250 years, and, in late rabbinical works, 4,231 years—400 years after the destruction of Jerusalem). But the most typical systems involved division into periods: twelve 'parts' (2 Esdras 14.11; *2 Bar.* 53ff.); twelve 'years' or 'hours' (*Apoc. Abraham* 29.2; 30.2); ten 'weeks' of various lengths (*1 Enoch* 92–93). The division into four periods, which was attested already in Hesiod and later in Ovid, recurs, as we have seen, in Daniel. Here we do not have to do with the whole of world history, as is the case in the Persian system, but only with the time from the fall of Jerusalem in 587 BCE until the Day of Judgment. To achieve greater precision in the determination of the time of Judgment Day, these four periods were in turn divided into seventy 'year weeks', that is, periods of seven years, on the basis of the figure seventy in the book of Jeremiah. Sixty-nine of these 'weeks' cover the period from the beginning of the Babylonian exile to Antiochus Epiphanes' first outrage. The last period of seven years is accordingly the critical time in the 160s, when the temple service was discontinued. And it was precisely at this time that Daniel was composed. The way the authors played with several different calculations, which do not agree mutually, is palpable. The reason for this is probably that, as time went on, it became necessary to change the calculations, just as modern apocalyptic sects have been forced to change their equations when Judgment Day has failed to materialize at the calculated moment. In any event, Dan. 7.25 operates with a half year-week, that is, three and a half years. This agrees with the last half week of Dan. 9.27, and agrees reasonably well with the 1290 days in Dan. 12.11, although it conflicts with the mysterious 1150 days in Dan. 8.14, and with the 1335 days of Dan. 12.12.

All of this is terribly complicated, and so very much in the spirit of apocalyptic. We have previously observed the interest of the apocalypticists in astronomical calculation, which is really just another side of the same issue. But as we have just seen above, it is dangerous to commit oneself to exact figures. Once a figure has been written down, it becomes painfully embarrassing when the predicted event does not occur. An alternative was to depict in vague generalities the sort of events which were expected immediately to precede the end of days. Then it would be possible for everyone to interpret the signs of the time, after which they could wait and see if expectations were fulfilled. If nothing happened, then it was possible to claim that one had interpreted wrongly! Enumerations of such sorts of 'messianic travails', that is, the world's birth-contractions preliminary to the birth of the Messiah and the end of days, are frequent in the apocalyptic literature.

The imagination of the authors was virtually unlimited when they decided to portray the horrors of the last times. Such descriptions, each more gruesome than the last, could fill many pages. It was a feature of apocalyptic dualism, as expressed in the teaching about the two ages, that the evil which dominates this age will grow continually, culminating just prior to the Day of Judgment. It was this culmination which the apocalyptic writers strove to describe: the breakdown of world order, seen as the beginning of the end of the

world. Nature, social existence, family life, all will collapse; by
way of illustration, a few quotations will suffice:

> In the days of the sinners the years will become shorter, and
> their seed will be late on their land and on their fields, and
> all things on the earth will change, and will not appear at
> their proper time. And the rain will be withheld...And the
> moon will change its customary practice, and will not
> appear at its proper time (*1 Enoch* 80.2, 4).

> The sun will suddenly begin to shine in the middle of the
> night, and the moon in the day-time. Trees will drip blood,
> stones will speak, nations will be in confusion, and the
> courses of the stars will be changed...Chasms will open in
> many places and spurt out flames incessantly. Wild beasts
> will range far afield, women will give birth to monsters,
> fresh springs will run with salt water, and everywhere
> friends will become enemies (2 Esdras 5.4-5, 8-9).

A later apocalypse represents the disasters as a repetition of
the ten plagues of Egypt:

> The first plague will be great distress through want; the
> second, the burning of cities by fire; the third, destruction of
> cattle by pestilence; the fourth, universal starvation; the
> fifth, destructions among rulers by the ravages of earth-
> quake and sword; the sixth, deluges of hail and snow; the
> seventh, lethal attacks by wild animals; the eighth (to vary
> the mode of destruction) famine and pestilence; the ninth,
> retribution by the sword and flight in terror; the tenth,
> crashing thunder and destructive earthquakes (*Apoc.
> Abraham* 30.5-7; cf. *2 Bar.* 27).

It would also be appropriate to continue with a couple of
quotations from the New Testament, which contain some
descriptions of the 'messianic travails' which were doubtless
adopted directly from Jewish apocalyptic and brought into
relation with Christ's return:

> When you hear the noise of battle near at hand and the news
> of battles far away, do not be alarmed. Such things are bound
> to happen; but the end is still to come. For nation will make
> war upon nation, kingdom upon kingdom; there will be
> earthquakes in many places; there will be famines. With
> these things the birth-pangs of the new age begin (Mk 13.7-
> 8).

> But in those days, after that distress, the sun will be darkened, the moon will not give her light; the stars will come falling from the sky, the celestial powers will be shaken. Then they will see the Son of Man coming in the clouds with great power and glory... (Mk 13.24-26; cf. Rev. 6.12-17).

> But when you see Jerusalem encircled by armies, then you may be sure that her destruction is near. Then those who are in Judaea must take to the hills; those who are in the city itself must leave it, and those who are out in the country must not enter; because this is the time of retribution, when all that stands written is to be fulfilled (Lk. 21.20-22).

'The noise of battle and the news of battles'—these, too, are part of the last, trying times; in the last seven-year period, 'until the end', there will be war, or so we read in Daniel (9.26). Peoples will turn against one another, they will turn against the land of the Jews and their holy city and will inflict indescribable sufferings on each other and on the chosen people. Instead of quoting such materials, we shall now turn to the texts from Qumran. When we consider the extent to which both cosmic dualism and anthropological-ethical dualism form the basis of Qumran theology, it is hardly surprising that eschatological dualism was also an integral part of the self-understanding of the congregation. After all, the Qumran congregation was quite simply an eschatological phenomenon; its existence was predicated on the conviction that the last times were at hand. Imminent expectation of the end ran in the blood of the congregation, and they only found it possible to bear their existence in the desert because they knew that it would only be a short while before the end arrived:

> In the mysteries of His understanding, and in His glorious wisdom, God has ordained an end for falsehood, and at the time of the visitation He will destroy it for ever. Then truth...shall arise in the world for ever (1QS 4.18-19).

The people of Qumran observed the signs of the times more perspicaciously than others did; they also knew that the trials of the world were fated to increase until their culmination on the Day of Judgment:

> The torrents of Belial shall reach
> to all sides of the world.

In all their channels
a consuming fire shall destroy
every tree, green and barren, on their banks;

The land shall cry out because of the calamity
fallen upon the world,
and all its deeps shall howl.
And all those upon it shall rave
and shall perish amid the great misfortune.

The war of the heavenly warriors shall scourge the earth;
and it shall not end before the appointed destruction
which shall be for ever and without compare (1QH 3.29-30,
    32-34, 35-36).

The last passage seems to indicate that the 'war of the heavenly warriors', being a part of the tribulations of the last times, would last until the advent of the Day of Judgment. This war is more throughly described in one of the more remarkable documents of the Qumran community, the *War Scroll*, or, as it has also been called, 'The War between the Children of Light and the Children of Darkness'. The work is a strange mixture; on the one hand it pretends to be a set of regulations governing the mobilization of the army of the Children of Light, who are to be deployed against the Children of Darkness. The latter appear in the guise of Israel's historical enemies, the Philistines, the Moabites, the Assyrians, and so on, concluding with the Seleucids and, presumably, also the Romans. On the other hand, the scroll depicts a war which is elevated above the sphere of human and historical activities: angels take part on one side, while Belial and his hosts rage on the other. We have come back to the cosmic dualism of the Qumran theology. It is all-encompassing, and in reality the battle is the last conflict between the good and evil forces in existence. This lends the conflict an eschatological perspective, so that it represents not only the phenomenon encountered, previously, the time of troubles immediately prior to the end of the world, but also the execution of the judgment, through which all evil is destroyed so that the Kingdom of God may be established:

At that time the assembly of gods and the hosts of men shall battle, causing great carnage; on the day of calamity, the sons of light shall battle with the company of darkness amid

the shouts of a mighty multitude and the clamour of gods
and men to make manifest the might of God. And it shall be
a time of great tribulation for the people which God shall
redeem; of all its afflictions none shall be as this, from its
sudden beginning until its end in eternal redemption (1QM
1.10-12).

Once again, the familiar 'messianic travails'. Another passage
shows unambiguously that the battle is to take place, so to say,
on the Day of Judgment:

For this shall be a time of distress for Israel, and of the
summons to war against all the nations. There shall be eternal deliverance for the company of God, but destruction for
all the nations of wickedness. All those who are ready for
battle shall march out and shall pitch their camp before the
king of the Kittim (the Roman emperor?) and before all the
host of Belial gathered about him for the Day of Revenge by
the Sword of God (1QM 15.1-3).

The matter is somewhat differently expressed in the following 'commentary' on the Old Testament book of Habakkuk
(1.12f.):

Interpreted, this saying means that God will not destroy His
people by the hand of the nations; God will execute the judgement of the nations by the hand of His elect. And through
their chastisement all the wicked of His people shall expiate
their guilt who keep His commandments in their distress
(1QpHab 5.3-6).

Here it might, at first sight, seem confusing that there appears
to be a coincidence between the 'messianic travails' and the
execution of the judgment itself. However, this was entirely
intelligible to the congregation of Qumran. As we have already
seen, the congregation held that the Children of Light (the
members of the congregation) were the only ones who were to
be saved and so enter into the Kingdom of God, while the
Children of Darkness (the rest of humanity) were destined to
destruction. In this context, a juridical confrontation would
have been superfluous. When the end of time arrives, one has
merely to begin the slaughter of the Children of Darkness.

But there are numerous other apocalyptic writings in
which the relationship between the tribulations preceding the

end of days and the decisive eschatological events is not entirely clear. In fact, it would prove overly problematical to attempt to reduce all the 'doctrines' of the various apocalypses to a single formula. There are differences and nuances between the various documents, and even within the framework of one and the same treatise. Some of these differences resulted from the development of ideas over the two to three hundred years which our period covers. It would be impossible here to attempt an analysis of the many eschatological ideas and their subsequent evolution. However, there are certain complexes of ideas which, albeit in quite various forms, are common to apocalyptic: the figure of the Messiah, the resurrection of the dead, the judgment, the dissolution of the world, the creation of the new world. This sequence might seem to be natural; nevertheless it is to some extent an abstraction. Apocalyptic is, after all, a genre in which there is no reason to expect that things follow the order of nature! Nonetheless, we shall attempt briefly to say a few words about these ideas in the stated sequence.

We are inclined to regard *the messianic motif* as the most central element in Jewish eschatology. This is only natural, since we regard ancient Judaism as the background of early Christianity, in which this motif assumes vast importance. But in reality the idea of the Messiah was not particularly central to ancient Judaism, or, for that matter, to the Old Testament. Among the Old Testament prophets, it was really only Isaiah who emphasized the expectation of a coming ideal ruler of the line of David, and the reasons for this probably lay in Isaiah's peculiar background in the Jerusalemite ideology. Thus it is in Isaiah that we find the famous messianic assurances about 'Immanuel', and the proclamations: 'to us a child is born, to us a son is given', and: 'a shoot shall grow from the stock of Jesse' (Isa. 7; 9; 11). The other prophets we quoted earlier when we discussed the prophetic concept of the coming kingdom of glory just manage to mention a new king of the line of David, but they do so more or less *en passant*, as if referring to an obvious component of the kingdom to come.

At all events, there was a prophetic expectation of an ideal king reigning over an earthly kingdom of glory, and this concept naturally continued to survive into the antique period;

but it did not do so primarily in apocalyptic. It is almost as if the messianic figure did not quite fit into the apocalyptic concept of a supra-terrestrial Kingdom of God. In fact, it is only in one of the least apocalyptically coloured writings among the Pseudepigrapha that we discover a well-defined picture of the royal Messiah, namely in the *Psalms of Solomon*. In this work, the seventeenth psalm expresses a traditional Jewish expectation of a king of David's line in a language which is rife with prophetic formulas:

> Behold, O Lord, and raise up for them their king, the son of
>   David,
> for the time which thou dist foresee, O God, that he may
>   reign over Israel, thy servant.
> And gird him with strength, that he may shatter
>   unrighteous rulers;
> and purify Jerusalem of the nations which trample her
>   down in destruction.
>
> And he shall gather together a holy people, whom he shall
>   lead in righteousness,
> and he shall judge the tribes of the people which has been
>   sanctified by the Lord his God.
>
> For he will smite the earth with the sword of his mouth for
>   ever:
> he will bless the people of the Lord with wisdom and joy;
> and he himself is pure from sin, so that he may rule a great
>   people,
> that he may rebuke rulers, and remove sinners by the might
>   of his word (*Pss. Sol.* 17.21-22; 26; 35-36).

This Messiah is a man of David's line, and his function is to establish the coming kingdom of glory, to defeat the heathen and rule over the world with righteousness. This is a recurrence of the prophetic expectation. The same is the case with the Davidic Messiah who is portrayed in the *Testament of Judah* ch. 24, and in quite a few passages in later rabbinical works.

But in the apocalyptic works it is a commonplace that it is God himself who establishes the supra-terrestrial Kingdom of God. What place, then, is assigned to the Messiah? As we have seen, the apocalyptic writers had difficulty locating a messianic figure in the Kingdom of God, so that in the large majority of the apocalypses the Messiah is either absent or plays only a remote role. In some cases, his advent is merely the signal for the establishment of the Kingdom of God, while he himself seems to have no function. For example, the *Syriac Apocalypse of Baruch* first describes the 'messianic travails', after which we read, 'The Messiah shall then begin to be revealed'. Further, however, the author proceeds to describe the spendours of the Kingdom of God:

> The earth shall also yield its fruit ten thousand-fold; and on each vine there shall be a thousand branches, and each branch shall produce a thousand clusters, and each cluster produce a thousand grapes, etc.

And, a little later:

> And it shall come to pass after this, when the time of the presence of the Messiah on earth has run its course, that he will return in glory to the heavens: then all who have died and have set their hopes on him will rise again (*2 Bar.* 29–30).

Here the duration of the messianic time seems to be limited to the period between the cessation of the travails and the Resurrection and Judgment. A similar idea appears to be expressed in *2 Bar.* 40.3, and perhaps in 74.2 as well. But it is in any case clearly stated in 2 Esdras:

> My son the Messiah shall appear with his companions and bring four hundred years of happiness to all who survive. At the end of that time, my son the Messiah shall die, and so shall all mankind who draw breath (2 Esdras 7.28-29).

Thus some of the writings attempt to solve the problem of the relationship between the Messiah and the Kingdom of God by reducing the Messiah to a transitional figure who disappears before the Day of Judgment and the real advent of the Kingdom of God. The intermediate period thus arrived at plays a certain role in later Jewish speculations about the last times, and, thanks to Revelation (ch. 20), the idea of the millennium was accepted by Christians as well.

This evolutionary course represents a degradation of the figure of the Messiah. But something else occurs as well. Some apocalyptic writings in Early Judaism took the opposite course and endowed the Messiah with divine, supernatural features. In this fashion the writers managed to ensure that he, so to speak belonged naturally to the Kingdom of God. We have here to do with the messianic 'son of man'. The point of departure for these speculations is Daniel 7, which we have repeatedly discussed. This chapter is one of the most famous and interesting in the apocalyptic literature. There are the four animals from the sea, each representing a world empire; the 'Ancient in years', on his flaming throne; the destruction of the animals, and the 'one like a son of man' on the clouds of heaven, the one of whom it is said:

> Sovereignty and glory and kingly power were given to him, so that all people and nations of every language should serve him; his sovereignty was to be an everlasting sovereignty which should not pass away, and his kingly power such as should never be impaired (Dan. 7.14).

The entire scenario is so magnificent that it is hard to blame anyone for taking the 'son of man' for a messianic figure. Already the first Christians did so (cf. Mt. 24.30; 26.64), along with the later rabbis. But above all, *1 Enoch* and *2 Esdras* did so. However, this interpretation of Daniel 7, which is, incidentally, a composite text, is probably fallacious. There seems to be ancient Canaanite-Israelite mythology underlying both the 'Ancient in Years' and the 'Son of Man', and perhaps also the animals, of which many peculiar things are said in the text. We have previously characterized the speculations about time periods as deriving from Persian influence, and some scholars have similarly wondered if Persian ideas are not somehow behind the concept of the human figure on the clouds of heaven, namely the idea of the 'primeval man'—the first man and first king who returns at the end of time.

However, if such ideas were in fact known within Early Judaism, they are hardly to be found in Daniel 7. In this chapter the human figure merely plays a symbolic role; just as each of the animals represents a godless world empire, so the 'son of man' represents the Kingdom of God. The point of it all resides in the antithesis animal vs. man, which expresses the absolute distinction between the Kingdom of God and any merely earthly kingdom. In reality, the suggestive English rendering 'son of man' is misleading, not least when we consider the use of the expression in the New Testament. In both Hebrew and Aramaic (the first half of the book of Daniel is in Aramaic) 'son of man' means simply 'man'. The expression was especially weak in Aramaic, signifying something like 'every' or 'one', so that Dan. 7.13 is probably best translated 'and behold, on the clouds of heaven a manlike figure appeared'.

But this figure did, however, come on the clouds of heaven in Daniel's vision, and he was accorded sovereignty over the Kingdom of Heaven. Probably these facts, rather than the expression itself, explain why this passage in Daniel was later interpreted messianically. In the apocalypses, this interpretation is confined to two works. The Parables in *1 Enoch* 37–71 are an integral section in the book which is probably later than other parts of it; some scholars regard the section as post-Christian, but there is much to suggest that they derive from the time just prior to the birth of Christ. Here we cannot deal with the whole problem of the messianic features of the Parables. In them, the Messiah has many designations and a wide variety of characteristics. However, in the passages in which the Messiah is designated 'son of man', recalling Daniel, he is characterized as a heavenly being. It is not only the case that his face 'was full of grace, like one of the holy angels' (46.1), but we are also told that he has existed from the beginning of eternity:

> Even before the sun and the constellations were created, before the stars of heaven were made, his name was named before the Lord of Spirits.

> All those who dwell upon the dry ground will fall down and worship before him, and they will bless, and praise, and celebrate with psalms the name of the Lord of Spirits. And because of this he was chosen and hidden before him before the world was created, and for ever (*1 Enoch* 48.3, 5-6)

He is the one who is destined to judge and eliminate evil, after which he will rule over the Kingdom of God:

> And he sat on the throne of his glory, and the whole judgement was given to the Son of Man, and he will cause the

sinners to pass away and be destroyed from the face of the earth (*1 Enoch* 69.27).

In the somewhat later 2 Esdras, the Son of Man is equipped with fantastic features. He emerges from the sea with the clouds of heaven, and when all the kingdoms of the earth gather against him, he takes his stand on Mount Zion:

When he saw the hordes advancing to attack, he did not so much as lift a finger against them He had no spear in his hand, no weapon at all; only, as I watched, he poured what seemed like a stream of fire out of his mouth, a breath of flame from his lips, and a storm of sparks from his tongue... and burnt up every man of them; suddenly all that enormous multitude had disappeared, leaving nothing but dust and ashes and a reek of smoke (2 Esdras 13.9-11).

To return to *1 Enoch*, something striking appears in chs. 70–71. The account of Enoch's heavenly journey is summarized in brief; in it, Enoch arrives at God's dwelling and is confronted with the 'ancient in years', archangels, and 'thousands and thousands of angels without number'. Then one of the archangels says to Enoch:

You are the Son of man who was born to righteousness, and righteousness remains over you, and the righteousness of the Head of Days will not leave you (*1 Enoch* 71.14).

The episode appears unexpectedly and lacks a proper conclusion; it would be reasonable to suppose that the two chapters were later additions to the *1 Enoch*. But the expression of the idea that one of the great ones of the past will return at the end of time, in the form of a messianic saviour is decisive. Particularly, the rabbis stressed not merely that a messianic king of the line of David would reign, but that David himself would one day return; others expected that such prophetic figures as Elijah or Moses would return as precursors of the royal Messiah, and so forth. At Qumran, the congregation apparently expected that the Teacher of Righteousness, that is, the leader of the congregation in the early days of the community, would return at the end of time as a priestly Messiah. It is characteristic of the priestly-led Qumran community that its members did not expect just a royal Messiah on traditional lines (he is called 'the Messiah of

Israel'), but also a priestly messiah alongside him ('Aaron's Messiah'), just as the *Testaments of the Twelve Patriarchs* expect both a royal and a priestly Messiah (1QS 9.11; *T. Levi* 18; *T. Judah* 24). Both works regard the priestly figure as the superior of the two; this is most clear in the fragmentary 'Messianic Rule':

> When the Messiah shall summon them, the Priest shall come at the head of the whole congregation of Israel with all his brethren, the sons of Aaron the priests, those called to the assembly, the men of renown; and they shall sit before him, each man in the order of his dignity. And then the Messiah of Israel shall come, and the chiefs of the clans of Israel shall sit before him (1QSa 1.11-15).

A future ideal king, a future ideal priest, a future ideal prophet, and in fact, somewhat later we also find the expectation of a future ideal warrior, Messiah ben Joseph. And alongside all of these, the heavenly Messiah. The messianic expectations of Early Judaism were manifold; what we have is a rather diffuse motif, frequently overblown in accounts of the religious ideas of the epoch. Nevertheless, the motif illustrates a typical feature of contemporary eschatology which might well be termed 'projection': the greatness of the past is projected far out into the glamorous future. Or, to use the Greek expressions, *ta prota* is identified with *ta eschata*, the first things are equal to the last things.

A newcomer in the conceptual world of early Jewish religion was the expectation of *the resurrection of the dead*. Back in Old Testament times there were few things which interested the Israelites so little as the question of man's condition after death. The dead were in the Kingdom of Death, *sheol*, where they led a grey, uninteresting and shadowy existence. Yahweh was regarded as the god of life, and the realm of the dead was beyond his sphere of influence. Thus the psalmist asks, 'Dost thou work wonders for the dead, shall their company rise up and praise thee?' (Ps. 88.10). And Ecclesiastes offers the following advice to those who are still among the living: 'Whatever task lies to your hand, do it with all your might; because in Sheol, for which you are bound, there is neither doing nor thinking. Neither understanding nor wisdom' (Eccl. 9.10).

But the Israelite saw the realm of the dead as other than just weary and grey; it could also be dangerous, in the event that the evil powers it contained escaped. Plague, disease, drought and disaster were the messengers of death, and they ravaged at will. A tragic death was one which struck down a young man before he had managed to get offspring; he was like Abel, whose name means 'puff of wind', that which disappears and is no more. But death was not tragic for the old man who died in the height of age; he descended with his grey hairs to his fathers in the Kingdom of Death, with a considerable posterity to bear him to the grave. He continued to live on in his descendants, so there was no reason to wonder how he himself was doing.

This reasonably harmonic relationship with death seemed primitive to the early Jews. New ideas had appeared on the scene; the rise in individualism brought with it an interest in the question of reward and punishment in this life or the next. The ancient concept of collective punishment of the nation was now seen to be inadequate. In one way or another, and even if he had been dead for ages, the individual had to be held accountable for his actions. Some contemporaries explained the matter in such a way that the dead did not enter the Kingdom of Death in undifferentiate fashion, but rather that the righteous went on immediately to blessedness, while the godless were instantly subjected to the torments of the punishment. This seems to be Josephus' view on the matter, although he combines the idea with a doctrine of transmigration of souls (*Bell.* 7. 374f.). A few passages in the New Testament also point in this direction (Lk. 16.22ff.; 23.43). Many rabbis held that judgment was pronounced upon the individual immediately after death.

If the ancient concept of the Kingdom of Death was perhaps a little oversimplified, then on the other hand one discovers that Early Judaism contained surprisingly many and diverse views, even to the extent of revealing numerous contradictions within one and the same document. A thorough German scholar (Volz) has attempted to systematize the materials, and the resulting survey shows more than a dozen different understandings. Nevertheless, the most widely diversified view, at least as far as the

apocalyptic writings are concerned, was that a judgment
would take place at the end of time, and that before this the
dead would be resurrected so as to be able to receive their
judgment. It is not completely clear whether it is this idea that
underlies the only unambiguous statement about the
resurrection of the dead in the Old Testament, Dan. 12.2:
'Many of those who sleep in the dust of the earth will wake,
some to everlasting life and some to the reproach of eternal
abhorrence'. But at all events, it became a common view in
apocalyptic that the dead would be preserved in the Kingdom
of Death until the Day of Judgment. In many contexts we
hear of the Kingdom of Death as divided into several
subdivisions; the righteous were sent to a paradise-like region,
while the sinners went to a different place, where they were
granted a foretaste of the tortures of judgment. But the whole
arrangement has in any case only a temporary character.

Thus we see that the idea of the resurrection of the dead was
subordinated to the notion of judgment at the end of time; the
dead are to arise only because they are to be ushered into the
presence of their judge:

> For after death will come the judgement; we shall be
> restored to life, and then the names of the just will be known
> and the deeds of the godless exposed (2 Esdras 14.35).

> The earth shall give up those who sleep in it, and the dust
> those who rest there in silence; and the storehouses shall
> give back the souls entrusted to them. Then the Most High
> shall be seen on the judgement-seat... (2 Esdras 7.32-33).

The expression *judgment* encompasses a number of the
events of the end of time, both the pronouncement of
judgment and its execution. Already several of the
descriptions of God's coming to sit upon the seat of judgment
anticipate the destruction of nature and the world which is to
follow the judgment:

> And the earth will tremble:
> it will be shaken to its farthest bounds;
> and high mountains will collapse
> and hills be shaken and fall.
> And the sun will not give its light;
> and the horns of the moon will be turned into darkness

and they will be broken,
and it will be turned wholly into blood;
and the orbit of the stars will be disturbed (*Ass. Moses* 10.4-
5).

Terror seizes everyone, and not least the godless, Satan, and
his demons; they know what awaits them. But the judgment
applies to both righteous and sinful people, the heathen world
powers and the evil powers of existence. The judgment
arrived at is not difficult to guess. When we studied the Law in
the section dealing with the basic religious structure, we also
touched on the criteria for condemnation and for being found
innocent; there is no need to repeat this here. At all events as
Matthew 25 informs us—a chapter which presents a picture
of the judgment of the world which owes many of its details to
Jewish apocalyptic—the sheep will be separated from the
goats, the righteous shall go on to eternal life, the sinners to
eternal punishment.

Those who do not survive the judgment are condemned to
either destruction or to *eternal punishment*. In his heavenly
vision, Levi sees in the third heaven, 'the warrior hosts
appointed to wreak vengeance on the spirits of error and of
Belial at the day of judgment' (*T. Levi* 3.3). The priestly
Messiah who is described in chapter 18 is to bind Beliar, but
God himself will incinerate him on the Day of Judgment
(*Sibylline Oracles* 3.73). In other texts, both Beliar and his
spirits are condemned to eternal punishment in 'the abyss of
fire; in torment and in prison they will be shut up for all
eternity' (*1 Enoch* 10.13). Similar fates are visited on both the
heathen world powers and on the godless, both in and outside
of Israel: either annihilation or eternal punishment. It is
tempting to quote some examples, as the apocalyptic works do
not lack imagination when they try to describe the sufferings
the godless are to undergo. On the other hand, quotations
would be virtually superfluous, as most of the descriptions
have survived in our Christian tradition in the various
conceptions of Hell.

The place where the enemies of God are to suffer their
punishment is often simply called the Kingdom of Death,
sheol, although some works prefer the Greek designation,
Hades. It was mainly the rabbis who used the name *Gehenna*,

which became the classical Jewish designation for hell. There was plenty of room in Gehenna; the Talmud claims that it is 216,000 times greater than the earth. It lies under the earth, and its entrance is in the Valley of Hinnom outside Jerusalem, which has also given the place its name.

But the godless and the evil powers will not be simply removed or destroyed; the culmination of it all occurs when this entire *world is destroyed,* so that a new one can be created:

> Everything corruptible will pass away,
> and everything mortal will disappear:
> no memory of it will endure,
> for it is defiled with evils (*2 Bar.* 44.9).

But not only the sinful earth will disappear; rather,

> the first heaven will vanish and pass away, and a new heaven will appear, and all the powers of heaven will shine for ever with sevenfold light (*1 Enoch* 91.16).

The *Sibylline Oracles* describe things more dramatically; here we see the dissolution of heaven and earth as a single event:

> God whose dwelling is in the sky shall roll up the heaven as a book is rolled. And the whole firmament in its varied forms shall fall on the divine earth and on the sea: and then shall flow a ceaseless cataract of raging fire, and shall burn land and sea, and the firmament of heaven and the stars and creation itself it shall cast into one molten mass and clean dissolve (*Sib. Or.* 3.81-87 [Charles' edn]).

Several other apocalyptic works conceive of the end of the world as an all-consuming fire (*The Life of Adam and Eve* 49.3), which is probably yet another idea of Persian origin.

When at last we turn to the various views on *the eternal life of the saved in the Kingdom of God,* we encounter the previously mentioned projection of the relationships and conditions of primeval time into the future. The idea is of a return to Paradise, to the first fresh day of creation. We characterized earlier the prophetic eschatology by noting that, for the prophets, salvation history began anew after the judgment. The apocalyptic writers took a further step backwards and maintained that it was the creation of the world and of man which began anew. Everything was to be as it once had been when it emerged from the hand of the Creator. We have previously quoted a few passages in the apocalyptic literature which describe the glorious future (pp. 195f.); here we shall look at one of the many descriptions of the Kingdom of God which emphasize man's return to the time before the Fall:

> For all of you, paradise lies open, the tree of life is planted, the age to come is made ready and rich abundance is in store; the city is already built, rest from toil is assured, goodness and wisdom are brought to perfection (2 Esdras 8.52).

One of the texts from Qumran says it all even more concisely: after the judgment, the righteous man will once more possess, 'all the glory of Adam' (1QS 4.23). This means that the external forms of men will be changed: 'they are to shine like stars, never to fade or die, with faces radiant as the sun' (2 Esdras 7.97). But it also means that they will live in eternal peace, sinlessness and plenty, as we saw in the texts cited on pp. 195f. The idea of newly saved men dwelling in Paradise is not solely dominant; other texts suggest that they will dwell in a glorified Palestine, in heaven, or in a heavenly Jerusalem. The various concepts tend to run together; thus Jerusalem is to be transformed into Paradise, and the Tree of Life will be planted at the temple (*1 Enoch* 25.5); while still other texts simply identify heaven and Paradise. Here, too, creative imagination was lively. Most interesting of all is perhaps the notion of the heavenly Jerusalem, which recurs, incidentally, in Revelation 21. One text mentions the strange idea that Jerusalem was created together with the world and preserved in heaven. At the end of time, the city will 'be renewed in glory and be made perfect for evermore' (*2 Bar.* 4; 32.4), or, as Esdras has it, 'it will be revealed' (2 Esdras 10.54). Not only will the temple and its cult be restored, but God himself will descend and dwell in the midst of his people:

> And the Lord shall appear in the sight of all, and all know that I am the God of Israel and the father of all the sons of Jacob and king on Mount Zion for all eternity; and Zion and Jerusalem shall be established (*Jubilees* 1.28).

This closes the ring: the last things will be as the first. But a narrowing of the field of vision has also occurred. It is characteristic of apocalyptic that its dimensions are global; we have already noted its interest in world history and world order. But when we come to the restoration, we suddenly discover that the idea of election is determinative. It is the Jews, and only the righteous among them, who are to enter into the Kingdom of God. The heathen who have oppressed Israel and the Jews in the course of time are to be annihilated, although other heathen will be allowed to share in salvation if they will subordinate themselves to the Jews. Once again a recurrence of national aspiration. The world powers will be destroyed, and Israel will manifest herself as a new world power in the Kingdom of God.

For this reason we may ask whether the national-messianic idea is not more central to apocalyptic than we allowed ourselves to suppose a few pages ago. Then we noted that the figure of the Messiah itself is not prominent in apocalyptic. But we have seen that what might be termed *the messianic idea*—in a very broad sense—was so vivid in the Jewish imagination, ever since the time of David, that it simply had to manifest itself in apocalyptic. In this wise the 'salvation historical' viewpoint—which, as we have also seen, is otherwise remote in apocalyptic—also manifests itself. Admittedly, apocalyptic was a form of religious expression which absorbed much foreign material. But at the end of the day it tended to return to the ancient concepts, which were the inalienable property of any Jew desiring to remain faithful to things essentially Jewish.

Apocalyptic in Jewish Society

In the earlier section dealing with research into apocalyptic, we were confronted with a number of modern efforts to determine the relationship of apocalyptic to Jewish society. These attempts ranged from Bousset's view, that apocalyptic was a matter of the lower classes' wild and naive speculations about the future; via Plöger's theory about groups, occupied with the prophetic message, existing on the margins of society; to Hanson's hypothesis about oppressed and alienated groups who attempted to find an alternative ideology in apocalyptic. The question is whether it is possible to arrive at a more accurate definition of the circles in which apocalyptic speculation and literature developed.

The view of both Plöger and Hanson harmonize well with that understanding of apocalyptic which has won the most general adherence. On this view, there was some sort of connection between the Hasidim, who supported the Maccabees in the revolts of the 160s BCE, and the beginnings of apocalyptic speculation. This is an entirely natural supposition, primarily since the book of Daniel, one of the first apocalyptic works, made its appearance in the 160s, and, in the spirit of the Hasidim, was directed against Antiochus Epiphanes and the Jewish circles which supported him. The Hasidim may be reasonably described as 'oppressed' and 'alienated' with respect to the leading elements of Jewish society of their day. The only drawback to this position is that it is difficult to delimit it more precisely, as the Hasidim were not a very well defined group represented in certain strata or classes in society. Rather, the Hasidim were courageous men, 'every one of them a volunteer in the cause of the Law', as we read in 1 Maccabees,—hardly sufficient to qualify as a sociological definition.

Now in the section on the Pharisees (p. 116) and the one on the Essenes (p. 150) we saw that both of these movements seem to have emerged from the Hasidim. We concluded that a partition took place later in the second century BCE into a Pharisaic and a priestly-Essene wing. Further, considering that apocalypticism was the constitutive religious foundation of that branch of the Essene movement which established itself at Qumran, it becomes inviting to suppose, as several scholars have recently done, that apocalyptic may have originated in priestly circles within the Hasidic movement.

Some objections may be raised against this suggestion. At least some of the roots of apocalyptic were in Old Testament prophetism, and it has long been a scholarly dogma that priests and prophets were oppositionally related in Old Testament times. Nor is there any particular evidence to suggest that the priesthood were especially concerned with eschatology. Indeed, according to Plöger's model, the priesthood represented the very 'establishment' against which the apocalyptic writers protested. If, furthermore, it is correct that other apocalyptic roots lay in the Wisdom tradition, it would not be any easier to argue for a priestly provenance.

And yet...once one considers the idea, there are good reasons for attempting to retain and to offer a plausible explanation of the idea of priestly circles behind apocalyptic. It was, after all, not only at Qumran that there is tangible evidence of connections between apocalyptic and the priesthood. If we examine certain sections of the apocalyptic literature closely, we note that there are many examples of the fact that both priestly and cultic interests are well represented. To begin with Daniel: what is the decisive event that, for the authors, triggers the 'time of the end'? It is the cessation of the temple sacrifices (Dan. 8.11, 14; 9.27). And even more basically: who initiated the Maccabean revolt which called forth the first apocalyptic literature? The lesser priesthood, represented by Mattathias and his sons. Nor is it difficult to find signs of priestly interests in subsequent apocalyptic literature. The cult is the centrepiece of a semi-apocalyptic work like the *Jubilees*, while the *Testament of Levi*, which is the most apocalyptical of the *Testaments of the Twelve Patriarchs,* is thoroughly based on priestly concerns. *2 Enoch,* too—otherwise dominated by the apocalyptic heavenly vision—concludes with an extensive legend about the origins of the priesthood.

But the decisive argument in favour of priestly circles being behind apocalyptic is the following: it is a thorough-going feature in apocalyptic literature that speculations about and calculations of the time of the end are combined with astronomical considerations. And who were the astronomers in Jewish society? The priests, of course; their interest in astronomy was dictated by the need for accurate calculation of the annual sequences in order to ensure the correctness of the calendar and the dates of the year's religious festivals. The astronomical materials, numerological speculations and periodic division of time, which are characteristic of such large parts of the apocalyptic literature, clearly reveal it to be an erudite literature. Nothing could be more wrongheaded than to assume, like Bousset, that it all emerged from popular imaginings. Rather, the particular type of Wisdom teaching, called 'mantic Wisdom', which was the province of the priesthood, namely the knowledge of the secret forces underlying nature and existence, was activated during the rebellions and their attendant end-of-the-world climate in the 160s, only to crystallize in the apocalyptic writings. This is a very clear example of the interrelationship between politics and religion which we have repeatedly witnessed in this study, and which might even be described as its actual theme.

As far back as we can pursue the history of Israel, the close connection between politics and religion is strikingly obvious. David managed to create his Israelite empire by plucking the political and religious strings in a masterful way. Solomon endowed this empire with a strong centre when he built the temple on Zion in Jerusalem. Throughout the period of the monarchy, until the Babylonaian exile in the sixth century BCE, there was a close relationship between royal power and the Jerusalem priesthood. And after the exile, when there was no king, the temple and its priesthood formed the religious and political focus of the Jews.

Now we have been accustomed to suppose that the power of the priesthood was broken with the destruction of the temple in 70 CE, and that from then on it was the laity, represented by Pharisees and rabbis, who bore Judaism onwards, with the Law as its central point. This is, naturally, not incorrect, as we have attempted to show several times in the course of this study. But there remains one thing that must not be overlooked. If it is correct that priestly circles were behind the apocalyptic school of thought, then the influence of the priesthood on further developments was much greater, albeit indirectly, than is usually imagined. The groups which broke off from Judaism, that is, the community of Qumran and the early Church, lived in the universe of apocalyptic. The Qumran community disappeared, but it would be impossible to over-estimate the importance of Jewish apocalyptic for the formation of the conceptual world of the first Christians. Like the Qumran community, the earliest Christianity was an apocalyptic-eschatological phenomenon. And Christianity would not have become a world religion, had it not been borne along by Jewish apocalyptic.

Bibliographical Note to pp. 157-222
The Appendix (pp. 225ff.) accounts for those ancient Jewish writings which have been quoted in this section. The classical studies on Jewish apocalyptic are two German works, both of which originally appeared in 1903, and of which later revised editions have been used here: W. Bousset, *Die Religion des Judentums* (3rd edn; Tübingen, 1926); and P. Volz, *Die Eschatologie der jüdischen Gemeinde* (2nd edn; Tübingen, 1934). I have drawn particularly on the latter work in my section on eschatology and it is indispensable for those who wish to orient themselves in the apocalyptic literature. More recent works on apocalyptic as such are: G.F. Moore, *Judaism in the First Centuries of the Christian Era*, I-III (Cambridge, Mass., 1927-30); J. Bonsirven, *Le Judaïsme palestinien*, I-II (Paris, 1934-35); H.H. Rowley, *The Relevance of Apocalyptic* (rev. edn; London, 1963); D.S. Russell, *The Method and Message of Jewish Apocalyptic* (London, 1964); M. Hengel, *Judaism and Hellenism*, I-II (London, 1973); W. Schmithals, *The Apocalyptic Movement* (Nashville, 1975); J. Schreiner, 'Die apokalyptische Bewegung', in: *Literatur und Religion des Frühjudentums* (Würzburg, 1973); K. Koch, *The Rediscovery of Apocalyptic* (Naperville, 1972); E.W. Nicholson, 'Apocalyptic', in: *Tradition and Interpretation* (Oxford, 1979), pp. 189-213; J.J. Collins, *The Apocalyptic Imagination* (New York, 1984); M. Stone, *Scriptures, Sects and Visions* (Oxford, 1980); C. Rowland, *The Open Heaven. A Study of Apocalyptic in Judaism and Early Christianity* (London, 1982). The problem of Persian impact on Jewish apocalyptic has been competently dealt with by A. Hultgaard, 'Das Judentum in der hellenistisch-römischen Zeit und die iranische Religion', in: *Aufstieg und Niedergang der römischen Welt*, II.19.1 (Berlin, 1979), pp. 512-90. Collections of shorter articles on apocalyptic: K. Koch and J.M. Schimdt (eds.), *Apokalyptik* (Darmstadt, 1982); D. Hellholm (ed.), *Apocalypticism in the Mediterranean World and the Near East* (Tübingen, 1983); J.J. Collins (ed.), *Apocalypse. The Morphology of a Genre*, *Semeia* 14 (1979); P.D. Hanson (ed.), *Visionaries and their Apocalypses* (Philadelphia, 1983).

Plöger's account of the post-exilic period and the background of apocalyptic is: O. Plöger, *Theocracy and Eschatology* (Richard, 1968). Hanson's view appeared in P.D. Hanson, *The Dawn of Apocalyptic* (Philadelphia, 1975), and in his article 'Apocalypticism', in *The Interpreter's Dictionary of the Bible. Supplement* (Nashville, 1976), pp. 28-34. Gerhard von Rad's final understanding of the matter is to be found in *Wisdom in Israel* (London, Nashville, New York, 1972), pp. 263-83 (cf. the revised section on Daniel and apocalyptic in the 5th edition of von Rad's *Theologie des Alten Testaments*, II (Munich, 1968), pp. 316-38). P. von der Osten-Sacken's booklet, *Die Apokalyptik in ihrem Verhältnis zu Prophetie und Weisheit* (Munich, 1969), may be regarded as an attack on von Rad's position. F.M. Cross has a short section on the origins of apocalyptic in *Canaanite Myth and Hebrew Epic* (Cambridge, Mass., 1973), pp. 343-46. A survey of recent research into Daniel has been presented by K. Koch, *Das Buch Daniel* (Erträge der Forschung, 144; Darmstadt, 1980). The heavenly visions have been studied by H. Bietenhard, *Die himmlische Welt* (Tübingen, 1951), and I have dealt with the problem of the Old Testament background of the apocalyptic heavenly visions (and also touched on the question of priestly apocalyptic) in 'Heavenly Visions in Early Judaism. Origin and Function', in: *In the Shelter of Elyon. Essays in Honor of G.W. Ahlström* (Sheffield, 1984). Dualism and demonology: H.W. Huppenbauer, *Der Mensch zwischen zwei Welten* (Zürich, 1959); P. von der Osten-Sacken, *Gott und Belial* (Göttingen, 1969); B. Otzen, 'Old Testament Wisdom Literature and Dualistic Thinking in Late Judaism', *Congress Volume Edinburgh* (Leiden, 1975), pp. 146-57. The apocalyptic understanding of history: B. Noack, *Spätjudentum und Heilsgeschichte* (Stuttgart, 1971). The Messiah: S. Mowinckel, *He that Cometh* (Oxford, 1956). The question of the possibility of priestly circles behind apocalyptic has been best treated by J. Lebram, 'Apokalyptik und Hellenismus im Buche Daniel', *Vetus Testamentum* 20 (1970), pp. 503-24.

APPENDIX

Jewish Writings from Antiquity

This survey covers only Jewish writings mentioned or quoted in the book. In addition, to the general reference works, information has been obtained in the following, where further details may be found: O. Stählin, 'Die hellenistisch-jüdische Literatur', in: W. Christ, *Griechische Literaturgeschichte* II.1 (6th edn, Munich, 1921), pp. 405-698; L. Rost, *Einleitung in die alttestamentlichen Apokryphen und Pseudepigraphen* (Heidelberg, 1971); A.-M. Denis, *Introduction aux Pseudépigraphes grecs* (Leiden, 1970); J.H. Charlesworth, *The Pseudepigrapha and Modern Research* (Missoula, Montana, 1976); G.W.E. Nickelsburg, *Jewish Literature between the Bible and the Mishnah* (London, 1981). Further: the introductions to the various writings in the following modern translations of the Apocrypha, Pseudepigrapha and similar literature: R.H. Charles (ed.), *Apocrypha and Pseudepigrapha of the Old Testament*, I-II (Oxford, 1913); *De gammeltestamentlige Pseudepigrafer* (København, 1953-76); *Jüdische Schriften aus hellenistisch-römischer Zeit* (Gütersloh, 1973ff.); H.F.D. Sparks (ed.), *The Apocryphal Old Testament* (Oxford, 1984); J.H. Charlesworth (ed.), *The Old Testament Pseudepigrapha*, I-II (New York and London, 1983-85).

In the following survey, references are made using the following signatures:

Charlesworth: work mentioned above (1983-85)
Sparks: work mentioned above (1984)
Vermes: G. Vermes, *The Dead Sea Scrolls in English* (rev. edn; Harmondsworth, 1968; Sheffield 1987)
NEB: *The New English Bible. The Apocrypha* (1970)
Other references are given by full title.

Aboth
see: *Pirqe Aboth*

Abraham, The Apocalypse of
Apocalyptic writing from the first century CE. The first part relates how Abraham was converted from idolatry. The second part takes its point of departure in Genesis 15 in connection with Abraham's sacri-

fice, and records his assumption to the seventh heaven. Preserved only in Slavonic; the tradition presumably derives from a now lost Greek or Semitic text. *Sparks* pp. 63-91; *Charlesworth*, I, pp. 681-705.

Adam and Eve, The Life of

Legends about Adam and Eve and their children after the expulsion from Paradise. The book is related to the Greek Apocalypse of Moses, the Slavonic Book of Adam, and to the later Christian legends about Adam in Syriac and Ethiopic. *The Life of Adam and Eve* is extant in Latin only, but is based on Greek and perhaps Semitic works that go back to the first or second centuries CE. *Sparks*, pp. 141-67; *Charlesworth*, II, pp. 249-95.

Antiquitates
see: Josephus

Apocrypha

A collection of Jewish writings from the centuries preceding and just after the time of Christ. The books were not accepted into the Jewish Hebrew Bible, but they have been transmitted in the Septuagint, partly as additions to canonical writings. They are also found in the Vulgate and enjoy canonical status in the Roman Catholic Church. Most of them originally existed in Hebrew or Aramaic; some Hebrew fragments of one of them (The Wisdom of Sirach) were discovered during the last century. The number of books to be included in the collection of the Apocrypha varies. For example, the English collection numbers thirteen writings, whereas the corpus acknowledged by Lutheran tradition numbers only eleven (excluding 1 and 2 Esdras). In this book the Apocrypha are quoted from the New English Bible; the individual apocryphal writings mentioned are treated separately by title in this survey.

Aristeas, The Letter of

An account of the translation of the Pentateuch into Greek. The story takes place in Egypt about 250 BCE; the book itself was composed among Egyptian Jews in the 2nd or 1st centuries BCE. The original language was Greek, and the literary form is that of the 'historical novel'. *Charlesworth*, II, pp. 7-34.

Asher, Testament of
see: *The Testaments of the Twelve Patriarchs*

Baruch, The Book of

An apocryphal book of admonition and consolation dating from the 2nd or 1st century BCE; attributed to Baruch, the scribe of Jeremiah,

who is said to have sent it from Babylon to Jerusalem during the exile.
NEB, pp. 192-97.

Baruch, The Syriac Apocalypse of (2 Baruch)
The work dates from ca. 100 CE. The visions in the piece are notionally
attributed to Jeremiah's scribe Baruch, who is said to have received
them just after the fall of Jerusalem in 587 BCE. However, the visions
reflect the sentiments of Jews following the second fall of Jerusalem in
70 CE. Baruch tries to comprehend the fate of Jerusalem and is convinced that the end of days is imminent. Preserved only in Syriac,
although a small Greek fragment confirms what the book itself says,
namely, that it is a translation from the Greek. The Greek version
may have been a translation of a Hebrew original. *Sparks*, pp. 835-95;
Charlesworth, I, pp. 615-52.

Baruch, The Greek Apocalypse of (3 Baruch)
An apocalyptic work composed ca. 100 CE. After the fall of Jerusalem
in 587 BCE, Jeremiah's scribe Baruch is shown through the five
heavens. The original language was Hebrew or Aramaic, but only the
Greek and some Slavonic versions are extant. *Sparks*, pp. 897-914;
Charlesworth, I, pp. 653-79.

Bellum
see: Josephus

Benjamin, Testament of
see: *The Testaments of the Twelve Patriarchs*

Community Rule (1QS)
Writing from Qumran. A well-preserved parchment scroll, 11
columns in all. Contains rituals, dogmatic-ethical instruction, and
rules for community life. It ends with a poetic section which is related
to the Qumran *Hymns (q.v.)*. *Vermes*, pp. 71-94.

Contra Apionem
see: Josephus

Damascus Rule, The (CD)
A work originating in Qumran, but found in 1896 in a Cairo
synangogue in two medieval copies. Tiny fragments of the work were
found at Qumran c. 1950. The first part includes a religious
interpretation of the history of Israel and of the Qumran Community.
Vermes, pp. 95-117.

Dan, Testament of
see: *The Testaments of the Twelve Patriarchs*

Eighteen Benedictions, The
A Jewish Prayer consisting of 18 (later 19) sections. Parts of it may go back to the temple service, but in its final form it was a prescribed prayer in the synagogal service. It is also used in private prayer three times daily. Hebrew text and translation in the *Jewish Daily Prayer Book*.

1 Enoch (Ethiopic Enoch)
An apocalyptic work in several parts, perhaps completed in the years immediately preceding the birth of Christ. It is a kind of apocalyptic anthology containing sections on angelology, heavenly journeys, astronomy, history and the last days. In the *Book of Parables* (chs. 37–71), the 'Son of Man' of Daniel 7 is interpreted as a Messianic figure. In its complete form, the book is known only in Ethiopic, but fragments of earlier Greek and even earlier Semitic versions exist. *Sparks*, pp. 169-319; *Charlesworth*, I, pp. 5-89.

2 Enoch (Slavonic Enoch)
An apocalypse presumably dating from the time preceding the second fall of Jerusalem in 70 CE. The first part is about Enoch's heavenly journey, while the second part contains a legend about the birth of the priest Melchizedek. The work is only preserved in Slavonic, and there is both an early, short version and a later, longer one. The Slavonic text seems to have been translated from Greek, and a Hebrew or Aramaic original may underlie the Greek. *Sparks*, pp. 321-62; *Charlesworth*, I, pp. 91-213.

2 Esdras (4 Ezra)
An apocalypse from ca. 100 CE. The visions in the book are attributed to Ezra during the Babylonian exile in the 6th century BCE, but, like those in the *Syriac Apocalypse of Baruch*, they reflect the feelings of the Jews after the second fall of Jerusalem in 70 CE. The questions of the sceptical Jews are rejected by reference to the imminent advent of the Divine Kingdom. The original Hebrew version is lost, and the book is extant in Latin, Syriac and other languages in translations from the Greek, a version which is, however, also lost. NEB, pp. 19-53.

Gad, Testament of
see: *The Testaments of the Twelve Patriarchs*

Habakkuk, Commentary on (1QpHab)
Biblical commentary from Qumran consisting of a fairly well-preserved parchment scroll of 13 columns. The commentary 'actualizes' the first two chapters of the biblical book of Habakkuk, taken as a prediction of the history of the Qumran Community. *Vermes*, pp. 235-43.

Hymns (1QH)
A collection of poetical texts from Qumran, consisting of a somewhat damaged parchment scroll that once encompassed about 20 columns. The hymns imitate the biblical psalms of lament and thanksgiving, but they also include many allusions to the prophetic literature. At the same time, they express the theological views of the Qumran Community. *Vermes*, pp. 149-201.

Isaiah, The Ascension of
In its final form, this book is a Christian apocalypse, but it is composed of partly Christian and partly Jewish materials. Most of the first five chapters is a Jewish legend about the martyrdom of the prophet Isaiah which dates from about the 1st century BCE. The apocalyptic section (chs. 6–11) describes Isaiah's vision of the seven heavens; it is Christian and cannot be earlier than the end of the 1st century CE. The original language of the Jewish part was presumably Hebrew, but only fragments of a later Greek translation are known. The whole book is extant only in Ethiopic and Latin. *Sparks*, pp. 775-812; *Charlesworth*, II, pp. 143-76.

Issachar, Testament of
see: *The Testaments of the Twelve Patriarchs*

Josephus
Jewish historian born in Jerusalem in 37 CE; died in Rome c. 110 CE. Of aristocratic descent and well educated, J. had visited Rome already in the 60s. He participated in the revolt against the Romans in Palestine, but eventually went over to the Roman side. After the war he lived in Rome as a man of letters under imperial protection. He wrote (in Greek) four works: an autobiography, a defence of the Jewish religion (*Contra Apionem*), an historical record of the Jewish war against the Romans (*Bellum*), and a history of the Jews from the earliest times, mainly based on the Old Testament (*Antiquitates*). Quoted from: *Josephus with an English Translation I–IX* (The Loeb Classical Library; Cambridge, Mass., London, 1926-1965).

Jubilees
A reproduction of Genesis supplemented by a summary of the
beginning of Exodus, with sections on angelology and apocalyptic,
and, above all, cultic rules and laws. An important feature is the
chronological calculation in the work: the time covered is divided into
50 'jubilees', i.e., periods of 7 x 7 years. A Hebrew original goes back to
the 2nd or 1st cent. BCE, and fragments of it have been found at
Qumran. Part of the book is extant in Latin, although the whole work
is preserved only in Ethiopic. *Sparks*, pp. 1-139; *Charlesworth*, II, pp.
35-142.

Judah, Testament of
see: *The Testaments of the Twelve Patriarchs*

Levi, Testament of
see: *The Testaments of the Twelve Patriarchs*

1 Maccabees
A record of the history of the Jews from 175 BCE to 135 BCE, i.e., from
Antiochus Epiphanes to the first Hasmonean kings. The work seems
to have been written about 100 BCE, originally in Hebrew. Now
preserved only in the Greek of the Septuagint. NEB, pp. 210-47.

2 Maccabees
A historical work that claims to be a digest of a five-volume work by the
North African Jew, Jason of Cyrene. The record covers only the
beginning of the Maccabean Revolt; on the other hand it gives a very
thorough account of the conflicts between the various high priests in
the years before the revolt. It contains a couple of legends about
martyrs (chs. 6–7). Jason's work may be from the 2nd century BCE,
and the digest of it from the 1st century BCE. Both were originally
written in Greek; the digest has been incorporated into the Septuagint.
NEB, pp. 248-75.

3 Maccabees
A legend about the Jews in Egypt in the 3rd century BCE. The work
was written among the Jews of Egypt just before the birth of Christ as
a contribution to the debate about the status of the Jews in the country
in Roman times. The legend may contain some correct details about
conditions in Ptolemaic times. The original language was Greek, and
the writing was included in the Septuagint, for which reason it is
sometimes considered as a part of the Apocrypha. However, as it is not
in the Vulgate, it should rather be included among the Pseudepigrapha. *Charlesworth*, II, pp. 509-29.

Messianic Rule (1QSa)

A Qumran work consisting of fragments of parchment containing two columns that were originally stitched together with the *Community Rule* (q.v.). The contents are rules for the Community at the end of days. *Vermes*, pp. 118-21.

Mishnah

Earliest collection of rabbinic teaching. The final redaction took place ca. 200 CE, but many of its traditions go back to pre-Christian times (e.g., statements by Hillel and Shammai). The language is Hebrew, and the text is divided into six sections with 63 tractates in all, including the *Pirqe Aboth* (q.v.). Most sections include cultic and ritual laws. The Mishnah and later commentaries, taken together, make up the medieval rabbinic collection called the *Talmud*. Quotations from: *The Mishnah*, translated by Herbert Danby (Oxford, 1933).

Moses, The Assumption of (The Testament of Moses)

An apocalyptic work from the years just after the birth of Christ. Moses reveals to Joshua the events from the invasion of the tribes in Palestine to the end of days. Extant only in Latin, but both Greek and Hebrew editions presumably existed. *Sparks*, pp. 601-616; *Charlesworth*, I, pp. 919-34.

Naphtali, Testament of
see: *The Testaments of the Twelve Patriarchs*

Nahum, Commentary on (1QpNah)

A Qumran work, of which only fragments have been preserved; it contains actualizing commentary on the prophetic book of Nahum, which is treated as a prediction of the history of the Qumran Community. *Vermes*, pp. 231-35.

Philo

Jewish-Egyptian philosopher, born in Alexandria c. 20 BCE, died c. 45 CE. Philo is a representative of hellenistic Judaism; in his writings (in Greek), he attempts to combine Greek philosophy with the Jewish faith. Most of his works are allegorical commentaries on biblical writings and treatises about biblical figures and notions. Quoted from: *Philo with an English Translation* I–XII (The Loeb Classical Library; Cambridge, Mass., London, 1929-62).

Pirqe Aboth

Literally, 'The Chapters of the Fathers'; the name is used to designate a tract in the section *Nezikin* in the Mishnah (q.v.). It mainly contains utterances of an ethical character which can be traced back to

Pharisaic and rabbinical teachers in the centuries around the birth of Christ. Cited from: *The Mishnah*, translated by Herbert Danby (Oxford, 1933), pp. 446-61.

Pseudepigrapha

Ancient Jewish writings which were not accepted into the Hebrew Bible. In contradistinction to the works in the Apocrypha (*q.v.*), with only a few exceptions the Pseudepigrapha were not incorporated into either the Septuagint or the Vulgate. Their use was perpetuated within various oriental church communities, where some of them have, or once enjoyed, canonical status. They are thus preserved in a diversity of languages (Greek, Ethiopic, Syriac, Latin, Armenian, Slavonic, etc.), but most were originally composed in Hebrew or Aramaic. 'Pseudepigraphon' means 'with a false heading', and in fact the authorship of many of the Pseudepigrapha is attributed to biblical figures from the remote past. However, this does not apply to all of the works, and the collection has no fixed limits. The Danish edition ('De gammeltestamentlige Pseudepigrafer') numbers 17 works; *Sparks* has 23, *Charlesworth* 47, while the new German edition contains 31 writings. Thus 'Pseudepigrapha' has become a general designation for ancient Jewish writings, excluding the Apocrypha, Philo, Josephus, and the Qumran texts. In this book these writings are quoted from *Sparks*, and are treated separately by title in this survey.

Qumran, Writings from

Hebrew texts found since 1947 in the district at the Northwest end of the Dead Sea. The non-biblical texts from Qumran date from the period between ca. 150 BCE and 70 CE. Editions and literature are mentioned in the bibliographical note on pp. 155f. See: *Community Rule*; *Damascus Rule*; *Commentary on Habakkuk*; *Hymns*; *Messianic Rule*; *Commentary on Nahum*; *Temple Scroll*; *War Rule*.

Reuben, Testament of
see: *The Testaments of the Twelve Patriarchs*

Sibylline Oracles, The

Collection of oracles ascribed to the legendary Sibyl. The Jewish parts of the oracles were apparently produced in imitation of earlier Greek and Roman collections. Its place of origin may have been 2nd- and 1st-century (BCE) Egypt. The Christians collected and adapted both pagan and Jewish oracles and published a collection of 12 Books of Oracles. Most of the Jewish materials are found in Books III–V; the section is accordingly called the 'Jewish Sibyl'. *Charlesworth*, I, pp. 317-472.

Sirach, The Wisdom of

Sapiential work from c. 180 BCE. The instruction takes the form of aphorisms and admonitions; wisdom is its central ethical idea. Chapters 44–50 contain a praise of the great figures in the history of Israel. The work survives in Greek, although fragments of the greater part of the original Hebrew version have been found. The author, Jesus, the Son of Sirach, apparently came from learned and aristocratic circles in Jerusalem. The Greek text is in the Septuagint. NEB, pp. 117-92.

Solomon, The Psalms of

Collection of 18 poems attributed to King Solomon. They date from the middle of the 1st century BCE, and seem to have been composed in Palestine. They imitate the biblical psalms of consolation, admonition and instruction, and were probably originally written in Hebrew or Aramaic. Now extant only in Greek, the text is included in modern editions of the Septuagint. *Sparks*, pp. 649-82; *Charlesworth*, II, pp. 639-70.

Solomon, The Wisdom of

Sapiential work which presumably dates from the 1st century CE. It contains mainly Jewish Wisdom instruction, although hellenistic influence is evident in both the contents and the characteristic presentation of the material as separate tractates. The book no doubt derives from Egyptian Jews; some of its views are affiliated with those of Philo (*q.v.*). The Greek text is preserved in the Septuagint. NEB, pp. 99-116.

Temple Scroll, The (11QTemple)

A Qumran document consisting of a parchment 9m long and divided into 67 columns, though unfortunately only poorly preserved (only about half the text is legible). It contains laws governing the organization of the temple and the temple service in the reconstituted Israel of the end of days. J. Maier, *The Temple Scroll* (Sheffield, 1985).

Testaments of the Twelve Patriarchs, The

A collection of 'testaments' attributed to Jacob's twelve sons. On his death bed, each admonishes his descendants and predicts coming events. The work thus combines ethical instruction with apocalyptic. At least some of the *Testaments* were originally written in some Semitic language (parts of the Aramaic text of the *Testament of Levi* have been found in Cairo and at Qumran), but the collection as such is known only in Greek, Armenian and some other ancient languages. The collection seems to have been composed in Palestine in the 2nd or 1st century BCE. *Sparks*, pp. 505-600; *Charlesworth*, I, pp. 775-828.

War Rule, The (1QM)
Text from Qumran, also called 'The War between the Children of Light and the Children of Darkness'. Scroll of parchment consisting of 19 columns; 4-5 lines lacking at the bottom of each page. The writing is of an apocalyptic character and gives the rules for and a description of the war at the end of times between the good and evil powers. *Vermes*, pp. 122-48.

INDEXES

INDEX OF AUTHORS

INDEX OF SUBJECTS